"WHY WRITE A BOOK ABOUT RADIOHEAD?"

For me, the answer lies mainly in the excitement I felt on that first hearing of "Planet Telex." But there are other reasons. Both as musicians and as people, Radiohead are fascinating because they diverge strongly from the rock norm. Well educated, almost unfailingly polite but unmistakably reserved, they don't often engage in silly booze- and drug-fueled antics or spend much time schmoozing at industry affairs, preferring to head for the comforts of home whenever possible. Instead of celebrating the end of a tour by getting zonked at a strip club, they'll host a book party. Far from smashing up hotel rooms, they've actually been known to clean up after their more destructively minded opening acts. And although they're aware as only rock stars can be of the public nature of their profession, they guard their privacy all the more zealously for it. For all the hundreds of thousands of words that have been written about the band in publications across the globe, it is striking how little is actually known about their lives, which, I'm sure, is just the way they like it.

EXIT MUSIC

tHe raDioHEAd stoRy

MAC RANDALL

DELTA
Trade Paperbacks

A Delta Book
Published by
Dell Publishing
a division of
Random House, Inc.
1540 Broadway
New York, New York 10036

Some portions of this book have previously appeared, in
altered form, in *Musician* and *Guitar World* magazines.

Dell books may be purchased for business or promotional use
or for special sales. For information please write to:
Special Markets Department, Random House, Inc.,
1540 Broadway, New York, N.Y. 10036.

Library of Congress Cataloging-in-Publication Data
Randall, Mac.
Exit music: the Radiohead story / Mac Randall.
p.   cm.
Includes bibliographical references (p.).
ISBN 0-385-33393-5
1. Radiohead (Musical group) 2. Rock musicians—England—Biog-
raphy. I. Title
ML421.R25 R36 2000
782.42166'092'2—dc21
[B]   00-029037

BOOK DESIGN BY JENNIFER ANN DADDIO

Manufactured in the United States of America

Published simultaneously in Canada

September 2000

10 9 8 7 6 5 4
BVG

INTRODUCTION

My first exposure to Radiohead, like that of most Americans, was the hit single "Creep," first released in the band's native England in September 1992 but not heard widely on U.S. airwaves till early the following year. No doubt about it, the song attracted attention, but at the time I felt that most of its distinguishing features—the miserable, self-torturing lyrics, the mock-anthemic quality of the music, the dynamic shifts between the quiet, brooding verses and the loud choruses splattered with grungy guitars—had been used earlier, and better, by bands like Nirvana and the Pixies. I was aware that Radiohead had an album in the stores (their debut, *Pablo Honey*) but wasn't interested enough to investigate the matter any further.

The reaction I had to "Creep" was not an uncommon one. It was shared by most of the rock critical establishment, who wrote Radiohead off early and often as a shallow flash-in-the-pan sensation. In all honesty, they had good reason for doing so. "Creep" was the kind of song that practically cries out "one-off," and the band had nothing similar to back it up with. Given the fickle nature of pop music buyers, it seemed quite likely that Radiohead would never be able to match their early success and would quickly fade from view. That the Oxford quintet would instead evolve into arguably the most accomplished and forward-looking British rock group of the '90s was a prediction that few sane people would have made.

About two years later, in April 1995, I was on vacation in England when, by chance, I happened to see the same band, whose name I only vaguely remembered from the "Creep" era, playing a new song, "Just," live on MTV Europe. It was an eye-opening three minutes and fifty-five seconds. The Nirvana and Pixies influences were still there but weren't as obvious. More to the point were the kaleidoscopic complexity of the song's structure, the devilish intricacy of its three-guitar arrangement, and the incredible energy of the performance, especially on the part of lead singer Thom Yorke, who wriggled and shook as if a combustion engine were perpetually backfiring inside him.

To pique my interest even further, flying Virgin Atlantic back to the States a couple of days later I caught a video for another new Radiohead song, "High and Dry" (the English rain-in-the-desert version, not the American *Pulp Fiction* pastiche). A bit more traditional-sounding, perhaps, but still damn catchy. I made a mental note to look into the band a bit more when I got home, and it wasn't long before I'd picked up a copy of their latest album, *The Bends*.

What I heard when I slipped that CD into the player captivated me immediately. First, setting the tone, a brief collage of howling wind-tunnel effects. Then the staticky drum groove and ominously echoing piano chords that open "Planet Telex." A few seconds later, the drums cut out to reveal a lone, forcefully strummed electric guitar. Yorke began the first line of the song; his voice, electronically distorted, sounded like he was singing through clenched teeth: "You can force it but it will not come. . . ." And then the rest of the band came crashing back in, with even greater power and volume this time. Yes, there was still some life left in the aging corpus of rock music. Radiohead, the new heroes of the genre, had proved it.

Now intrigued, I made it my business to go back and catch up on what I'd missed. I gave *Pablo Honey* the listening time I hadn't given it back in '93 and hunted down the earlier Radiohead singles. Though I didn't find anything as exciting as what I'd heard on *The Bends*, I was pleased to hear some of the previous pieces of the puzzle, the promising hints of what was to come. The first time I saw the band perform live—a surprise club show at New York's Mercury Lounge in the fall of '95, following their tour with R.E.M.—was a revelation, and subsequent shows have been nearly as stellar.

Within a few months, I turned from a Radiohead detractor to an ardent proponent. In my capacity as senior editor at *Musician* magazine, I did what I could to gain the band more recognition, interviewing various members in late '95 and early '96. And I was privileged to be one of two American journalists attending the festivities that accompanied the European release of their 1997 album *OK Computer* in Barcelona, Spain. By this time, the great majority of rock critics had come around just as I had, hailing Radiohead as groundbreakers. *OK Computer* would not only cement the band's critical reputation, but it would also foster the type of commercial success that had been lacking for them since "Creep."

Finally, in June 1999, I traveled to Oxford to see for myself where the band had gotten its start. I visited the school where they had all first met, searched out the places where they'd played their earliest shows, and talked to several people who had known them before they were superstars. The observations and insights I picked up along the way have done much to shape the content of the book you are now reading.

Why write a book about Radiohead? For me, the answer lies mainly in the excitement I felt on that first hearing of "Planet Telex." But there are other reasons. Both as musicians and as people, Radiohead are fascinating because they diverge strongly from the rock norm. Well educated, almost unfailingly polite but unmistakably reserved, they don't often engage in silly booze- and drug-fueled antics or spend much time schmoozing at industry affairs, preferring to head for the comforts of home whenever possible. Instead of celebrating the end of a tour by getting zonked at a strip club, they'll host a book party. Far from smashing up hotel rooms, they've actually been known to clean up after their more destructively minded opening acts. And although they're as aware as only rock stars can be of the public nature of their profession, they guard their privacy all the more zealously for it. For all the hundreds of thousands of words that have been written about the band in publications across the globe, it is striking how little is actually known about their lives, which, I'm sure, is just the way they like it.

To some degree, Radiohead have always been outsiders. It was their outsider status at the private boys' school they all attended in the '80s that brought them together in the first place, and it is their need to stand apart from the music-business machine that has distinguished them in the years since. One could argue that at the beginning the band was less a musical endeavor than a support group, reinforcing mutual interests and talents in the face of widespread nonrecognition from parents, teachers, and classmates. That it remains together after nearly 15 years shows that it has succeeded not merely as a creative outlet for its members but also as a means of insulation from a hostile world.

Of course, there are still many people who think of rock music as essentially an outsider's game, the product of an unruly gang of miscreants. There is just enough truth in this view to keep it popular, but only barely enough. In reality, rock at the end of the twentieth century is less an art than a business, with its own code of conformity, its own rules of behavior that must be adopted in order to get ahead. The five members of Radiohead have never fit into this system very comfortably. Not that they ever wanted to; they're proud of their misfit stance, and at times they've consciously cultivated it. For example, they never moved to London, which is where most aspiring English musicians go when they want to show they're serious about their career. Instead, all five remain in the Oxford area, close to their families, a situation that seems unlikely to change any time soon.

Geographically, Radiohead are a British band, but musically, they bear few obvious allegiances to their native land. Like their early idols U2 and R.E.M., they are international, or perhaps more accurately, supernational. They've never figured into the South vs. North ideological battle that periodically sweeps the English music world (exemplified by the largely press-manufactured Blur/Oasis showdown of 1995). They even keep their distance from the burgeoning crowd of excellent bands that have emerged from their hometown. The message is clear: Whatever your scene may be, we're not part of it.*

---

*This doesn't mean that the band has no loyalty to the Oxford scene or hasn't put anything back into it. Quite the contrary, as later chapters will prove.

This sense of not belonging, of being somehow separate and apart, is strong in all five members of the band. It affects the way they live their lives and it affects the music they make, lending their songs an emotional power that connects to listeners on an intense, visceral level. The music of Radiohead, like so much great rock music before it, appeals to the outsider and the misfit in all of us, the part of us that is constantly adrift, unsure, questioning what our existence means. At its best, rock has always provided not only feelings of hope and strength in the face of uncertainty but also glimpses beyond the surface drudgery of the world. These visions are at the core of Radiohead's art too.

This book's title, *Exit Music*, is taken from the name of a song on *OK Computer*, "Exit Music (For a Film)." In the lyrics to the song, the "exit" is a literal one; a young couple prepare to leave their homes and their parents behind, with the shady implication of a possible suicide pact. Yet one can also apply the term "exit" to all of Radiohead's music in a figurative sense. For Radiohead themselves, making music presents a way out, a means of avoiding "normal" lives that might be comfortable but would inevitably prove dissatisfying. And for Radiohead's audience, the music is an open door to another emotional territory. Sometimes the landscape is depressing or morbid, but in the end we are uplifted. The exit that Radiohead offer is not a negative exit, an escape from life, but a positive one, a means toward more fully appreciating life in all its aspects.

Exit Music is not an authorized biography. Though the band has in the past been gracious in granting me interviews, they respectfully declined my request to take part in this project. Lack of further access to the band has made my task more difficult in some ways but easier in others. Nailing down the accuracy of certain facts, especially those pertaining to the band's early years, has occasionally been frustrating, but I have also been spared the necessity of procuring the group's approval of my every word. For better or worse, although the raw material for this book has come from a variety of sources besides my own interviews, the opinions and conclusions presented here are my own.

"You should never assume that people are paying attention to you because of who you are," Radiohead's bassist Colin Greenwood once said. "If you think that, you're damned, you're doomed. . . . Nobody knows who we are, and I hope they never do, on one level, obviously."[1] Though this book does not purport to do anything so bold as to reveal the true identities of Radiohead, I hope it will bring the curious reader to a better understanding of what lies behind some of the most captivating rock music produced in the 1990s.

1 The day was Monday, June 9, 1997, and a concert was about to begin near New York City's Union Square. Over the weekend that had just ended, thousands of music fans had made pilgrimages much farther uptown, to Downing Stadium on Randalls Island in the East River between Manhattan, the Bronx, and Queens, to witness the second annual two-day Tibetan Freedom Concert. An all-star event organized by New York's own hip-hop kings the Beastie Boys, the concert would attempt to focus world attention on Tibet's plight under harsh Chinese rule and would raise money for the cause of Tibetan independence. Performers had included such rock luminaries as U2, Patti Smith, Michael Stipe and Mike Mills from R.E.M., Alanis Morrissette, and the Beastie Boys themselves.

Another band in that distinguished lineup was set to play again on this evening, in the far cozier confines of Irving Plaza (capacity approximately 1000 people). Their Tibetan Freedom performance had been one of the festival's highlights. Their name was being mentioned more and more often in the same breath as those of rock's most lauded superstars. And whereas over the weekend they had played a short set, sharing the stage with several other artists, tonight would be theirs alone, without even an opening act. They were a quintet from Oxford, England, and they were called Radiohead.

Earlier in the year, the band—made up of singer and guitarist Thom Yorke, guitarist and keyboardist Jonny Greenwood, guitarist Ed O'Brien, bassist Colin Greenwood, and drummer Phil Selway—had put the finishing touches on its third album, *OK Computer*. The album wouldn't be released in the United States until July, almost a month after the Irving Plaza show, but many of the music-industry types in the audience had heard advance copies; some were already using words like *masterpiece* to describe it. And nearly everyone in attendance had either heard the album's leadoff single, a six-and-a-half-minute, three-part epic called "Paranoid Android," or seen its quirky animated video on MTV. That June night, Radiohead planned to air several songs off the new album. They may not have been fully conscious of it, but they were also preparing to join the ranks of the rock aristocracy.

The VIP section of Irving Plaza, on the right side of the balcony above the stage, was roped off to prevent anyone without a special pass from entering. It overflowed with some of the most respected and successful people in popular music. Michael Stipe and Mike Mills hobnobbed with Bono, the Edge, and Adam Clayton from U2. Oasis' Noel Gallagher quietly sipped his beer while his brother Liam pranced goonishly through the crowd. Blur's Damon Albarn sat sulkily by the bar, at a distance from his bandmate Alex James.

Most of these artists, like Radiohead, had performed at the Tibetan Freedom Concert and had stayed over into the following week. But many other celebrities who hadn't played during the weekend had caught wind of this particular evening's mega-event and had gotten their names on the guest list too. Madonna showed up; so did Courtney Love. Lenny Kravitz made it, along with Marilyn Manson. Sheryl Crow was supposed to have been on the VIP list but wasn't for some reason or other, and when she got to the club she was nearly turned away at the door before somebody recognized her and let her pass. Ben Folds, all four members of Teenage Fanclub . . . it seemed everyone who was anyone wanted in on this party. Of the less distinguished crowd standing on the floor downstairs, quite a few spent more time during the show ogling the celebs in the balcony than watching the band onstage. As Ed O'Brien later cracked, "If a bomb had been let off in that building, we'd have seen the resurrection of Jim Kerr from Simple Minds."

Of course, the five members of Radiohead had known in advance about all the special people who'd be watching them that night. And the most special of them all was Ed O'Brien's mother. "It was the first time she'd seen us in four years," Ed says. "Before the doors opened, I went round looking at the VIP section, as it were. Madonna had the best table in the house and my mum's table was way in the back. I thought, 'I'm not having this,' so I swapped my mum's and Madonna's tables around. So," he continues with a giggle, "Madonna was at the back, and my mum had the best table in the house, sandwiched in between U2 and R.E.M. And that's exactly how it should be—I'm sure Madonna would have done exactly the same. You know, it's great that all those people are there, but if your mum is there, your mum is the most important thing."

Now that the real priorities had been straightened out, it was time for Radiohead to take the stage. Although the prospect of playing in front of such a group of people (including at least two bands—U2 and R.E.M.—that the fivesome had idolized in younger days) was incredibly intimidating, the band weren't about to let on anything of the sort. "We were nervous," O'Brien admits. "But there was also a sense of, like, we're still the underdogs. There was this kind of rock 'n' roll hierarchy there—U2 and R.E.M. and Lenny Kravitz and Madonna, et cetera, et cetera—and there were Oasis as well, our peers, but they're obviously bigger than us. And we knew beforehand that if we were able to get into it, relax a little bit and do a good gig, we could give everyone a good run for their money."

As the lights in the house darkened, a computer voice boomed through the P.A. speakers, dispassionately intoning what seemed to be random phrases and observations, by turns ambiguous, ironic, and disturbed: "Fitter, happier, more productive . . . getting on better with your associate employee contemporaries . . . no longer afraid of the dark or midday shadows . . . at a better pace . . . no chance of escape. . . ." Tall, lanky Ed O'Brien took his place on the left side of the stage and began scraping the strings above the nut of his Fender Stratocaster, summoning the ghostly sonic atmosphere that opens "Lucky," the first song recorded for *OK Computer*. On the opposite side of the stage, Jonny Greenwood hunched over his Telecaster, his chiseled cheekbones hidden by a curtain of jet-black hair. Behind those two, Phil Selway, head newly shaven, manned the drumkit with consummate cool, while Colin Greenwood, Jonny's older brother, held down a subdued yet warm bassline, bobbing slowly back and forth but never moving out of the drummer's sight for long.

In the center stood Thom Yorke, diminutive, spiky-haired, intense, a Fender Jazzmaster loosely slung over his shoulder. Eyes nearly closed, he sang, quietly at first, words that seemed beyond optimism, hinting at a mysterious change of luck and at the same time conjuring up images of air crashes and bodies at the bottoms of lakes. When the band paused between the chorus and the verse, Yorke raised his right hand and waved it three times. The gesture kept the rhythmic count steady in the absence of drums, but it also resembled the last hopeless wave of a drowning victim. As the song progressed, Yorke's singing gradually gained momentum. On the climactic line, "It's gonna be a glorious day," his voice swelled up and out before spiraling gracefully down, achieving an almost operatic grandeur. The band's playing matched the mood perfectly, their deep minor chords echoing across vast spaces.

The set continued with energetic runs through "My Iron Lung" and "Nice Dream," from the band's previous album, *The Bends*, released in 1995. Another new song, "Exit Music (For a Film)," followed. Yorke started it off alone, strumming an acoustic guitar. The crowd yelled over the music; Thom ordered them to shut up. But the aggravation in his voice wasn't completely serious. He was smiling too broadly for that.

"It was kind of heads down for the first three songs," Ed recalls, "but we were really, really on the money. We were playing really well. And it was nice after that, 'cause we were able to relax and get a little . . . not cocky, but like, 'Yeah, we can cut the mustard as well.' In front of that kind of audience, it was really nice to be able to know that. Normally as a band, we freak ourselves out a bit and put on some rubbish show, but we actually controlled ourselves, we didn't let the tempos get too quick, fly off and then become this express train. We were able to sit back and enjoy it."

Indeed, Radiohead appeared to be absolutely in control of both themselves and the illustrious crowd. As far as tempos were concerned, even when the band seemed to rush (on the explosive midsection of "My Iron Lung") or slow down (the thudding transition parts on "The Bends"), they did it together, with all five members moving seamlessly in tandem. While Thom held the audience's attention front and center, Ed and Jonny went about their work like old-fashioned alchemists. Ed bounded restlessly around his corner of the stage, as if jockeying for position against an invisible opponent. During "Bones" (off *The Bends*), Jonny squatted over his homemade tremolo pedal, turning the rate knob manually to speed up and slow down the pulsating effect. The act seemed invested with magical significance. On several songs, particularly the new ones, the younger Greenwood would shift from guitar to keyboard or more unusual instruments—xylophone on "No Surprises," transistor radio on "Climbing Up the Walls." When he did step out on six-string, he snapped his picking arm back violently after every gutsy stroke; no wonder he was wearing an arm brace for repetitive stress syndrome. Without exception, each time all three guitarists played at once, their parts meshed beautifully, as Ed, Thom, and Jonny stayed out of each other's way and each other's frequencies.

A clear sign that something was up, that the band was on top of its game and knew it, was the big goofy grin that kept reappearing on Thom's face. Several songs in, Ed picked up on his bandmate's obvious high spirits and made a comment that couldn't be heard offstage. "Thanks, Ed," Thom said into the microphone. "Yeah, I'm having fun. I don't know about anybody else."[1] To which the crowd whooped en masse. Thom's beaming response: "That's good. This is a song called 'Paranoid Android.'" As Bono, Stipe, Madonna, and company looked on from the balcony, Radiohead dug into the tricky new minisuite with relish. The audience's roar at the end left no doubt in anyone's mind that they'd nailed it.

But the biggest response of all was saved for a song played toward the end of the set. Thom prefaced it with a brief announcement: "We're going to do this next song 'cause we still like it, and we don't have a problem with it. Sing along if you feel like it." The song was "Creep."

"Creep," Radiohead's second single, had been their first hit and the song that brought them their notoriety. Like Nirvana's "Smells Like Teen Spirit" before it and Beck's "Loser" soon after, it had encapsulated the attitude of a generation uncomfortable in its own skin. "I wish I was special," Thom crooned, "you're so fucking special/But I'm a creep, I'm a weirdo/What the hell am I doing here?/I don't belong here." Attached to a classic, Hollies-worthy chord progression and one of the indisputably great non-melodic hooks in rock history—Jonny attacking the muted strings of his Tele three times to make a sound *(chu-chunk, chu-chunk, chu-chunk)* as ominous as the loading of a rifle—Yorke's socially maladjusted ditty had touched a general nerve. It also put his band onto the worldwide charts, made his sleepy-eyed, Johnny Rotten–meets–Martin Short visage an MTV staple, and helped sell several millions' worth of Radiohead's debut album, 1993's *Pablo Honey.*

Unfortunately, this type of notoriety wasn't what Radiohead wanted. "Creep" hadn't been written to establish them as anthem makers or generational spokesmen. In fact, it hadn't even been one of their favorite songs. Overwhelmed to the point of disturbance by the tremendous response it had received, the band felt the need to move in a different musical direction following *Pablo Honey*'s release. But as they tried to branch out, they found that their big hit had already pigeonholed them. Subsequent singles failed to catch on commercially. Attention-deficient casual listeners recognized Yorke only as "the 'Creep' guy." A hostile press readied itself to label them one-hit wonders. The result was a crisis of confidence that nearly destroyed this tightly knit band of old school chums. Only by closing ranks, ignoring the expectations of others, and responding solely to their own muse did Radiohead finally prevail, undergoing a creative breakthrough that would eventually be heard on *The Bends* and *OK Computer*.

"Creep" had been both Radiohead's salvation and their albatross. But now, tonight, on this darkened stage in New York City, at the beginning of a bold new phase in the band's career, it was just another part of the repertoire, though still an important part. Jonny's overamped shotgun guitar hook rocked the hall, and the white stage lights flashed on and off in time with it. The band burst into the distorted chorus with a combination of sly wit and brute force. And as Yorke's singing reached a crescendo, the others stopped playing, leaving him to sustain one pained, tremulous, fervent note. The crowd erupted in hollers and applause.

Several months later, when asked by the British music magazine *Mojo* to submit a year-end best-of list, R.E.M.'s Mike Mills sent them a photograph of himself holding a large cardboard sign that read RADIOHEAD, JUNE 9, IRVING PLAZA, NYC: BEST SHOW OF THE YEAR. By this time, *OK Computer* had been nominated Album of the Year by a host of worldwide publications, was in the running for several international music-industry awards, including two Grammys, and was set to become Radiohead's biggest-selling album so far. Radiohead had won the support of the public, the critics, and their peers, and at Irving Plaza that night they'd made believers out of their own heroes as well.

But most importantly, what did Ed O'Brien's mum think of her first Radiohead show in four years? "She loved it," Ed reports. "She thought the gig was fantastic. And she had Madonna's table, which is lovely."

2

Ask just about anyone to list the most prestigious institutions on our planet, and chances are Oxford will figure prominently. All around the world, the name of Britain's oldest university is recognized as a symbol of the highest academic achievement. But Oxford is not just a university. It's also a city in its own right. And as is the case with so many university towns, the relationship between the university and the town is not always close or easy. The five members of Radiohead, who have lived in or around Oxford for most of their lives and who fall squarely on the town side of the town-and-gown dichotomy, can attest to that.

"Too many people, not enough space," Thom Yorke once said of his hometown. "It's very oppressive because the university owns 90 percent of the land and the public haven't got access to it."[1] The large transitory student population, mainly privileged youth from parts elsewhere, has never endeared itself to Yorke, who has in the past described Oxford students as "these fuckers walking around in their ball gowns, throwing up on the streets, being obnoxious to the population. The little guys in the bowler hats will clean up their puke and make their beds for them every night. They don't know they're born [British slang for being clueless] and they're going to run the country. It's scary. Of all the towns in the country it's one of the most obvious examples of a class divide."[2] The countless waves of tourists that throng the city's streets can be a considerable nuisance as well.

Yet even after achieving great success, none of Radiohead have chosen to make their home anywhere other than Oxford. The reasons for this are varied—family ties, an affection for familiar comforts, a healthy disregard of city congestion and pollution, maybe even plain old inertia—but the effects that the band's surroundings have on their music can't be discounted. Yorke, for one, has frequently claimed that living in Oxford influences his writing, although the degree of that influence is unclear. Perhaps the mere experience of having been longtime observers of an intellectual community from the outside, close to it geographically but never a part of it, has helped inform the character of the band's art: intelligent but not elitist, sensitive but guarded, emotional but too perceptive to avoid a certain skepticism.

"They obviously like living here," says Dave Newton, former manager of Ride—another local band made good—and current head of Oxford-based independent label Shifty Disco. "In fact, they all live closer to the center of the city now than they did when they were coming up. You'll still see them at the local clubs sometimes, or in the record shops. Nobody hassles them, except for a few tourists, and they appreciate that. I think that the fact they've stayed here is great for the younger Oxford bands as well—it offers them a good example of how to conduct yourself, knowing that that guy who you saw in the supermarket the other day picking out the best cauliflower might be on the cover of the *NME* next week."

These days, there are a lot more young Oxford bands to benefit from that example. Ten years ago, when Radiohead were still in their infancy, the local music scene was tiny, oriented around a handful of clubs and a few dozen groups. Now, at least 200 bands are based in the area. Why this dramatic upsurge? Location is part of it. An hour's train ride from London, Oxford is conveniently close to England's acknowledged music-industry capital, but not close enough to be ruled by its dictates. The remarkable camaraderie of the Oxford scene is another reason. Bands openly support one another here, a far cry from the divisiveness so common in music circles of other British cities—Manchester, for instance.

But more than anything else, the growth of Oxford's pop music community can be attributed to the widespread influence of the many local bands who've made names for themselves in the past decade. The list is sizable, including Ride, Swervedriver, the Candyskins, Supergrass, and the trio led by Thom Yorke's younger brother Andy, Unbelievable Truth. And out of these, the band to achieve the greatest global recognition is Radiohead. "Their success has definitely had a ripple effect," says Dai Griffiths, head of the music department at Oxford Brookes University. "People not only love their music but are also very aware of where the band came from. It's a source of pride, and it's also been encouraging to a lot of young musicians here."

The influence they've had on their hometown has been substantial, but it's not something Radiohead tend to acknowledge. That's not much of a surprise. Private and reserved as they are, the band have never been keen on drawing attention to themselves, even for acts of generosity. While the visibility of Oxford as a source of creative contemporary music continues to grow, the five people who have done more than anyone to put that city on the rock map remain what they have essentially always been: interested observers.

As Thom Yorke says, "Oxford is a place where you have a plan and then you go out and never achieve it. You just walk around in circles. I've always been able to walk round and round Oxford for days and watch people and be perfectly happy. I used to have favorite places to sit and watch. I still do."[3]

The members of Radiohead don't like to talk much about their childhoods, at least not to interviewers. When pressed on the issue, they'll usually say something along the lines of this quote from a 1997 interview with Thom: "It's fairly flat. I didn't get kicked around as a kid. Sorry to disappoint."[4] Wary of turning their lives into press fodder, the band shy away from deep analysis of their early years. They prefer to maintain that the households in which they grew up were unremarkable and that it isn't necessary to know what they were all like as kids to properly appreciate the music they make. Fair points, to be sure. But in fact, the childhood experiences of at least one member of the band were decidedly unusual, perhaps traumatic, and arguably had a great deal of bearing on what was to come.

Thomas Edward Yorke was born on October 7, 1968, in Wellingborough, Northamptonshire, with his left eye fixed shut. The doctors quickly determined that the eye was paralyzed and that the condition appeared to be permanent. Searching for solutions to this unfortunate defect, the Yorkes took their son to an eye specialist, who suggested that a muscle graft might be of assistance. The course of treatment agreed to by Thom's parents resulted in his undergoing five operations before his sixth birthday. "The first operation I had," he later remembered, "I was just learning to speak, and apparently I asked, 'What have I got?' I didn't know. I woke up and I had this huge thing on my eye, and according to my parents, I just doubled up and started crying."[5] These operations did eventually change matters for the better— the left lid opened successfully (though to this day it droops lower than the right one), and Thom was able to see through two eyes for the first time in his life—but the physical and, more importantly, emotional difficulties they caused would leave a lasting mark of their own.

Shortly after Thom's birth, his father, Graham, a supplier of equipment to the chemical engineering industry, was hired by a firm in Scotland, and so the family moved north, where they were to remain until Thom was seven. They lived near the beach, close to an abandoned World War II sea defense fortification surrounded by barbed wire barricades, a bleak scene that Yorke has occasionally recalled in interviews. During this period, Thom spent an entire year wearing a patch over his damaged eye. "They fucked up the last [eye operation]," he once explained, "and I went half blind. I can kind of see. I can judge if I'm going to hit something, but that's just about it. They made me go around with a patch on my eye . . . saying, 'Oh well, it's just got lazy through all the operations,' which was crap because they'd just damaged it."[6]

The patch and his understandable self-consciousness about it were reportedly the two features that distinguished him most at the first schools he attended. The situation was worsened by the fact that in 1976, the year the Sex Pistols roared onto the British charts with "Anarchy in the U.K.," the Yorkes moved back south to England, again following Thom's father's work. Within six months, they moved a second time. For young Thom, this meant a rapid succession of new schools, new classmates, and new insecurities. (Leaving Scotland also meant saying good-bye to his first girlfriend, Katie Ganson, whom the seven-year-old had romantically pledged to marry. The two would never see each other again.) Though he later claimed that "the only thing that affected me really badly was . . . everyone taking the piss out of me"[7] because of his eye problems, that was bad enough. In the face of the other boys' taunts and jeers, Thom soon learned to withdraw into himself and his own creative projects.

"My mother has always said that I was a very quiet, happy kid who just worked all the time," Yorke told *Q* in October 1997. "Using my hands. Building stuff out of Lego, taking care of my bike—I was obsessed with my bike—designing and drawing cars . . . I never got bored as a kid." He may not have been bored, but he was never perfectly content either: "There's a pervading sense of loneliness I've had since the day I was born. Maybe a lot of other people feel the same way, but I'm not about to run up and down the street asking everybody if they're as lonely as I am. I'd probably get locked up."[8] Though it's arguable that the emotional effects of Thom's childhood have had a deep influence on the tenor of Radiohead's songs, it's also worth noting that he has never dealt explicitly with the events of his early life in his music. "I wish I was actually able to write more about how I felt when I grew up," he once said. "I don't find I can that well. That would probably be a really good way of dealing with it."[9]

By 1978, the Yorke family had finally settled down for good in Oxfordshire. From September of that year to July of 1980, Thom attended the Standlake Church of England Primary School in Witney, a few miles west of Oxford. His equally artistic younger brother Andy would also eventually become a Standlake student; perhaps not coincidentally, their mother, Barbara, taught at the school (as she does to this day). Despite the close family connections, Thom was again teased relentlessly by his classmates due to his ocular irregularity. The constant schoolyard jibing, instead of thickening his skin, made him even more sensitive. He began getting into fights regularly, most of which he lost. ("I was into the *idea* of fighting," he once said.[10]) No longer merely wary of others, he now expected people to give him trouble—sometimes to the point that he could be accused of actively looking for an argument—and he became unwilling to back down, the first signs of a stubbornness and suspicion of outsiders that would be increasingly apparent as the years went on.

"I'm like my dad" is how he explains it. "I have the sort of face that people want to punch me. That means I get into fights easily." Indeed, Thom's father, a prizewinning boxer when he was in college, took it upon himself to teach his son the pugilistic art—for purposes of self-defense, of course. His attempts were not incredibly successful. "One of the first things he ever bought me was a pair of boxing gloves," Thom remembered in *Rolling Stone*.[11] "He used to try to teach me to box, but whenever he hit me, I'd fall flat on my ass."

Offsetting all this everyday unpleasantness, though, was a new interest, in which the young Yorke found both consolation and a creative outlet. For his eighth birthday, Thom's mother and father had given him a cheap Spanish guitar as a present. He'd discovered rock music not long before, and his parents, encouraging the enthusiasm, no doubt hoped that learning to play an instrument could help boost his overall confidence. (Four years earlier, Yorke had had a steel-string guitar, but his initial musical experimentations were short-lived; the strings hurt his fingers, and so he impatiently threw the guitar against the wall, breaking it to bits.)

Tellingly, it wasn't the raw three-chord punk sweeping the English scene at the time but the far more ornate, theatrical, and conspicuously accomplished stylings of Queen that first ignited Thom's passion. In particular, he idolized the perfect mix of melody, bombast, and campy humor in the playing of their guitarist Brian May, which he first heard on a friend's copy of the band's 1975 album *A Night at the Opera*. "I wanted to be Brian

May," he later recalled. "I went into a guitar lesson when I was eight and said, 'I want to be Brian May.' I'd never wanted to be anything else. Before that, it was Legos."[12] Though certainly diluted by exposure to other music over the years, that early influence of Queen can still be heard in Radiohead's work, particularly in more ambitious songs like "The Bends" and "Paranoid Android."

Legend has it that Thom was convinced early on that he would be a rock star, perhaps not exactly like Brian May but close enough, and that he advised his parents to this effect. His father duly passed the information on to his friends, who no doubt got a chuckle or two out of it. At this point, the only song the youngster could play on the guitar was "Kumbaya."

Wasting little time, Yorke formed his first band at age ten. (Actually, it wasn't a band but what might be more aptly described as an experimental duo, consisting of Thom on guitar and another Standlake student whose primary duty apparently consisted of miswiring TV sets so that they'd explode.) By age 11 he'd written his first song, a cheery little number about the atomic bomb called "Mushroom Cloud." The composer has since explained that the song was "more about how [the mushroom cloud] looked than how terrible it was."[13] Still, it stands as evidence that the morbid world view so commonly found in the songs of Radiohead was already well in place at a tender age.

At the dawn of the 1980s Thom Yorke entered Abingdon School, a "public" (the English term for private) single-sex institution located, as the name indicates, in the smallish (population approximately 32,000) suburb of Abingdon, just a few miles down the Thames from the city of Oxford. One of the oldest public schools in England, Abingdon has been in existence since at least 1256. In 1563, the school was re-endowed by John Roysse, a London mercer, or dealer of fine fabrics; in 1870, it moved to its present beautiful 37-acre site on Park Road in the heart of the market town, which until 1980 was also the head-quarters of the MG automobile company. Thom joined a student body of about 750 boys between the ages of 11 and 19, of whom one-fifth were either full or weekly boarders. Pupils are expected to put in a grueling class schedule by American standards—six days a week, 8:35 A.M. to 5 P.M. weekdays, 8:35 A.M. to 1 P.M. Saturdays—but the school prides itself on the results: Nearly every Abingdon graduate goes on to university (which is still a far less automatic career path in Britain than in the U.S.), with an average of 15 to 25 per year winning places at Oxford or Cambridge.

Though the people and surroundings of Abingdon were different from Standlake, the teasing—about both Thom's looks and his attitude—wasn't about to let up. A particularly caring classmate gave him a new nickname, "Salamander." The brawl that ensued between the two boys didn't stop the name from spreading. "I didn't like it," Thom would later vouchsafe, adding that "it was a very malicious school and everyone had very malicious nicknames, so 'Salamander' was par for the course."[14]

Much of Thom's personal malice was saved specifically for Abingdon's headmaster, one Michael St. John Parker, who also had a student-devised nickname, "the Beak," a reference to his unusually long nose. A historian by training, Parker is the co-author of the splendidly written and highly informative *The Martlet and the Griffen: An Illustrated History of Abingdon School* (London: James & James Publishers, Ltd., 1997). Yet it isn't his scholarship that most of his students seem to remember, but rather his allegedly peculiar mannerisms and dress sense. Another former Abingdonian, Rick Clark, interviewed by author Jonathan Hale for his book *Radiohead: From a Great Height*, remembered that Parker "constantly prowled the school grounds in his Dracula robes, trying to look like a slice of early nineteenth-century English school folklore."[15]

Parker also presided over the twice-weekly morning chapel services that were, along with school uniforms, mandatory for all students. (One of the principal aims in the official Abingdon School mission statement is to "give boys an understanding of the Christian heritage.") According to Thom, Parker's sermons to the boys were sabotaged by the fact that he wasn't an ordained minister; in the young Yorke's eyes, the headmaster was simply impersonating a man of the cloth. "I really grew up with hatred for [Parker] because he was one fucked-up guy," Thom later said. "He was a power-crazy, lunatic, evil, petty little man with ridiculous sideburns who used to flick his hair across his head to hide his bald patch."[16]

This deeply held loathing has lasted long enough to come through in the lyrics to several Radiohead songs, the most obvious being "Bishop's Robes," released as a B-side in 1996. The words leave little to the imagination. Yorke curses a "bastard headmaster," confesses that he's still terrified by his mental image of the man (wearing the titular robes; no mention of sideburns, though), and bewails the British system of cultural indoctrination ("Children taught to kill/To tear themselves to bits/On playing fields") in which the headmaster is a major participant. But just in case you still have any doubts about the meaning of the song, here's how Thom introduced it one of the few times Radiohead has played it live, in Stockholm in 1995: "This is about an old headmaster that we had. . . . He suddenly decided he was close to God 'cause he was a useless headmaster. The guy was a fascist idiot, and this is about him."[17]

Clearly, there is no love lost between Thom Yorke and his alma mater, but the reasons for this, at least pertaining to Thom's first couple of years at the school, remain unclear. His academic performance, though not exceptional, was far from miserable. Abingdon's teachers were no doubt overly concerned with discipline, but it also seems likely that Yorke had already developed an inherent mistrust of authority figures that went beyond any actual loathsome behavior on the part of his headmaster. In any event, Thom went through what he later characterized as "a really bad period . . . [M]y parents worked themselves into this state and were convinced I was going to get expelled. They got things slightly out of proportion."[18]

It would seem so, if Abingdon geography and athletics instructor Jeff Drummond-Hay's testimony is to be believed. Interviewed by the *Mail on Sunday* in 1997 about his experience teaching the future members of Radiohead, Drummond-Hay painted a rosy picture. "They kept their heads down and worked hard. They were quite popular, but they weren't the rowdiest bunch that we've had here."[19] Indeed, the ways in which Thom chose to rebel against his school's rigid strictures were far more constructive than those of some other classmates. During his time at Abingdon, a few of his contemporaries gained notoriety by allegedly hijacking a local bus and attempting to set off a homemade bomb in the park adjoining the school. Jonny Greenwood recalled that the students had built the bomb "by collecting chemicals every week from [chemistry] lessons over a whole term until they had a whole bottle full, and then they laid it next to a statue. . . . [It's] bizarre for this sleepy town in the middle of Oxfordshire, very hard to imagine."[20]

Still, there were good points to Thom's attending Abingdon, for it was there that he would meet the other four boys with whom he'd forge a future in rock 'n' roll. The first to join the gang was Colin Charles Greenwood. Born several months after Thom, on June 26, 1969, he had lived in the Oxford area all his life. Like Thom, he had suffered from teasing and self-consciousness about his appearance (in Colin's case, an oddly shaped head and somewhat sunken facial features). Also like Thom, he'd been drawn to music as a youngster, following the death of his father, Raymond, a major in the Royal Army Ordnance Corps, when Colin was seven years old.

Encouraged at the beginning by his mother, Brenda, who wasn't a musician but had some appreciation for light classical and show tunes, Colin started taking guitar lessons around age nine, but he was by now more interested in playing bass, inspired by the late-'70s and early-'80s post-punk that he found in his older sister Susan's record collection. Bassists like Magazine's Barry Adamson and Joy Division's Peter Hook had an aggressive style, simple yet melodic, that appealed to Colin and had the added benefit of being relatively easy to duplicate. (The work of more experienced bassists like Motown's great James Jamerson and Stax's Donald "Duck" Dunn was also a formative influence on young Colin.)

Another trait Thom and Colin had in common was a love of outrageous dress. Thom once explained that he started a band with Colin because "we always ended up at the same parties. He'd be wearing a beret and a catsuit, or something pretty fucking weird, and I'd be in a frilly blouse and crushed velvet dinner suit and we'd pass round the Joy Division records."[21] Lest we forget, this was the early '80s, heyday of the New Romantics, and dressing foppishly was a big pop trend. Of course, the music of Joy Division would have been far too raw and despairing to make it onto the turntables of most New Romantic enthusiasts, but these Oxford kids, none of whom could be mistaken for strict purists, were already mixing and matching their favorites with little regard for genre lines.

The first band these two disaffected Abingdon students both played in, at approximately age 14, was the school's resident punk outfit, TNT. Thom became the singer because, as he put it, "no one else would."[22] In possession of a cheap microphone but no stand, Yorke made do by tying the mike to a broomstick: "Everyone just started falling about laughing, and that was that. That was my introduction to singing."[23] By all accounts, the band made a horrible racket, which was the whole point, of course. But although TNT was an exciting proposition at first, by 1984 it had become a drag for Thom and Colin, who decided to leave the band's ranks and investigate other musical avenues.

Soon joining Thom and Colin in this new enterprise was another lifelong Oxfordite and would-be musician, Edward John O'Brien (born April 15, 1968). Son of John O'Brien, a local osteopath, Ed lived with his mother, Eve, after his parents split up in the late '70s, but he stayed on good terms with both sides of the family. Though he first became interested in pop music around the time of Elvis Presley's death in 1977, Ed's greater passion was for outdoor sports: cricket, football, and field hockey. Of all the future members of Radiohead, he was the most athletically inclined, and because of this he was by far the most frequently mentioned in Abingdon School's yearly magazine, *The Abingdonian*. (In the 1984 issue, Jeff Drummond-Hay, who coached the Abingdon cricket team, praises O'Brien for "chancing [his] arm to good effect."[24])

Another major interest of Ed's was theater, and it was his frequent acting in school dramatic productions that led him to meet both Greenwood and Yorke, who were in the year below him. First he met Colin, who costarred with him in Gilbert and Sullivan's operetta *Trial by Jury*, and then Thom, who helped provide background music for an experimental, in-the-round, modern-dress version of *A Midsummer Night's Dream*. In an interview many years later, Ed recalled the first time Thom came across his radar. "There was this tense dress rehearsal, and Thom and this other fella were jamming freeform cod [British slang for weak or amateurish] jazz throughout it. The director stopped the play and shouted up to this scaffold tower thing they were playing on, trying to find out what the hell was going on. Thom started shouting down, 'I don't know what the fuck we're supposed to be play-ing.' And this was to a *teacher*."[25]*

Already towering over his classmates—he would eventually reach a more than respectable height of six foot four—O'Brien was recruited, Thom said, because "I thought he was cool and looked like [then-Smiths vocalist] Morrissey."[26] Ed was flattered by this comparison to the singer of one of his all-time favorite bands (he has since called the Smiths, and especially the playing of guitarist Johnny Marr, "an enormous influence—I realized re-cently that I'd been subconsciously ripping off their stuff for ages"), and a fast friendship was formed. Thom and Colin cer-tainly didn't take Ed into their inner circle for his guitar-picking abilities, which Ed claims were just about nonexistent. "I wasn't trained on the guitar at all," he says. "I could barely play a chord when I was first in the band." But in those early days, looks counted for a lot.

This is not to say that the future members of Radiohead lacked musical training entirely. On the contrary, all of them re-ceived formal instruction on at least one instrument in their youth. Thom took both guitar and voice lessons, but though he was an eager student at first, he was far less interested in learning to read and write music, a discipline he has yet to acquire: "My [singing] teacher . . . would give me things to practice and I'd come back and say, 'You have to sing this to me, 'cause I can't

*The "other fella" playing with Thom was a gifted keyboardist named Donald Gawthorne. Another Abingdon classmate, James Lister-Cheese, claims that Gawthorne's musical influence on Thom was considerable and that, for a time, the two musicians had a band together. The adaptation of *A Midsummer Night's Dream* for which they provided the music was performed at the school's Amey Hall on November 15 and 16, 1984. In a review that ran in the following year's edition of *The Abingdonian*, classmate Tom Hollander reported that Yorke and Gawthorne's music "seemed to be largely a matter of improvisation, providing pace and generally contributing to the atmospheric nature of the production," before concluding sourly, "It can't be very gratifying for the people involved in such a production when so few members of the school community can be both-ered to go and see their work." [*The Abingdonian*, July 1985, vol. 18, no. 3, 26] read it.' . . . I could never get the hang of [reading] at all."[27] Colin was classically trained on guitar. Ed studied trumpet for several years, but when he joined one of Abingdon's school orchestras, he was moved from his chosen instrument to the trombone. He claims that he was moved "because there weren't enough trombone players in the orchestra, but he [the orchestra leader] said my lips were too big for the trumpet." (To which Colin responds: "He was telling you porkies. He just wanted to throw you the 'bone, didn't he?")

Many of Thom, Colin, and Ed's early group activities took place in Abingdon's music department, which was one of the few parts of the school that Thom would later describe unequivocally as "great—no one came down there, and there were these tiny rooms with sound-proofed cubicles."[28] Music is an important part of the Abingdon curriculum, though not generally music of the pop variety. Over half the school's pupils receive instruction on an instrument, and there are three school orchestras, plus several brass and wind ensembles. The school also boasts a state-of-the-art concert hall, built in 1980 for amateur and professional recitals. Colin remembered Abingdon's music school as a place "where we would all run and hide away from the tedious conformity of timetables and uniforms."[29]

It wasn't long before this retreat from obligations took on a more constructive tone, and a more or less permanent band was soon formed with Yorke, Greenwood, and O'Brien at its core, along with a rotating cast of other members. For a while, that cast included three saxophone players, two of them sisters from the nearby girls' school of St. Helen's and St. Katherine's; a horn section would be a regular group feature until well into the late '80s. The band had a variety of names—Shindig, Dearest, and Gravitate were among the longest-lasting—but had difficulty finding a drummer, and so timekeeping duties were held down at first by a Boss Dr. Rhythm drum machine. Unfortunately, at one of the group's earliest performances, a birthday party for a fellow class-mate, the machine broke down in the middle of their first song. After a great deal of cursing, especially from Thom, the band de-cided that they had to get a real drummer right away.* Someone mentioned trying out a boy that everyone vaguely knew from one of Abingdon's upper forms (higher grades, in American terminol-ogy), and the next day Ed was sent to the local pub to recruit him. He was then playing in a band called Jungle Telegraph, and his name was Philip James Selway.

The only member of Radiohead besides Thom to have been born outside Oxford's environs (in Hemingford Gray, Cam-bridgeshire), Phil Selway is also the oldest member of the group, born May 23, 1967. Drumming had long been an interest of Phil's. "I found my first drum at three o'clock in the morning of my third Christmas," he reminisced in 1993. "My parents [Michael and Dorothea] never really encouraged me to play after that."[30] Nevertheless, Phil stuck with his original choice of instru-ment, except for a brief dalliance with the tuba. During his time at Abingdon, he studied classical percussion but stopped after two years of tympani instruction. (Colin comments, "If we ever head on into the progressive direction, we've got the guy who can play the tymps already." In response, Phil quips: "I was kind of thinking of transferring those skills to the gong, though.") Al-though several of Phil's friends had beaten Thom up in the past, this was overlooked when it came time to evaluate his drumming abilities, which were acceptable to all concerned. According to some reports, Thom's only comment to Selway at their first meet-ing was "Can't you play any fucking faster?"[31] The answer was

*The band ruefully remembers another part of that early birthday party show. After the music ended, a boy came up to Colin and complimented him on his bass playing, a compliment that Colin, who was still a relative beginner on the instrument, took with a great deal of satisfaction. It was only later that he discov-ered the fellow who'd praised his playing was completely tone-deaf.

evidently in the affirmative; many years later, Phil would remember those words with a chuckle and say, "I soon learned."[32]

In future years, the nondrumming members of the band would display their sense of irony by giving their unusually mild-mannered percussionist the nickname Mad Dog and warning their new acquaintances to watch out for Selway's ugly temper. "Phil is the antithesis of your normal drummer," Ed once put it. "He's very cerebral, he's very thoughtful . . . and he's not one to go smashing TV sets through windows. As none of us are. You know, that's all a bit old hat."[33]

Eventually, the fledgling band settled on a permanent name, On A Friday. There was no hidden meaning in the moniker—Friday was simply the day the band usually rehearsed—and not a tremendous amount of inspiration either, but it worked for the moment. The music they played, written principally by Thom, was the product of a mélange of influences: the aforementioned Joy Division, Magazine, and the Smiths, but also the Fall, Elvis Costello, Joe Jackson, U2, R.E.M., Japan (whose lead singer David Sylvian first inspired Thom to dye his hair blond), and many others. "Schizophrenic" is the word the other members of the band use most often to describe those early songs, which bore titles like "Fragile Friend," "Lock the Doors," and "Girl in a Purple Dress." A distinctive sound was slowly beginning to take shape, but one further addition to the lineup would be necessary before all the pieces fell into place.

Colin's younger brother, Jonathan Richard Gordon Greenwood (born November 5, 1971, in Oxford), was spending more and more time hanging around On A Friday's rehearsals. Originally, Colin had invited him along. He later claimed it was a way of keeping an eye on his sibling: "He was only thirteen, it was a difficult age."[34] Though Jonny (as he is generally known) was quiet by nature—Ed once joked that he didn't speak a word to anyone in the group for a year—his interest in joining the band had become clear. His age and his relation to Colin didn't weigh in his favor, but his obvious talent on a wide variety of instruments did.

Jonny showed signs of musical adeptness early on; he once claimed in print that his grandfather, the only previous member of the Greenwood family within living memory who'd exhibited any instrumental skill, had taught him show tunes on the banjo at the tender age of three. In their youth, Colin and Jonny shared a bedroom, and Colin remembers that around the same time he began playing the guitar, Jonny picked up the recorder. "I suppose that he was about age seven," the elder Greenwood says. (Jonny says he was five.) "And he learned to play the recorder a lot quicker than I learned to play the guitar. Then he went on to learn to play my guitar." (Colin had his revenge on his younger sibling by mixing up his crayons, a prank that Jonny, who is color-blind, would later claim retarded his development.) By this time, Jonny had gotten turned on to pop music—the first record he personally owned, at age six, was Squeeze's "Cool for Cats" on pink vinyl. Later, vintage jazz and modern classical music would become his main passions.

From guitar, Jonny progressed to piano and a number of other instruments, eventually manning one of the viola chairs in the Thames Valley Youth Orchestra. He was, without a doubt, the most versatile, knowledgeable, and musically literate member of the group. Except that he still wasn't really in the group. On A Friday already had two guitar players; they didn't need a third. What to do? The boys vacillated on the matter for nearly a year, during which time Jonny would frequently show up at band rehearsals toting a portable keyboard, ready to be called on when needed.

Those times when he was allowed to join in, unbeknownst to the rest of the band, Jonny would play with the volume turned to zero. "They'd had a previous keyboard player [probably Thom's friend and collaborator on the *Midsummer Night's Dream* music, Donald Gawthorne] who was into quite loud keyboards in a Genesis kind of way," he said. "So I thought, 'The way to stay in this band would be to be very quiet.' I'd be sat [*sic*] there, playing the right chords, but no one could hear a note I played. . . . The euphemism they kept coming up with was, 'Well, these keyboards sound like you can't hear them but if you took them away, then you'd notice they were missing.'"[35] This minimalist tactic had positive effects. Finally, grudgingly, Jonny was allowed a guest spot in the band—on harmonica.

With their final lineup nearly complete, On A Friday began making occasional live appearances around town at parties and the like. Fearing parental disapproval of his activities, Thom would make up stories for his mom and dad whenever the band played anywhere, telling them he was staying at a friend's house. Colin later recalled one of those early gigs with much good humor: "We all wore black and played very loud, because we thought that's what you had to do."[36]

The band has always maintained that at this time they were making music primarily for themselves and no one else. "It's not like we wanted to go play in London and be noticed straight-away," Colin said. "We've never done the music as paving the way to recognition or fame."[37] Even though their audience consisted mainly of Abingdon classmates, they professed not to be incredibly concerned with what their peer group thought. Yet at least some of their contemporaries at school held them in high regard. Rick Clark and Simon Cranshaw, two fellow Abingdonians interviewed by Jonathan Hale, claimed that Thom's musical proficiency impressed many students and that he got a lot of attention on campus because of it.

James Lister-Cheese, who came to Abingdon in the same year as Thom and Colin, told me much the same. Lister-Cheese's name is forever linked to Thom's in the pages of *The Abingdonian* due to a joint interview they conducted with master Charles Parker in 1986 on the fascinating subject of rewriting math textbooks. Now an investment consultant in London, Lister-Cheese confesses that he and all the Abingdon friends he's kept in touch with over the years are ardent Radiohead fans, owning all the band's albums and following their career with pride. "Thom Yorke was always very much a part of the music scene at the school," he says. "Whether it was mainstream or less so I don't think really mattered. Everybody was aware of his talent, and the fact that it was, and is, a very unique talent. Although it's fair to say that most of the guys in Radiohead were not part of the main school framework, there was no sense in which their obvious talent was subjugated to fit in with the mainstream view. I think everybody who's been at Abingdon has come away with the impression that no matter what their skills are, they're always there to be supported by the school."

Given that Abingdon School, despite its conservatism, offered plenty of opportunities for artistically inclined students to express themselves, and that the talents of the five future members of Radiohead seem to have been appreciated there to at least some degree, it may strike some observers as odd that in most of their later interviews the band have spoken about their Abingdon days dismissively, sometimes even disparagingly. Yet there's an easy explanation for this pronounced lack of fond reminiscence: Abingdon's beloved Headmaster Parker had a low tolerance for rock bands. In fact, he took it upon himself to ban electrically powered music from the school premises after another student band, one of TNT's punk descendants, got a bit too raucous at a function. All of a sudden, On A Friday needed a new place to play.

If Thom hadn't cared for Headmaster Parker before, this new affront added fuel to his fury: "It was when he banned music that I really knew I hated him. . . . I still hate him, and if I see or hear of him I get this deep sinking feeling."[38] Though Thom's anger may have been slow to subside, new rehearsal facilities were soon found. A nearby church hall looked like it would suit the purpose, and after the vicar had been assured that these youngsters were a serious jazz band, On A Friday were permitted to use the space. (It's uncertain whether the vicar ever realized the extent to which he had been duped by Yorke and company, but the group's inclusion of three saxophonists must have furthered the deception.)

By now, it was becoming clear that Thom, Colin, Ed, Phil, and Jonny had found something special in each other, something that they all wanted to contribute to and help develop. In Jonny's words, "I knew Thom was writing great songs and I knew what I wanted to do."[39] Yet On A Friday was fast approaching the crucial time that all bands of high school friends eventually reach, the time when high school ends and future directions are charted. Passing up college in favor of pursuing a career as a rock band simply wasn't an option for any of these five teenagers; they were all too talented academically, and besides, their families wouldn't have allowed it. (None of the Radiohead parents were incredibly supportive of the band in the early days, except for Ed O'Brien's father, whose interest in pop music reportedly borders on the maniacal: "[H]is dad will come in waving the music papers and want to discuss the new Primal Scream single," Colin once quipped.[40])

In the face of such postgraduation difficulties, most high school bands splinter forever, but this one would prove to be a remarkable exception. Phil, the first to leave the confines of Abingdon, had moved on in 1986 to Liverpool Polytechnic College, where he would major in English and history (in his spare time, he played drums in the pit bands of several musical productions). The following year, Ed enrolled at Manchester University, concentrating in economics, and Colin was accepted at Cambridge University's Peterhouse College, where he would major in English literature. But all three left no doubt of their firm allegiance to the band, continuing to rehearse and occasionally perform with the others when they returned to Oxford on weekends and holiday breaks. "The level of commitment, even when we were eighteen and nineteen, was pretty amazing," Ed recalls.

For his part, Phil puts his decision to attend university down to the need to keep himself occupied while the rest of the band finished their academic obligations. He downplays the role of parental pressure or any inner need to pursue a "straight" career path in case music didn't work out: "There was less design there, really. I mean, the age range in the band isn't huge, but at the time it made quite a difference. So when, say, I'd finished at school, everybody was still there. You know, I wanted to actually have something else to do at the same time, so I went on to university and then carried on through."*

To some observers, the members of On A Friday may have seemed to be going their own separate ways, but in reality, they were continuing to grow together as a band. By early 1987, they had begun to circulate their first demo tape, a limited-edition collection of six four-track recordings containing among others the now-forgotten numbers "Lemming Trail," "Fat Girl," and "Mountains (On the Move)." A copy of this tape made it into the hands of Dave Newton, who at the time ran a newspaper called *Local Support*. Started in the mid '80s, the paper was Oxford's first to be devoted solely to the local music scene. Based on his stewardship of *Local Support*, Newton was asked at the beginning of 1987 to head the music section of a new college publication called the *Oxford Enquirer*. The venture lasted for less than a

*Another, more amusing effect of the band's age range was the sometimes vast appearance differential between its members. As Colin put it in 1997, "We're still in our same classes and years, really. The thing about having been together for such a long period is that there are some heinously embarrassing group shots from ten years ago when we were in adolescence with varying styles of haircut and demeanor which would now be openly laughed at in the street. . . . You'd literally take a photograph of Morrissey to the barber and say, 'I want it like that.'"[41]

month before funding dried up and Newton went back to his previous job, but it was in the pages of the *Enquirer*'s February 24 issue that he gave On A Friday their first press notice, in the form of a brief demo tape review. "From the band's name and song titles I expected some dour bedroom Goth music," Newton wrote, "but happily I enjoyed the experience." Citing R.E.M., Green on Red, and the Prisoners as audible influences, he concluded, "Certainly a band worth hearing, and from what I hear a band worth seeing."

Not long after this encouraging review was published, Thom Yorke began his final term at Abingdon School. Even though he had been in frequent trouble in previous years, he'd never given up completely on his school work, and in his last year, he concentrated enough on it to excel in several subjects, winning class prizes in art and music. "I became a good boy and started working," he later commented sarcastically, adding that even during the earlier, more fraught times at Abingdon, "I didn't mind getting told off because I probably deserved it."[42]

After taking his A-level exams, though, Yorke elected to postpone college and take the next year off. He worked for a while in the menswear section at a local department store but quickly earned disfavor for being argumentative; he also served a stint as a bartender, during which time he made the acquaintance of a woman whose comments on his appearance he'd repeat several years later in a *Rolling Stone* interview: "You have beautiful eyes, but they're completely wrong."[43]

Like many teenage boys, Thom was interested in cars, and now that he was old enough to drive, he took full advantage of the opportunity. But his youthful auto infatuation would come to an abrupt halt following a nasty accident that took place during his time between Abingdon and college. Details on the accident are fuzzy, but we do know that Thom wrecked his car and that his girlfriend at the time, who was riding with him, suffered whiplash. Luckily, no one was seriously injured. Still, the crash colored Thom's outlook from that day forward. He became very wary on the road, and nursed a growing fear not just of cars but of any mechanized form of transport, a fear that would find its way into several future songs.

Mainly, Thom continued to work on music and to evade his father's bigger plans for him. "He felt I had talent for advertising," Thom said. "It was very embarrassing. He was always calling up advertising agencies for me, saying, 'Do you need anybody to wipe the floor for three months?' But Dad, I want to rehearse! Or, Dad, I want to sit at home and feel miserable!"[44] At the same time, Phil and Ed were busy with their classes up north. Colin was ensconced in his first year at Cambridge, and his brother was still more than three years away from leaving Abingdon, where he would eventually be cited in the school magazine as one of several students who "have . . . given untold service to school music throughout their time here."[45]

It was at this point of relative dispersal, ironically, that On A Friday played their first official club show, at Oxford's Jericho Tavern in the summer of 1987.

From the nominal center of Oxford at Carfax, the medieval tower that marks the spot where High Street (or the High, in city parlance) meets Cornmarket, it's approximately a fifteen-minute walk northwest, past the Ashmolean Museum and the splendid Georgian houses that line Beaumont Street, to the section of the city that's long been known—though why, no one can say—as Jericho. Immortalized by author Colin Dexter in the pages of his Inspector Morse mystery *The Dead of Jericho*, the area's two principal landmarks are the Radcliffe Infirmary and the headquarters of the Oxford University Press. On the whole, Jericho is a quiet residential neighborhood, its commercial outlets confined largely to Walton Street, the meandering avenue that forms its spine.

On the north corner of Walton and Jericho streets stands an unassuming two-story stone building that houses a pub, now called the Philanderer and Firkin. One of a chain of pubs owned by the Firkin brewery, it's notable mainly for its fake Edwardian décor and the cutesy placards on the walls that boast an array of groan-inducing puns: MIND YOUR FIRKIN HEAD, HAVE A FIRKIN BEER, and so on. Behind the bar on the ground floor, at the back of the building, a narrow flight of stairs leads up to the second floor, which contains a smaller bar and a midsized stage. The large windows facing the street help make the place look bigger than it actually is; capacity is approximately 120 people. Though this room is still referred to as the Jericho and local bands play here to this day, the Jericho Tavern as On A Friday knew it is long gone.

For nearly a decade, up until the middle of the 1990s, the Jericho Tavern was a central part of the Oxford scene, one of a handful of area venues that regularly offered live rock music. Its proprietor, Bob Woods, was friendly with many of Oxford's up-and-coming bands (including the members of On A Friday), and during his tenure, he transformed the place from a dingy, infrequently visited dive into a still-dingy but well-loved musicians' hangout. But in 1995, Woods' run of luck came to an end when the Firkin chain took over the Jericho and promptly got rid of the proprietor, claiming that they wanted their pub to have a "younger image." Their plan backfired. What once was an admittedly rough-and-ready but always crowded neighborhood linchpin is now a plastic pub, bright and clean but soullessly garish, and one that the youth of Oxford have not flocked to in anywhere near the numbers for which the new owners must have hoped.

Besides the outside shell of the building itself, little of Bob Woods' Jericho is left in the present-day Philanderer and Firkin. The stage is significantly smaller, and the dressing room that used to be behind the stage has been replaced by an unbecoming set of emergency doors. Yet on the ground floor, one architectural element from the Jericho's glory days remains: a beam stretching across the length of the ceiling to the left of the main bar, running directly underneath the floor of the music room. This beam was installed by friends of Woods as a safety precaution. On those frequent nights when a band would pack in over 200 people upstairs (well beyond official capacity), the movement of the crowd's feet made the floor shake. Downstairs, the undulations of the ceiling were clearly visible, and patrons of the main bar were justifiably nervous that the whole thing might come crashing down at any time.

It's unlikely that the Jericho's floor was shaking too much on the night that On A Friday made their debut there. Since this was the first show they'd played to an audience not composed completely of Abingdon classmates, the turnout was sparse. Fifteen-year-old Jonny, still not regarded as a full-time member of the band, sat onstage, harmonica in hand, "waiting for his big moment to arrive," as Phil later recalled.[46] Jonny and his older colleagues may have been excited about their bow as professionals, but at least one local musician who saw On A Friday around this time wasn't too impressed. Known only as Mac, he would in a few years provide an invaluable service to the band as the talent booker for the Jericho, but in 1987 he saw little talent there. "They were terrible," Mac remembers. "They obviously didn't know what they were doing. They had the three sax players, and they sounded like a bad version of Haircut One Hundred."

Mac wasn't alone in his lack of enthusiasm. Even Dave Newton of *Local Support*, who'd had positive things to say about the band's first demo tape, couldn't find much to recommend on their second. (It didn't help that the tape contained a whopping 14 songs.) "The horns certainly help to keep the attention," he wrote, "but the tape has very few outstanding tracks and those that did grab me were ruined by [Thom's] American accent. . . . It was hard work listening to this lot," Newton added with a trace of exasperation.[47]

Despite such reactions, the group continued to hone its live act over the next year whenever its members' class schedules allowed. Their most notable engagements included a date opening for the Icicle Works at Exeter College, Oxford; a gig at the London School of Economics; and a February 1988 show at the Old Fire Station on George Street in the center of Oxford, supported by a band called the Illiterate Hands, whose members included Jonny Greenwood and Andy Yorke. (As he had at Standlake Primary, Andy followed his older brother to Abingdon, where he and Jonny, both aspiring guitarists, had formed a fast friendship.) Dave Newton attended this show and wrote an amusing review of it in *Local Support* that's worth quoting at length:

An Old Fire Station packed to the hilt with boatloads of babycham/cider-drinking 14-year-old schoolgirls/boys left me feeling quite geriatric: especially as the bar shut at 9:30 and the evening faded before 10—so that they didn't miss the last bus back to Abingdon, I guess.

Not long after 8, on came the Illiterate Hands: the six of them looking like those nauseating kids from that Xmas Casio ad, and their accents and equipment perhaps showed that their parents had indeed been filling their Christmas stockings with the said Casio gear (from £200 to £2000). . . .

But still, the sound was anything but immature or pampered, walking a straight line through rock's past (and future?). The best thing this lot have got going for them is their songs—punchy, poppy, memorable tunes, neatly touched up by the lyrics. If they last past the sixth form, then the Illiterate Hands may well find a niche in pop's future.

Following this bunch, just after 9, were On A Friday, playing a rare gig in town. R.E.M. vocals (highlighted by the west-coast "Jumpin' Jack Flash"), neat pace, a touch of Stax and a touch of sax (three saxophones, to be precise!). Tight, entertaining, powerful, melodic, driving pop and most certainly foot-tapping (at least). . . .[48]

Soon after this gig, Jonny was finally rewarded for his perseverance by being accepted into the fold at long last as On A Friday's permanent keyboardist. (Following the demise of the Illiterate Hands, Andy Yorke would eventually put the lessons he'd learned with Jonny to good use in his own band, Unbelievable Truth, whose other members, Jason Moulster and Nigel Powell, had previously served time in a group called the Purple Rhinos.)

However, this change in personnel dynamics would not be noticed for some time by anyone outside the band's inner circle for the simple reason that the band was about to enter a long period of near invisibility. After much deliberation, Thom had decided to sign up for the coming academic year as an undergraduate in English and art at Exeter University, a decision that reportedly startled his parents. ("They were really shocked that I actually wanted to go to college," he remembered in *Option*.[49]) When he left Oxford for Exeter in the fall of 1988, any plans that On A Friday might have had for world domination were put on indefinite hold. Although they would continue to rehearse during holiday breaks, they would remain strangers to the stage for most of the next three years.

Did you already think in college that music was something you were going to carry on with?

COLIN: There wasn't anything else that was exciting at the time.

ED: That's really true.

PHIL: Yeah.

ED: Well, we were pretty certain . . . we didn't want to study music at college. I mean, *[laughs]* they wouldn't have us to study music at college. But you know, you don't have to be in a rock band and study music necessarily, although some great ones have, like John Cale.

PHIL: The fact that we actually kept on getting back together during that time . . .

ED: Was more important.

PHIL: Yeah. We all went off to different parts of the U.K., but we'd all still come back and actually get together and write new songs and just keep practicing, really. I mean, that's a good indication that we wanted to do something with it.

So you felt pretty certain that you were going to try and do something as a band.

PHIL: We did.

ED: Yeah, well, I mean, we'd talked about it for so long that we really had to. Otherwise, it would have been embarrassing, really.

(from an interview with Colin Greenwood, Ed O'Brien, and Phil Selway in Barcelona, Spain, May 21, 1997)

It wasn't long before Thom Yorke, in his new position as Exeter University undergraduate, began having his doubts about the true meaning and worth of higher education. His classes in English literature frequently drove him to despair, and as he would later remember, "[M]ost of my essays came to the conclusion: It's useless studying this work, who needs it? Matthew Arnold said literature was the new religion, and going to university and studying it means you worship these great works, which is a load of wank."[1] The art side of his major wasn't instilling great feelings of confidence in him either, although at least it allowed him to paint: "I was into Francis Bacon, so it was all red, white, and black. The only good painting I did during the first year was this guy blowing his brains out."[2] Increasingly bored, Thom spent more and more time away from class.

Such lack of enthusiasm about college could have been predicted, given Thom's previous tendencies toward skepticism, quick disillusionment with ideas, and hatred of authority. The immediate environment probably didn't help. Exeter, though home to one of England's great Gothic cathedrals and close to some of the country's most beautiful scenery in the wilds of Dartmoor, is one of the many British cities that "modernized" their centers in the post–World War II years, resulting in a distinct loss of character; take away the few major landmarks, and you could be in just about any midsized town in the United Kingdom. In so many of these sleepy English towns, the sense of aimlessness in the populace and lack of connection to the outside world (especially among the young) are almost palpable, feelings that the ultra-sensitive Yorke would have been certain to pick up on.

And yet the time spent in another city as a student did help Yorke come to better grips with something that had rankled him for years: the distaste he had felt growing up for the privileged young men and women who had arrived from elsewhere to attend university in his hometown. Now that he himself was one of those outside usurpers, the distaste only deepened. "I was embarrassed to be a student because of what the little fuckers got up to," he said in a *Q* interview[3] about his Exeter classmates. "Walking down the street to be confronted by puke and shopping trolleys and police bollards. Fucking hell, I used to think, no wonder they hate us. . . . If I was going to throw up, I did it in the privacy of my own room."

Vomiting wasn't the principal activity of Thom's stay at Exeter, of course, but the prodigious amount of alcohol he was consuming made it a more regular one than had previously been the case. Booze and drugs were easily found on campus, and Yorke indulged himself no less than most of his "embarrassing" fellow students—no less, for that matter, than his Oxford bandmates, who displayed similar tendencies toward dissipation during their college years. Drunkenness did have its creative benefits, however, as Thom's frequent alcoholic stupors often triggered the beginnings of songs. One such song was about being unable to communicate with others and hating yourself for it, about feeling like an outsider, a weirdo, a creep. It had promise, but Thom didn't like the lyrics much, so he set it aside for possible future work.

He may have been drinking more, but in other respects, Yorke's character hadn't changed at all—specifically when it came to his taste for bizarre apparel and argumentativeness. A combination of the two got him in trouble yet again early on in his undergraduate years. "In first year at college," he later remembered, "I went through this phase where I was into this granddad hat and coat I had. They were immaculate and I was into dressing like an old man. But I went out one night and there was these three blokes, townie guys, waiting to beat someone up and they found me. They said something, I turned around, blew them a kiss and that was it. They beat the living shit out of me. One was kicking me, one had a stick and the other was smashing me in the face."[4] This experience led Thom subsequently to tone down his confrontational nature and do his best to avoid getting into fights, a tactic that he employed more or less successfully through the rest of college.

Yorke has occasionally had positive things to say about his Exeter years. "At art school, you spend your entire time unlearning what you learnt," he said in 1995. "The college I went to was like a combination of a finishing school for upper-class idiots and one of the most exciting environments I've ever been in. It was a really buzzing environment, and it was there simply for people to work and express themselves. It was the first time I'd seen anything like that, other than in bedrooms with tape recorders. . . . You're totally left to your own devices, there's no substance to any of it unless you create it yourself, and I actually got a real buzz out of that." Even so, the experience left him with plenty of questions: "Art college is a wonderful environment, but I came out the end of it thinking, 'Why do you have to artificially set up an environment in which to work like that?'"[5] In the future, Thom would find himself asking similar questions about recording studios.

As it had been for more than a decade now, Yorke's real passion was invested in making music. At college, he got involved with an ad hoc student band called at first Headless Chicken and then simply Headless (after it was discovered that a band from New Zealand had already laid claim to the former name). The group, a sort of experimental punk/techno hybrid, played a total of 30 shows around Exeter and put out a limited-edition single, "I Don't Want to Go to Woodstock." By 1991, Headless had morphed into an even weirder project called Flickernoise, but Thom's membership in that outfit lasted for only one gig before he returned to Oxford. Headless' leader, who later went on to form the semi-industrial band Lunatic Calm and now goes by the enigmatic moniker sHack, was disappointed but not surprised by Yorke's departure. "It was always quietly asserted that [Thom's] loyalty was towards what he would call his 'Oxford band,'" he told Jonathan Hale.[6] Yet the legacy of Headless would not end in Exeter. One of the band's other members, violinist John Matthias, would eventually guest-star on Radiohead's second album, *The Bends*, the same album that included "High and Dry," which had originally been part of Headless' regular repertoire.

Thom had also become interested in dance music at college, informing himself about the acid house/rave craze that was beginning to sweep England in the late '80s and would only gather momentum in the next decade. Thom's occasional stints as a DJ in a campus club called the Lemon Grove became more common; within four months, the number of people attending the club on his nights mushroomed from around 200 people a week to over 1000. "That was an excuse to spend loads of money on records and be a cult figure," Yorke said. "It was great for my ego."[7]

Yet whenever it was time to go back home to Oxford, Thom would always reunite with the rest of his old Abingdon mates in On A Friday. And ironically, considering how long it had taken for the others to fully accept him into the band, Jonny Greenwood was becoming the person Thom most looked forward to seeing. In a short time, Jonny had progressed from relative exile as a part-time harmonica player to being Yorke's principal songwriting collaborator. The two spent a lot of time experimenting on Jonny's four-track cassette machine—a pleasurable experience that Thom would later express his desire to re-create during the recording of *The Bends* and *OK Computer*—and Thom was finding his junior partner to be a dab hand at putting the expert finishing touches on his sometimes rough compositions.

One event that helped turn Yorke away from solitary songwriting toward deeper collaboration with Jonny and the other members of the band was the reaction of one of his female friends upon hearing some early On A Friday demos. According to Yorke, this friend said, "Your lyrics are crap. They're too honest, too personal, too direct and there's nothing left to the imagination."[8] Instead of being cowed by these sharp comments, Thom came to a swift realization: His friend was right. "When I first started, I wasn't really interested in writing lyrics," he later explained, "which is strange in a way because if I don't like the words on a record, if it wasn't saying anything, I would never bother with it again. But at sixteen your own songs are half-formed and you don't really expect anyone to hear them, so you don't care what the words are. A big step for me was starting to work with Jonny and the others. And that would be a month after my friend said what she said. . . . I suddenly discovered that if I did concentrate on the lyrics I'd get much more out of writing and it would be easier to put a song together."[9]

During the infrequent school breaks when On A Friday would get together for rehearsals (and the odd gig, though there were very few of those), they would work on this new material, go over old songs, and perhaps most importantly, talk: about their favorite bands, about new music that was exciting them, and about their future plans as a group. Thom's long-held desire for rock stardom, which his parents had chuckled about when he was ten, had not abated in the slightest over the years, and the other four gave every indication that they would stand by him in his quest, though an element of pragmatism still governed their discussions to some degree. By 1989, they had begun to talk seriously about going for a record deal—but not until after everyone had finished college.

Inspiring them in this decision was the work of a group of "alternative" bands (a term that has been much abused in the years since the rise of Nirvana in 1991) that had quickly gained the affection of On A Friday's members. All of them were from the United States, and all of them had emerged from the network of American independent labels that had grown rapidly in the postpunk era. Everyone had his favorites. Thom adored the idiosyncratic stylings of Miracle Legion and Throwing Muses, while Colin leaned toward the morose musings of Mark Eitzel's American Music Club, and Jonny was a sucker for the protogrunge Neil Young–isms of Dinosaur Jr. Indeed, Jonny's taste for '80s rock bands to the exclusion of music from earlier eras would become the subject of much jesting by the others. As Ed puts it, "Jonny's always saying to us about these bands from the '70s: 'Who are the Who? Who are the Eagles? Who are the Stones? Oh, do you mean the Rolling Stones?' It's very endearing that someone should know Dinosaur Jr. better than the Who." Jonny's response: "Quite right, too. I'd rather listen to 'Freak Scene' than 'My Generation' or whatever."

There were at least two bands on whose importance every member of On A Friday could agree: R.E.M., from Athens, Georgia, and the Pixies, from Boston, Massachusetts. "When we were sort of getting our shit together in '89, '90," Ed remembers, "thinking about seriously trying to get a record deal once we'd finished college, R.E.M. and the Pixies were the two bands that we used to go down the pub and talk about after rehearsal. You know, 'They did it this way and that's how we want to do it.' There was an ethic there that we admired, and it extended to much more than the music as well."

By 1989, R.E.M. had become a mega-selling world phenomenon on the back of songs like "The One I Love" and "Stand"; they had also, to a large extent, left behind the Byrds-influenced "jangle-pop" that had once been their calling card. Though some stalwart fans of the band from the early days were beginning to lose interest, Thom Yorke and his bandmates saw the situation differently. R.E.M. had never ceased to grow artistically, and their move to a major label in the late '80s had done nothing to diminish their continuing development. Just as important, they hadn't let stardom change the way they behaved; they'd stayed close to their hometown and to the scene that spawned them. Such conduct was something the young Oxfordites wanted to emulate.

Similarly, the Pixies, led by the portly malcontent Charles Thompson (aka Black Francis), also brooked no artistic compromise, although they never managed to match the commercial success of R.E.M. Their music may have become somewhat smoother on the surface as their career went on, but the underlying dark humor and edgy non sequiturs in Thompson's lyrics, along with the band's love of extreme dynamic shifts (from soft to loud and back again) and making a good old-fashioned racket, were never lost. At their best, they were unsettling and liberating at the same time. "We all were very, very heavily into the Pixies," Ed says. "They were the most exciting band when we were at university. You always looked forward to a new album, and particularly when I heard *Doolittle* [released in the spring of 1989] for the first time, I remember thinking, 'Jesus, this is going to take a couple of listens to get my head round it.' And that's really important [a significant remark from one of the folks who brought you *OK Computer*], and then it's in there, and they're like nothing else." Thom's take on the band is more succinct: "The Pixies fucking rule. They were the best band ever, ever."*

The music of these and other American bands may have sparked schemes of stardom for On A Friday, but with everyone's studies still to be completed, any concrete action was still some time away. While Thom continued to labor at Exeter, the others polished off their degree requirements with little difficulty. Phil, the first to graduate, took a postgrad course in publishing at Oxford Polytechnic and signed on as a subeditor at a medical publishing house; he also briefly taught English to foreign-language students and became involved with the Samaritans, a group devoted to counseling troubled and suicidal teenagers (years later, he'd turn into something of a spokesman for the organization). Ed, the next to depart, spent time as a bartender and a photographer's assistant following the end of his course at Manchester.

Colin, meanwhile, had become the head entertainments officer at Peterhouse College, organizing parties and similar events that often involved the booking of musical acts; not coincidentally, quite a few of those acts included Colin as a member. After finishing at Cambridge, where his final thesis was on the short stories of Raymond Carver—a choice that, like his interest in the songs of Mark Eitzel, reflected his fascination with American writers who specialize in depicting ordinary people's damaged lives—he got into retail, working at an Our Price record store in

---

*Thom's particularly strong love of the Pixies may also have had something to do with Black Francis' pronounced lack of visual appeal as a frontman. For someone who was painfully self-conscious about his looks, the fact that a chubby, average-looking guy could make exciting, viable rock music *that people actually listened to* must have been an inspiration.

Oxford.* Like Phil and Ed, he worked primarily to make some extra cash and to kill time until the band was ready to go professional, but his choice of job would soon prove to be advantageous in a way that nobody could have foreseen.

The drudgery of Thom's time at Exeter was partly relieved in later years by an important acquisition by the university's art department: several new Apple Macintosh computers, with (at the time) state-of-the-art design software. Yorke, who had previously come to the conclusion that he wasn't much of a painter (a conclusion seconded by his teachers), was captivated by the technology and its possibilities, and it led him to embark on a rather droll senior project that would help him earn his degree in the spring of 1991: a virtual repainting of a Michelangelo classic. "I scanned the whole of the Sistine Chapel into a hard disk, changed all the colors and called it my own," he later reported.[10] With this playful gesture, Thom bade a not-so-fond farewell to the groves of academe and went back home to Oxford to start the next phase of his life.

Another bright spot enlivening Thom's Exeter years was his meeting with a fellow student named Rachel Owen. The two didn't get along that well at first, but Rachel eventually saw her way past the less pleasing aspects of Thom's personality, and they started going out seriously. "I pursued her," Yorke remembered, "but in all the wrong ways, because I was . . . terrified of her. You're always terrified of the ones you fancy, yeah? But in my funny way I was very tenacious. . . . She really thought I was a freak. She thought I was impossible to talk to, really moody, diffi-

*There were two branches of Our Price in Oxford at the time. The one where Colin worked was located in a shopping mall called the Westgate Centre and still exists to this day, while the other, on Cornmarket Street just a few doors down from the tourist-thronged Carfax Tower, has since become a Moss Brothers men's clothing store. It was apparently a rite of passage for Oxford scenesters to work at Our Price; Colin took a job that had previously been held by Dave Newton and by Ronan Munro, editor of the early-'90s music paper *Curfew*.

cult, unpleasant and idiotic. And I think I was. But she bashed a lot of that crap out of me."[11] Evidently so, because as of this writing, Thom and Rachel are still together.

Now that Yorke, On A Friday's central creative force, was finished with his studies and had rejoined his Oxford friends, it was time for the band to begin putting into action the plans that they had been talking about for at least the past couple of years. The three-piece horn section was by now ancient history, and Jonny was officially On A Friday's third guitarist and sometime keyboardist. Despite the fact that the younger Greenwood had yet to begin college (he was due to start a joint course in psychology and music at Oxford Polytechnic in the fall), it was decided that from this point on they would do their best to gain some local notice, which they hoped would lead to something more substantial down the road.

In April over the Easter break, the band had recorded a three-song demo tape at the Dungeon, a 16-track recording studio near Oxford. The demo included the tracks "Give It Up" (a light, dancy number, far from the mood of the music they'd make later but adding flesh to the early comparisons with Haircut One Hundred), "What Is That You See?" (a clanging, R.E.M.-ish tune, later described by Jonny as a "feedback frenzy"),[12] and "Stop Whispering" (a two-chord anthem along the lines of U2's "Bad"). Richard Haines, the Dungeon's owner and principal engineer, who has also produced the Candyskins and Dr. Didg, among others, remembers those sessions as "very comfortable, no problems. They were already a tight, accomplished band at that stage, though musically they were still finding their way to the direction that they wanted to go in. Even then it was fairly clear that Thom was a really together guy—he seemed to know what he wanted out of the songs and out of the session. By that I don't mean that the others were just sitting around doing his word, because they weren't. It's just that he had a vision of what the overall picture should be. That's quite rare in bands, to have one person that's got such a definite view and is unswerving in that view, and that helps focus the whole band."

Haines wasn't overly impressed with "What Is That You See?" or "Give It Up," though he admits that "by the end of the session, it was hard to judge because I'd heard them so many times." But "Stop Whispering" stuck in his head: "At that time, I was quite into U2, as a lot of people were, and that one track had a similar feeling which made it stand out. I wouldn't say it was completely obvious to me what would happen with them from just those few days of recording, but it wasn't a surprise when things started to firm up for them later on." If Colin Greenwood can be believed, the band had a great time recording at the Dungeon. "I bumped into Colin after they did *The Bends*," Haines remembers, "and I hadn't seen him since they did that demo. He said that they had the best memories of that session, because it was their first time, I suppose—there often is a sort of romantic attachment to the first time you record as a band. He may have said it just to be polite to me as well, but it was sweet of him to say that."

Simply called *On A Friday*, the Dungeon demo tape was duplicated and passed around to anyone who exhibited half an interest, including some Oxford-area club owners and members of the press. Handling the day-to-day business side of the band— sending out tapes, getting gigs, making contacts—had become principally Ed O'Brien's territory. John Harris, at the time an Oxford University student and sometime correspondent for *Melody Maker*, later to become the editor of the British music magazine *Select*, remembered: "There's always someone in a band that takes on a quasi-managerial role and for them it was Ed. He sent me a couple of letters—on On A Friday notepaper—saying, 'I'm in this group, come and see us.' To be honest, I ignored them."[13] It was a common reaction.

Around this time, the members of On A Friday also decided that if they were going to be a band, they should all live in one house. After all, the annals of rock history teem with well-known bands that at one point or another, usually early in their careers, pooled their resources and lived communally. (The late '60s, of course, fostered an inordinately large number of such domestic arrangements, from the group houses of Haight-Ashbury outfits like the Grateful Dead and Jefferson Airplane to Big Pink, the legendary upstate New York home of the Band.) By not only playing together but also living together, the band could strengthen its interpersonal bonds, which could in turn help them make further creative strides. Or at least that was the idea. In any case, Phil, Colin, and Ed were already jointly renting a semidetached house on Ridgefield Road near the center of Oxford, and so it seemed only logical that Thom, who'd taken a job selling secondhand clothes, and Jonny, who'd just graduated from Abingdon, should move in as well.

This communal living experiment turned out to be far from ideal. At times, it veered toward utter disastrousness. "At first it was quite a nice house," Yorke later remembered, "but we turned it into a complete fucking hole. We'd just begun taking the band seriously, so there were musical instruments everywhere. We ripped half the wallpaper off taking the Hammond organ in and out. There was always fag ash everywhere. Plus, the carpet would roll down the stairs every time you went up them."[14] Jonny was silently excused from most types of house maintenance due to his youth. Unfortunately, the others weren't crazy about keeping the place up. Phil was rarely home, and when he was around, he'd usually accuse the others of eating his food, an accusation that was completely true but that rankled nonetheless.

The choice of tunes with which to regale the house on the group stereo also became a frequent source of conflict. The affection for dance music that Thom had developed during his Exeter years and continued to cultivate with occasional engagements as a DJ around Oxford was not shared by his bandmates. Colin, who was already forced to listen to a fair amount of disco fodder during the day while working at Our Price, was particularly incensed by Yorke's listening tastes: "All I wanted to do in the evenings was sit around and listen to the Pale Saints, but Thom would stick on this horrendous techno music. He got pretty short shrift from the rest of us."[15]

Making matters worse was the fact that none of the band were exactly inspired cooks. According to Thom, it was a case of all pesto sauce, all the time. "All the things we cooked had to have pesto in. . . . A month after I moved out I ate some pesto and started feeling really sick. I haven't eaten it since."[16] To top it all off, the house was haunted, in a sense. "It was a bit eerie," Colin said later, "because the woman who'd lived there before had died. I think she died in the house. And Ed and I kept on finding things which had obviously belonged to her. Combs, half-empty fag packets, stuff like that. One day we found this half-eaten porkpie down the back of the sofa. It must've been there for months but you could still see the teeth marks. Of course, being morbid people, we managed to convince ourselves that she'd choked on it."[17]

On A Friday's new living situation didn't last long; the lease on the Ridgefield Road house ran out in a year, and only Thom and Colin mustered the stamina to stay there till the bitter end. But the band did manage to successfully relaunch itself onto the Oxford music scene in the summer of 1991. That scene was a small but fertile one, composed mainly of what were just starting to be called "shoegazer" bands—vaguely psychedelic-sounding combos like Ride and Swervedriver, whose live shows featured lots of dense guitar noise and band members resolutely staring at the floor. It centered around three main institutions: the Jericho Tavern (where On A Friday had made its official concert debut four years earlier), a record store called Manic Hedgehog (which would soon find its name closely connected to On A Friday's), and the local music paper *Curfew* (which published the first ever interview with the band in December of '91—and a cover story to boot). On A Friday's music didn't quite fit in with the prevailing trends, but they were interesting enough to attract at least occasional attention.

Many people, Americans in particular, may assume that in an urban community, the presence of a great university and a healthy music scene go hand in hand. But such has not been the case in Oxford, where local musicians and university students almost never mix. John Harris, one of the few notable exceptions to this rule, posits that the Oxford music community's rapid growth in the late '80s and early '90s owed more to the city's small size than to any kind of college crowd. "One of the reasons why there were so many local groups in Oxford was that it was very rare that a national tour by a name band would ever call there, because there was nowhere medium-sized to play. Unless you played the Jericho, which was very small, or the Polytechnic could fit you in, which wasn't often, there was nowhere for you to go. Since no national names ever played in Oxford, it was kind of 'make your own entertainment.'"

The three-song demo Ed had been passing around helped get the band a few gigs around town, most notably at the Jericho. Their first show after Thom's return from Exeter, however, was at a club called the Hollybush on North Street in Osney, near Oxford, on July 22, 1991, to an audience of six. Those early shows were well received by the few who attended; Yorke's dramatic singing style and frighteningly intense onstage demeanor—one moment tightly focused, the next seemingly ready to burst open—were already coming to the fore, and while the band's sound was still somewhat rudimentary garage, the sheer visceral appeal of three loud electric guitars playing in tandem made up for many of the less developed musical moments. Barry Beadle, owner of the Hollybush, particularly remembered the striking differential between Thom's onstage and offstage personae: "I remember the veins used to stand out onstage. . . . [H]e really went for it, but when he wasn't onstage he was quite passive. There was a major contrast between the two characters."[18]

Between gigs and rehearsals that summer, Thom and Jonny would occasionally engage in a kind of musical side project, venturing out onto the streets of Oxford with their guitars and playing for spare change. It was a humbling experience. "Tramps started throwing two pences at us," Jonny later recalled, "and we knew the only way we'd make money was if we played R.E.M. songs. . . . [O]ne time Ride, who were big local stars, walked past and actually stopped to listen. . . . Well, erm, it wasn't that much of a big thing."[19] Actually, according to *Curfew*'s Ronan Munro, the early interest of local bands like Ride played a major part in getting On A Friday noticed. "I first heard about them because other Oxford bands liked them and mentioned them to me," he remembers. "The Candyskins and the Purple Rhinos were big fans early on. Bands rated them more than punters. They were lucky to get fifty people to their gigs, but most of those fifty would have been in other bands, which I always think is quite a good sign."

Getting regular gigs at this stage of the game was crucial for On A Friday, and so in a sense their demo had already served its purpose well. But far more importantly, the tape also wound up in the hands of a local musician and producer who'd been looking for a break for years and whose entrance into the band's lives would dramatically affect his and their future course.

Though he was now making his living (barely) operating a recording studio, Chris Hufford had once had bigger plans. In the '80s, he and his longtime colleague Bryce Edge had both been members of a New Romantic band called Aerial FX, in which Bryce played keyboards while Chris switched between guitar, bass, and vocals.

For a time, they'd been signed to a major label (EMI, no less, a fact which would later prove significant), but their synth-pop stylings hadn't attracted many fans, and so Hufford and Edge detoured into other areas. In 1987, they got into the real estate game, becoming partners in a new development called Georgetown, named after its principal developer, George Taylor. The mixed residential/business complex was located in the village of Sutton Courtenay, just down the road from Abingdon and best known to nonlocals as the place where George Orwell is buried. As something of a nod to the partners' musical interests, the complex included a 24-track recording studio. Acoustically designed by Bryce, who'd been trained as an architect, the facility, originally called Georgetown Studio, opened in February 1988.

The new studio had been intended as a souped-up replacement for Chris' previous eight-track setup, located in a rented barn from which he'd been evicted for making too much noise. The principal purpose of the studio at first was to indulge Hufford and Edge's creative whims; bringing in outside clients ran a distant second and was only even considered in order to subsidize the owners' activities—"a bit naïve really," as Chris later recalled.[20]

Unfortunately, the Georgetown complex was no more a financial success than Aerial FX had been. The cost of the project escalated rapidly, and revenue was slow to come in. By 1990, Hufford and Edge had to sell off their share of the development to keep their heads above water, but the new owners were gracious enough to let the duo keep control of the studio as renters. Turning this kind gesture to their advantage, Chris and Bryce began actively soliciting local musicians to come in and use their recording facilities. "I realized that I had to run the place on a strictly businesslike basis and couldn't afford to subsidize bands," Hufford said.[21] While Bryce helmed the business side, Chris manned the console as needed; he produced several artists, the most notable being the darkly atmospheric Slowdive. None of them was more than a cult phenomenon, but they helped pay the rent.

One day sometime in late 1990, so the story goes, a fellow named John Butcher, a close friend of Hufford's assistant, came into Georgetown with a tape featuring two of his old classmates at Abingdon School, Thom Yorke (or Thom E. Yorke, as he billed himself back then, possibly inspired by the Fall's frontman Mark E. Smith) and Colin Greenwood. These were On A Friday's early, crude, rampantly schizophrenic four-track demos. "You couldn't hear any one band on it," Hufford later said of that first tape. "There were some good tunes but it was all obviously ripped off mercilessly."[22] One song stuck out, however, a track that Hufford remembered as "a weird looped-up dance thing which was completely mental but had something about it that was very different."[23]* Always on the lookout for new up-and-coming groups to bring into Georgetown (and thus make the place some money and maybe even raise his own profile), Hufford told Butcher to see if the band had any more songs they'd like him to hear.

No one has ever determined whether or not Thom and Colin actually asked Butcher to submit their music to Hufford, but it's hard to imagine that Butcher volunteered his services as an intermediary without the band's knowledge. Yorke and Greenwood certainly knew of their former classmate's studio connection, and they also couldn't help but be aware of how much it might cost them to make a professional demo. The bill for their April date at the Dungeon alone was over £300.† Continuing at that rate, the

---

*This song was probably an early Yorke composition entitled "Rattlesnake," which Jonny Greenwood later called "a drum loop that Thom did himself at home on a tape recorder with bad scratching over the top and kind of Prince vocals."[24]

†Richard Haines says that in 1991 his standard studio rate was £12 (approximately $20) an hour, and he recalls that On A Friday booked the Dungeon for three days, each day lasting approximately ten hours.

band would soon be deep in debt; in order to keep recording, they would have to find a sympathetic studio willing to cut them some slack. Maybe Georgetown, the only affordable 24-track facility in the area, could help.

About six months later, in the summer of '91, Butcher returned to Hufford's studio, recently renamed Courtyard, with a new tape, the three-song demo that On A Friday had recorded during Easter vacation. The band's sound was still rough and uncertain, but there was the germ of something there; the songwriting had improved tremendously, and the lead singer had definite possibilities. Hufford liked what he heard and was duly invited to one of their upcoming gigs at the Jericho Tavern.

This at least is the official story, and though there is no reason to disbelieve it, there are problems with it. First, it is extremely difficult to verify the existence of John Butcher; no one that I have spoken to in Oxford while researching this book can recall such a person, and the manner in which Mr. Butcher enters our tale and then disappears without a trace, as if on cue, is remarkable. One is reminded of the case of Raymond Jones, the mysterious leather-clad Liverpool youth whose alleged request for a hard-to-find German 45 one day in 1961 led Brian Epstein to discover the Beatles, and who was many years later revealed to have been a fiction, created for the convenience of the band's press agent.

Second, Dave Newton, an acquaintance of Chris Hufford's and a keen observer of the Oxford scene at this time, doubts strongly that Hufford had an assistant in 1991. His recollection is that although Chris may have heard On A Friday's demos before seeing them live, he was not directly invited to one of their gigs, having instead seen them by chance while escorting his clients Slowdive around town.* Of course, it doesn't matter much whose

---

*This opinion seems to be backed up by a feature on Hufford that appears in the February 1992 issue of *Curfew*.

account is closest to the truth, for the end of the story is the same: Chris Hufford was present at On A Friday's Jericho Tavern performance on August 8, 1991. Ronan Munro was there too, covering the show for *Curfew*. It was his first time seeing the band as well, and in his enthusiastic review, he made the prediction that On A Friday would soon be "extremely famous and you['ll] swear that you were there at the beginning."[25]

What Hufford saw and heard that midsummer night came as a pleasant shock. "I was completely blown away," he recalled. "All the elements of Radiohead were there. It was a lot rougher, a lot punkier, quite frenetic and a faster tempo. But they were still very musical, the songs were well put together, and Thom's stage presence was something else."[26] Indeed, even more than the songs and the sheer power of the band's three-guitar attack, it was Thom's performance that won Hufford over: "Out of all those Thames Valley bands of the time, there were no performers or great singers, but Thom was incredible. . . . I was so excited by them. They had fantastic energy. I could see it on a world level, even then."[27]

After the show, Chris approached the band and told them that, as Colin later remembered it, "we were the best group he'd seen in three years."[28] Hufford said he "made a complete buffoon of myself, bursting backstage saying, 'I've got to work with you!' "[29] Buffoonish or not, his offer was accepted. The price was certainly right; in exchange for doing whatever they could to help the studio, the five members of the band got unlimited time to record their demo for £100 each.

In October, On A Friday recorded a new five-song tape with Hufford at Courtyard, including three songs—"I Can't," "Thinking About You," and "You"—that would later appear on their debut album, *Pablo Honey,* albeit in re-recorded and less frantic form. The other two selections, "Nothing Touches Me" and "Philippa Chicken," were stage favorites at the time, but the band soon tired of them. The former is an aggressive, catchy number that was apparently based on the true story of a talented painter imprisoned for child molestation, while the latter is a goofy, country-flavored romp with a "Ticket to Ride" drumbeat and stream-of-consciousness lyrics.

This latest recording was released in cassette form and sold locally for £3 at Manic Hedgehog, the independent record store on Cowley Road that was one of the centers of the Oxford scene.* For this reason, it's been known ever since as *Manic Hedgehog,* even though those two words appear nowhere on the package. The spine of the cassette J-card actually bears the legend ON A FRIDAY *first tapes*—not strictly true, but how many out there would know?—while the front cover features a simple cartoon, probably by Thom, of an odd-looking creature with a stretched head similar to the aliens in Steven Spielberg's *Close Encounters of the Third Kind.* Next to this image is scrawled the pithy slogan WORK SUCKS.

The assistance that Hufford and Edge lent the band, first in recording the tape and then putting it out, was quickly moving them beyond the role of producers to that of managers, a direction that On A Friday went along with, gratified that people who understood the music business better than they did thought the band was doing something worthwhile. "Management had never been an ambition," Hufford once explained. "We'd always thought managers were complete tossers. But we'd learnt a lot. We thought, 'Let's be management where you put yourself in the artist's shoes.' We were naïve about a lot of the business but we totally believed in the band."[30] Yet the next major development for On A Friday had little to do with anyone's professional guid-

*Manic Hedgehog, which was run by a fellow whom most remember as an "unregenerate hippie," sold many local bands' demo tapes during the early '90s. The store went out of business a few years later after its proprietor forgot to pay his VAT taxes and fled town to avoid creditors. No one in Oxford has seen him since.

ance—it was something for which only the mysterious forces of chance can be held accountable.

In the summer of 1991, Keith Wozencroft, a sales representative for one of Britain's biggest and most fabled recording organizations, EMI, was making his last tour of duty around England's record stores. He was about to transfer to another part of the company, becoming an A&R man, or talent scout, for Parlophone, which had become famous in the '60s as the Beatles' British label. One of the main reasons for this trip was to say good-bye to his most faithful customers and wish them well. His list of faithful customers included the same Our Price store in Oxford at which Colin Greenwood worked. It just so happened that while Wozencroft was paying his visit, he struck up a conversation with Greenwood. When Wozencroft told Colin about his impending move to A&R, Colin saw an opportunity. "Oh, I'm in a band," he said, and he gave the rep a tape containing some of On A Friday's demos.

Of course, this kind of exchange—record company employee meets would-be rock star, who duly passes demo along for audition—happens all the time, with no results for anyone; most of the time, the tape never gets heard. But Wozencroft, about to start in a new position, was looking for any kind of tip he could find to get himself noticed. And so he listened. The tape, he later remembered, "had some really odd old stuff on it, but also a rough demo of 'Stop Whispering.'"[31] His interest piqued, Wozencroft caught the band at a Sunday open-air gig in Oxford Park: "There was no one there in this little tent apart from a couple of their girlfriends. But they played really well."[32] Though he had to leave the show early, Wozencroft left a message for the band with the soundman, saying that he thought they were great and that he'd keep in touch. Famous last words—but Parlophone's newest A&R man kept his promise.

Upon returning to EMI's London office and starting his new

65

job, Keith Wozencroft met with his boss Nick Gatfield, the director of EMI's A&R department (who'd once been the sax player in the brief '80s sensation Dexy's Midnight Runners), and made his first recommendation of an artist he felt the label should go for: On A Friday. At the same time, aware that the band's tape had made it into the hands of EMI personnel, Hufford and Edge began re-establishing the contacts they had at the label from their Aerial FX days.* Keeping all their bases covered, they also mailed out copies of the Manic Hedgehog tape to various people they knew at other British record companies. The result was a sudden industry buzz. By November, when Wozencroft finally enticed Gatfield and the rest of his A&R team to come up to Oxford and see On A Friday play at the Jericho (Wozencroft himself had seen nearly every show the band had played that fall), they were confronted by the sight of over 20 other record company representatives in the audience. Within a few months, On A Friday had gone from being complete unknowns to being the band every label wanted.

The EMI team loved the band's performance, but so did everyone else, and the contract offers came fast and furious. Wozencroft was a little surprised by it all. "Because I was new to the role," he later said, "it never occurred to me that the band might go with anyone else. [But] Gatfield put a good offer in straightaway and it was fine. We didn't mess around."[33] For their part, both On A Friday's managers and the band themselves found Gatfield's offer the most agreeable, feeling that of all their corporate suitors EMI would give them the greatest amount of artistic freedom. ("We wanted to stay in control like R.E.M.," Ed O'Brien explained in *Billboard*.[34]) They had also appreciated Wozencroft's early interest in the group. A deal was quickly put in motion.

Among the options Gatfield and Wozencroft discussed with Hufford and Edge was the possibility of issuing the band's music

*Dave Newton believes that Hufford and Wozencroft already knew each other well, which may have helped the band's cause.

on a nominally independent label that would in fact be EMI-controlled, perhaps even creating a label for this specific purpose. The reason for this was simple. British pop music at the time was dominated by indie labels like Alan McGee's Creation Records, and artists signed to the majors weren't getting a great deal of respect in the national press. Traveling the route of pseudo-independence could enhance On A Friday's perceived credibility and would also give EMI access to the indie charts. In the end, the band declined to participate in this mild form of subterfuge, resolving to take their chances as a major-label act. Ironically, this honest decision would later be derided in some quarters as a sell-out. "That sort of thing is such a British problem," Thom commented wearily. "The British hate success. . . . We're *not* an indie band. We write pop songs, but some people can't see that."[35]

In mid-November, while negotiations with EMI were still under way, the members of On A Friday sat down with *Curfew*'s Ronan Munro for an interview. Interest in the band had grown so quickly that Munro figured the paper might miss its chance if he waited much longer to talk to them. Luckily, the band, who liked *Curfew*, were happy to grant his request. By this time, Ronan had seen several On A Friday performances, including an ill-fated gig at Oxford Polytechnic that had permanently altered his opinion of the band: "Everything went wrong that night—no one was there, the sound was terrible, and Thom was having a tantrum. But they were fantastic. Thom would just go into this amazing sort of howl when he sang. Up to that point, I thought they were good but not particularly special. That show changed things for me." He'd also gotten to know Colin fairly well through his regular delivery of papers to the Our Price store in Westgate Centre where the bassist worked. "Colin had a reputation as being the nicest man in Oxford music, and deservedly so, although I used to think he looked a bit like Christopher Walken—eyes so deep that you can't quite see what expression's on his face."

Munro was less familiar with the other members of the band (the fact that he misspelled Thom's name in the final piece—leaving out the *h*—is evidence enough of this), so as he trudged over to On A Friday's communal house on Ridgefield Road for a brief chat, he wasn't sure what to expect. Once he got there, he was amused to find that, far from behaving like rock-stars-to-be, the first-time interviewees' reactions bordered on outright fear. "I was always really nervous about interviewing people," Ronan confesses. "I hated it. But they were *terrified* of me being there." Jonny, his hair cut unbecomingly short, "looked emaciated, like he'd been rescued from a concentration camp." Thom, similarly close-cropped, was "so incredibly shy. He still is—people think he's [stand-]offish, but he's not."

Yorke may have been shy, but in his quiet way he left no doubt of his drive to be successful. The *Curfew* piece closes with this revealing quote from him: "People sometimes say we take things too seriously, but it's the only way you'll get anywhere. We're not going to sit around and wait and just be happy if something turns up. We are ambitious. You have to be."[36]

On December 21, 1991, the five members of On A Friday and their management went down to London to sign their official recording contract with Parlophone. Wozencroft remembers the event as brief but happy: "[W]e went to this restaurant and then we went to a bar and got pissed and then they caught the bus back to Oxford."[37] While the band was still in the EMI offices, celebrating the signing with some champagne, Rupert Perry, one of the company's top executives, stopped in for a few friendly words. As Hufford recalled it, "He [Perry] told Jonny his favorite track was 'Philippa Chicken.' Jonny said, 'That's funny, because we've dropped it.' It was an indication that the band was always going to do their own thing."[38] Indeed, EMI's newest signing would prove to be stubbornly independent-minded and resistant to any attempts at direction. In the months and years ahead, there would be plenty of headaches on both sides.

The first major decision that followed On A Friday's signing had to do with the academic future of the group's youngest member, the one who'd talked back to Rupert Perry. At the time, Jonny Greenwood was in the middle of his first term studying psychology and music at what was then called Oxford Polytechnic College and has since been renamed Oxford Brookes University. A completely separate institution from Oxford University, its campus is located at the top of Headington Hill on the east side of town, boasting a commanding view of the city center's dreaming spires.

Jonny's principal tutor at the Polytechnic was an unusual fellow, it is said; in his earlier years, before ending up as a college professor, he'd apparently been the inspiration for the character of Charlie Kay in Hanif Kureishi's celebrated 1990 novel *The Buddha of Suburbia*. Kureishi portrays Kay as a well-bred product of an English public school whose life is transformed by rock 'n' roll. (Sound familiar?) Changing his name to Charlie Hero, he forms a punk band, moves to New York, and gets heavily involved in the decadent downtown scene of the late '70s. According to Colin, the story conforms quite closely to that of the real-life Charlie, his brother's teacher: "He used to live with Iggy Pop," the bassist said in wonder.[39]

Charlie's understanding of Jonny's interest in rock music was an unexpected benefit. When the EMI deal was in the works, Jonny deliberated about what to do, but his tutor, Colin claims, encouraged him to drop out of school and devote himself to the band with the simple words "Go for it." This encouragement helped ease the younger Greenwood's way from one career path to another more potentially exciting but far less certain one.*

Not everyone in the band fully endorsed Jonny's move. Ed

*As wonderful as this story sounds, it doesn't seem to be completely true. No one I spoke to in Brookes University's psychology or music departments recalled anyone from this era fitting Charlie's description. Dai Griffiths, the head of Brookes' music faculty, remembers Jonny fondly, but says, "Since he was only here for about three weeks, it's possible he never figured out who was actually a member of the faculty and who was just hanging around."

O'Brien was especially skeptical, repeatedly asking Jonny if he was sure about what he was doing. It's likely, though, that this had more to do with intraband competition between the guitarists than anything else. "He was trying to oust me," Jonny later said with a laugh. "I could see him, sharpening his plectrum behind my back."[40]

Jonny's decision to leave Oxford Polytechnic wasn't a decision the Greenwoods' mother liked very much either. Brenda Greenwood had never been keen on the notion of her sons becoming full-time rockers. "She thinks I should be getting into law or accountancy," Colin would later claim.[41] And she refrained from telling their elderly grandfather about the EMI signing for quite some time, thinking, in Colin's words, that "it would finish him off."[42] But hesitantly, she went along with her boys' choice. After all, they could always go back to school, or to real jobs, when the music didn't work out.

At the time On A Friday signed with EMI, the British music scene was still in the throes of the "baggy" movement. (General rule: Whenever a musical style becomes widely known by a term relating not to any element within the music itself but rather to a style of apparel favored by its listeners, one has to question that music's artistic relevance.) Manchester bands like the Stone Roses and Happy Mondays had harnessed derivative rock to house beats in the late '80s and started a sensation that had filtered down to all parts of the country. Now even new up-and-comers from the London area sounded like they'd just stepped off the latest train from the North. The most obvious example of this bandwagon-jumping, Blur, released their heavily

4

Manchester-influenced debut album, *Leisure,* in 1991, before going on to greater success in later years by putting their own ironic spin on classic Kinks-style British pop.

Bubbling under the Mancunian castoffs that headed the hit parade were the aforementioned "shoegazers." Many of them, like Ride and Slowdive, hailed either from Oxford or the surrounding Thames Valley area, but the kings of shoegazing were actually Irish. They called themselves My Bloody Valentine, and their 1991 release, *Loveless,* both summed up the genre and surpassed it, offering something of a dissertation on how epic waves of searing guitar noise could become melodic in the right hands. After making their case so well, MBV promptly dropped off the map, going more than nine years without a follow-up album.

In both the mainstream and the underground, 1991's British pop music was a triumph of style over substance. There didn't seem to be much place for a sincere, directly emotional band like On A Friday. But shock waves coming across the ocean from America signaled that a change might be afoot. For 1991 was also the year that Nirvana's epochal *Nevermind* was released. A mixture of punk and heavy rock with streaks of Beatlesque pop, the album took the U.S. charts by storm, fueling the stylistic phenomenon eventually known as "grunge" (and setting every record label in the country on a desperate quest to sign any band hailing from Nirvana's home base of Seattle).

Ed O'Brien remembers the excitement he felt the first time he heard Nirvana. "I thought, 'God, this is great, this has just taken the Pixies and moved on a bit.'" (Nirvana's frontman Kurt Cobain wasn't shy about acknowledging his debt to Black Francis and crew.) Musically speaking, On A Friday didn't have much in common with Nirvana—there was little about them that could be called grungy—but the fact that Cobain's songs seemed torn from his soul, and that his lyrics were by turns tortured and oblique, suggested that rock listeners were interested in something more emotionally affecting than they'd been getting for the past few years. Maybe there was a place out there for On A Friday after all.

Yet one opinion was swiftly growing among those close to the group: There was no place anywhere for a band that called itself On A Friday, no matter how promising its music might be. Although Thom Yorke, with perhaps just a touch of exaggeration, would later call On A Friday "the worst band name ever,"[1] it had served the band decently and gone largely unchallenged for more than five years. Dave Newton says that in a strange, perhaps unintentional way, the name had been a good choice: "It was such a stereotypical local band name that it stuck out in listings—you remembered it because it was so obviously parochial." Of course, for most of the time they'd been called On A Friday, Thom and his mates had been off attending college. Their music hadn't been made available to the general public during that time; it hadn't even been a top priority of the band members themselves.

But now the whole situation was different. On A Friday was signed to a major record label, and everything they did was under scrutiny. They'd already had to fend off the company's resident style experts—who, in a vain attempt to brighten up the band's image, ordered them to buy £300 worth of snappy secondhand clothes, most of which they never wore—and the hapless A&R assistant who insisted that what On A Friday needed most was a written agenda or manifesto of what they wanted to achieve in the music industry and who was allegedly sacked within two months for his trouble. The next necessary issue to address was the dreaded name question.

From the start of their dealings with On A Friday, EMI had made no bones about being unhappy with the band's name, but they hadn't forced the group to change it immediately. Keith Wozencroft and Nick Gatfield didn't want to get anyone's dander up so soon into the game, and they hoped that over time the band would come to see for themselves the disadvantages of an uninspired handle. The result was that for two months following their signing, the quintet dragged their feet, continuing to play shows under the familiar name while promising that a new one was on the way. In the end, it took pressure from the outside, in the form of a critical February 1992 concert review in the national weekly music paper *Melody Maker*, to make them act.

The review, which was the first national press exposure the band had received, was of a show On A Friday had played at a club called the Venue, formerly the Oxford Co-Op dining hall, supporting their longtime friends and fans the Candyskins. The writer was John Harris, who'd had to change his old habit of simply tossing out invites to On A Friday's shows, principally because of the frequent calls he was now receiving from their new press agent in London, Philip Hall, head of the Hall or Nothing agency.

"Philip phoned me up," Harris remembers, "and said, 'You're the local *Melody Maker* guy in Oxford, so when are you going to come and see this band?' At the time, even locally, there was a certain amount of bafflement about them, because they were signed after playing only about eight gigs. When I got to the Venue that night, I got the distinct impression that I was the first journalist to clap eyes on them. It was quite clear they were a good group even then. There were some songs that, perish the thought, actually sounded a bit '60s, partly because Ed was playing a Rickenbacker, which he still does. They played 'Stop Whispering' and 'Thinking About You' that night, and it was pretty impressive in places. Thom seemed to lose himself, whirling around with his eyes closed, and his voice, that thing he's got of moving from very low register to almost falsetto, he was doing that a lot. Don't forget that at that time, the idea of being a good singer was almost unheard of in British groups. Most people were mumblers. And secondly, music that was in any way fierce or confrontational was fairly thin on the ground; that year was the peak of the shoegazing bands. So it was like, 'Wow, this is different.' It became pretty obvious why they'd been signed."

Even though Harris' review was largely positive, concluding with the line " 'Promising' seems something of an understatement," its main gripe was right up front in the first paragraph: "Terrible name. Apt for beer-gutted pub rockers, but ill-suited to the astonishing intensity of this bunch. On A Friday swing between uneasy calm and crazed desperation, hinting at extremes that belie their moniker."[2] These comments were taken to heart by the band as soon as they read them. It became clear almost instantly to everyone that On A Friday was no kind of name for a group that wanted to be taken seriously, but it had taken the words of someone outside their immediate circle to make them acknowledge it for the first time.*

The next question that arose was obvious: If the name of this band couldn't be On A Friday, then what could it be? The answer was soon found on the back sleeve of Talking Heads' 1986 album *True Stories*, the companion to leader David Byrne's film of the same name. There lurked the two words "Radio Head," making up the title of a rather annoying pseudo-reggae number (though certain cheeky band members would later go on record as saying they picked the title because they felt it was the *least* annoying song on the album). After minimal discussion, the five soon-to-be-ex—members of On A Friday came to a firm decision: From this point on, they were to be Radiohead.

---

*Several years later, John Harris revealed to *Mojo* that the positive slant he'd taken in his review hadn't exactly mirrored what he felt about the band. In reality, "[t]hey looked awful. Thom was wearing a brown crew-necked jumper [*sweater* in American English], had cropped hair and looked very small, with none of the presence he has now. Musically they were all over the place. They started with something . . . that sounded like *All Mod Cons*–period Jam, then they'd flip it with something that sounded like the Pixies. All the raw material was there but they hadn't found their feet stylistically."[3]

The impetus for the band's name change and the source of the new name may be clear, but as to who first came up with the idea of using the title of one of Talking Heads' least admired compositions, that's a lot tougher to ferret out. No one within the band has ever officially owned up to suggesting the name Radiohead, which may be because the suggestion did not come from within the band. "The story I always heard," says Dave Newton, "is that Keith Wozencroft drew up a list of five names—all taken from other bands' song titles—and presented it to them, saying, 'Pick one of these, and do it soon.' And Radiohead was one of them. I never knew what the other four were, but it'd be interesting to see that list now." Several other Oxford acquaintances of the band at this time second Newton's account. Wozencroft has so far avoided comment on the matter.

Another question that's difficult to answer is: Why Radiohead? The most likely reason why the group picked that name in particular was that they intended it to be a conscious nod to Talking Heads, who had always been admired by On A Friday for their intellectual, artsy stance, their fondness for deep grooves, and the wide range of influences from which they drew. "They were one of the few bands that we all really liked," Ed O'Brien commented. "We admired their diversity, their musicianship, and their songwriting."[4]

In certain senses, Talking Heads and Radiohead had plenty in common besides a name. Both bands consisted of creatively inclined middle-class college students who didn't quite fit in with any particular social scene and so chose the role of keen observers rather than active participants. (David Byrne studied art at the Rhode Island School of Design, just as Thom did at Exeter.) Jonny Greenwood has also pointed out that there was a chronological significance in the choice of the name Radiohead and how it related to the band that had inspired it. For as the group that was to become Radiohead was just getting itself started, during the late '80s and early '90s, Talking Heads was rancorously dissolving. Under these circumstances, taking a name from the latter's catalog not only suggested that the newer band owed the older one an obvious debt but also bore the implication that the newcomers might in some way continue down the path established by those who had, in effect, named them. The connotations must have been agreeable.

Of course, there are other interpretations of what the name Radiohead means. Some of the more fanciful ones have been offered by Thom Yorke himself, who said in 1993: "It's just got loads of great connotations. . . . It's also about the way you take information in, the way you respond to the environment you're put in. You just become like a synapse in a long chain of other people's ideas. You receive and you consume, you know, you buy things you're told to buy, you read things you're told to read, or you don't read things you're told not to read. It's very much about the passive acceptance of your environment."[5]

Radiohead was definitely a better name than On A Friday. But it was still a somewhat unfortunate choice, given the growing abundance of pop artists in the '90s with the word *head* in their billing: Shinehead, Basehead, and Portishead, to name but three. (Among the other words that '90s bands gravitated toward in an astonishingly herdlike manner were *super*, *imperial*, *deluxe*, and *drag*.) Taking a name that was of only average interest would make it that much harder for Radiohead to stand out in the marketplace. Luckily, their songwriting and performing talents would prove to be more formidable than their skill at naming themselves.

The next order of business for Radiohead was to actually get some music out to the public. Before signing with EMI, the band had intended to put out an initial independent single funded by Chris and Bryce, but the interest generated by the five-song Manic Hedgehog demo had changed matters. Now that

Radiohead had a recording contract with a major label, that label wanted product to sell, and quickly. To that end, the band went back into Courtyard Studios with Hufford to record some new tracks that could be added to the already existing Manic Hedgehog material to form an EP. At first, the all-important leadoff track was planned to be a re-recorded version of "Nothing Touches Me," a frequent live set closer at the time. But according to Keith Wozencroft, "After it had been mixed it was all wrong."[6] And so the focus shifted to a newer song, "Prove Yourself," a lyrically bleak and musically powerful track whose jarring dynamic shifts owed a considerable debt to the Pixies.

The Courtyard sessions didn't go entirely smoothly. No longer just the man behind the board, Chris Hufford was now attempting a dual role as Radiohead's manager and producer, something the band was extremely conscious of and not always comfortable with. Hufford later admitted that he had set in motion "a huge conflict of interests. I think Thom was very unsure of my involvement. I'd had that happen to me as an artist when one of our managers acted as producer—it was fine until we wanted to develop and move on—so I was acutely aware of what he was feeling, but I can be quite overbearing and opinionated in the studio. There was definitely some friction on that front."[7]

In the end, Radiohead's first release on Parlophone, the *Drill* EP, featured two newly recorded compositions, "Prove Yourself" and "Stupid Car" (a number sung and played solo by Yorke on electric guitar, and the first of many Radiohead songs dealing with Thom's fear and suspicion of all mechanical modes of transport). The other two tracks, "You" and "Thinking About You," were taken off the Manic Hedgehog tape. Though the arrangement of the former was largely the same as what would eventually be included on *Pablo Honey*, the rendering of the latter was nothing like the introspective, acoustic ballad treatment it would later receive. The *Drill* version of "Thinking About You" was standard-issue up-tempo punk-pop, with rapid-fire strumming and drumming almost completely obscuring the delicacy of the singing and the personal nature of the lyrics.

Perhaps the most surprising thing about *Drill* is the way it camouflages what was at the time Radiohead's greatest asset. Even as early as 1992, Thom Yorke's graceful, arrestingly plaintive vocal style was well developed, far more so than the band's songwriting or overall sound. Yet all three tracks played by the full band on *Drill* are marred by a mix in which the singing is submerged beneath a dense layer of guitars. Maybe the band wanted to emulate the production style of post-punk bands like Hüsker Dü, who intentionally kept vocals low in an attempt to present vocals and instruments as one unified sound. Or maybe Thom felt self-conscious about his singing and/or lyrics.* In any case, the band's first outing was far from an unqualified success.

Colin Greenwood later described the whole process of issuing *Drill* as "a learning experience."[8] The design company hired to do the cover art charged a hefty sum for work that the band wasn't completely pleased with, and to make matters worse, the first 3000 copies of the EP were lost at the pressing plant, delaying the release date by two weeks. Some initial promo copies actually contained no Radiohead music at all; the mastering house had mixed up the *Drill* recordings with a bunch of Joe Cocker songs. It was an inauspicious start to a major-label career, to say the least.

Because of the two-week release delay, Radiohead began their first ever U.K. tour—supporting vaguely Pink Floyd–ish rockers Catherine Wheel—on April 28, 1992, with no music in the stores. Touring proved to be another learning experience for the band. Before getting signed, they hadn't exactly been road monsters. In

*Paul Kolderie, the coproducer of *Pablo Honey,* believes that the *Drill* tracks may have been recorded completely live and that the low level of the vocals was a result of excessive leakage from other instruments into Thom's microphone.

1991, the year of their signing, they'd played fewer than ten club shows. Regular concerts offered something of a rude awakening, indicating that they weren't always ready for prime time. At one early gig, the band was called back for an encore; during the interval while they were offstage, the road crew had turned the amplifiers off. Unaware of this, Jonny picked up his guitar and ripped into the opening chord of the next song, only to hear absolute silence. "He was so upset," brother Colin said. "We all just cracked up. . . . [What the road crew had done] was the professional thing to do, but we didn't know it 'cause we're not professionals."[9] Despite occasional embarrassments like this, the band were generally well received, both by audiences and by the other groups on the bill.

The *Drill* EP was finally released on May 5, and Radiohead got its first national radio exposure when BBC Radio One DJ Gary Davies played "Prove Yourself" on his show. It was a memorable moment for the band and their inner circle, as Ed later recalled: "We were completely excited—it was a mainstream weekend DJ on the national radio station. Some of our friends in Oxford phoned us up and said, 'You were played at eight o'clock this morning on the radio, and they're going to play it again on Sunday.' So we all tuned in and listened to it. It was wonderful."[10] Unfortunately, *Drill* didn't set off any corresponding whoops of joy in the EMI sales department. Its U.K. chart peak was an undistinguished 101. Chris Hufford was duly relieved of any further duties behind the recording desk and left to concentrate on managing the band. The hunt was on for a new producer.

At about the same time as this, the up-and-coming American production team of Paul Q. Kolderie and Sean Slade arrived in London looking for new business. Kolderie and Slade worked at a recording studio in Boston called Fort Apache, where over the last few years they'd made a name for themselves as choice "alternative" soundsmiths; the latest project they'd completed had been

Buffalo Tom's album *Let Me Come Over*. While in London, they met with about ten different record company executives, including EMI's Nick Gatfield, who'd recently been pitched by Slade and Kolderie's manager on a Nashville band called Clockhammer, whom Sean and Paul had produced. Shortly after the two producers entered his office, Gatfield gestured to the Clockhammer tape. "You did this?" he asked. "You got these guitar sounds?" When Slade and Kolderie answered in the affirmative, Gatfield said, "Well, maybe you might be interested in this new band we signed not too long ago. They have three guitar players, and we're having some trouble getting their sound on tape properly."

Gatfield played them a couple of the songs from Radiohead's most recent Courtyard sessions, "Prove Yourself" and "I Can't," plus the earlier demo of "Stop Whispering." Sean and Paul liked what they heard, and when Keith Wozencroft approached Radiohead about the prospect of working with Slade and Kolderie, the band responded enthusiastically. (The fact that Kolderie had engineered the Pixies' *Come On Pilgrim* couldn't have hurt. Another Pixies-associated producer, Steve Albini, had also been briefly considered, but, says Kolderie, "he was too scary for the record company, and he hadn't done anything big like Nirvana or Bush yet.") A series of dates to record the next Radiohead single with the Boston duo at the helm were booked at Chipping Norton Studios, not far from Oxford, to commence shortly after the band got off the road.

Before recording proper began, Sean and Paul met up with Chris Hufford and Bryce Edge for a chat. Kolderie remembers being more impressed by the managers than by the band. "Those guys are crafty mothers," he says now. "I don't think I've ever met two guys who had more of a plan. They knew they were on a major label, so they couldn't touch the [British] indie charts, which at the time ruled everything—bands like Ride and Chapterhouse and Blur. Back in 1992, you had to be on a cool indie label like Creation to get people to pay attention to you. It was almost impossible to crack in from the major side. So their strategy was like a reverse Stray Cats [the Brian Setzer–led '80s rockabilly revivalists who achieved success in their native America only after moving to England and becoming hitmakers there]: get American producers, go to America, tour really hard there, and then come back and work it at home."*

Following their meeting with Hufford and Edge, Kolderie and Slade sat in on some pre-production rehearsals at Radiohead's new central HQ, a disused shed on an apple farm in the Oxfordshire countryside that the band had recently rented and converted into a makeshift practice space. "We wanted a room that was completely ours," Jonny explained, "and also a room that wasn't like a rehearsal room."[11] With the two producers in attendance, the band ran through the numbers that EMI thought most appropriate to follow up *Drill.* The label's top pick was a manic, highly charged rocker called "Inside My Head," featuring more dark and desperate lyrics from Thom ("What have you put in that syringe?/What have you really said to him? . . . I'm holding on for dear life") and a brutal guitar part by Jonny. It was compelling, certainly, but it wasn't melodic enough to be a pop hit. The other two songs under consideration—"Million Dollar Question," which sandwiched a slow, plaintive middle section between two amped-up chunks of punk rock aggression, and the more expansive "Lurgee," which showcased Yorke's voice at its sweetest—were fine, but neither of them shouted out "single" either.

Kolderie later said of these rehearsals, "My first impression

---

*One wonders whether Chris Hufford would agree with this assessment. In practically every interview he's done, he's emphasized the fact that Courtyard has never had a secret game plan and that Radiohead's success was the product of sheer luck rather than strategy. Also, America is obviously a far bigger market than Britain, not the place you'd normally turn for an easy hit. Two possibilities suggest themselves: Either Hufford is being unduly humble, or Kolderie is over-interpreting history.

was that they were desperately inexperienced. The other was that we didn't like these songs Parlophone had chosen, and I don't think the band liked them very much either."[12] At one point during the rehearsals, however, more for variety's sake than anything else, the band spontaneously burst into a song that no one had heard before, a piece of high drama whose self-flagellating lyrics were matched by a grandiose guitar-crunch chorus and a soaring vocal by Thom. It was the song that the world would soon come to know as "Creep," but judging by the band's presentation of it on this particular day, they evidently saw it as little more than a throwaway number. Thom was even apologetic after they'd played it, mumbling something semiflippant about it being "our Scott Walker song" (Scott Walker being the deep-voiced American expatriate who achieved great fame in late-'60s England with lushly orchestrated ballads of existential dread).

The band's producers misheard Thom's remark and thought he'd said "Creep" actually *was* a Scott Walker song. "Now I was pretty familiar with Scott Walker," Kolderie said, "but jeez, there's a lot of albums and I could have missed something! We walked out of the rehearsal that night and Sean said, 'Too bad their best song's a cover.' "[13] Considering that the band was obviously uncertain about the new song, that their producers didn't know it was an original, and that their record company was unaware of its very existence, it seemed likely at this juncture that "Creep" would never be heard again.

The reason that it was came down to further tension in the studio as recording got under way at Chipping Norton. Neither "Inside My Head" nor "Lurgee" were turning out to anyone's satisfaction. (The released version of the latter is one of the few songs of the *Pablo Honey* era that weren't produced by Sean and Paul; dissatisfied with their take on it, the band returned to an earlier version produced by Hufford at Courtyard.) Hufford complained that Radiohead's music was being turned into "overblown bombastic rock,"[14] though to these ears, the Slade/Kolderie recording of "Inside My Head" is far more vital than that description implies. In fact, it's arguably the first real taste of Radiohead's power in performance, as Yorke's ungodly wails ride a forbidding up-tempo groove courtesy of Messrs. Greenwood and Selway. It's possible that Chris' comments stemmed less from the actual quality of the music than from a lingering case of sour grapes after being taken off production duty himself.

In an attempt to raise everyone's morale, Sean and Paul suggested that they run through that Scott Walker number again. Unbeknownst to the band, the tape was rolling. Radiohead nailed "Creep" in one searing take. "At the end," Kolderie recalled in *Mojo,* "everyone in the place was silent for a moment and then they burst into applause. I'd never had that happen before."[15] Listening back to their work in the control room, Thom asked Jonny, "What do you think?" Jonny replied, "I think it's the best thing we've done in ages." Once Kolderie had been reassured that the song was in fact an original, he got on the phone to Keith Wozencroft and told him that EMI might want to reconsider its choice for the next single. Wozencroft drove up to the studio that night to give "Creep" a listen. As he entered the building, he was greeted by a gale of laughter from the live room, where the band was situated. Eyebrows raised, he turned to Kolderie and commented, "A rather relaxed atmosphere here, isn't it?"

"Yes, well, that's what we try for," Paul responded. Immediately suspicious that not enough serious work was being accomplished and that Slade and Kolderie were pushing this new song solely to milk more money out of EMI, Wozencroft listened to the track with a certain skepticism. "After it was done," Kolderie remembers, "he said, 'Well, it's good, but it's not a single.' I said,

'Give it a chance.'" Wozencroft agreed that he'd spend some more time with the song and wouldn't rush to judgment, but he stressed that the band still had to finish the tracks they'd been assigned to record in the first place. "I don't blame him for not changing his mind immediately," Kolderie says. "He had an idea and he wanted to stick with it. That's not unusual."

Wozencroft stuck with his idea for another week or so, but by the time two weeks had gone by, he'd altered his opinion, and "Creep" was officially designated Radiohead's next single. As the new song made the rounds at EMI, enthusiasm grew rapidly. "Everyone who heard 'Creep' just started going insane," Kolderie said. "So that's what got us the job doing the album."[16] The rest of *Pablo Honey* was recorded with Sean and Paul at Chipping Norton in a brief three weeks, following a few days of pre-production rehearsals at an Oxfordshire facility owned by one-hit wonder Mungo Jerry ("In the Summertime") and initial sessions at Arpad Toth's studio in the countryside near Reading (where a flock of sheep occasionally looked in on the proceedings through the control room windows).* Putting forth such concentrated effort in such a short period of time, a method of working that the band wasn't used to, seems to have generated a fair amount of stress. "I was unbearable, apparently," Thom later said, "according to my girlfriend."[17] However, Paul Kolderie's memories of the recording sessions are mostly fond ones.

"We didn't use an assistant engineer at Chipping Norton," Kolderie says, "so it was just the seven of us, which was great. We shared a sense of humor—there was a lot of joking. Each night after

---

*"Arpad Toth," Paul Kolderie remembers, "was the stereotypical sad-sack studio owner who nothing ever goes right for. Marillion booked his studio for a reunion record with singer Fish, who had gone solo. The group arrived and spent days setting up, but just hours after Fish arrived there was a huge argument. Fish left. The session was cancelled, and they loaded up the semis." That said, we did actually use a couple of the drum tracks we recorded there on the finished album."

dinner, we'd watch this cheesy soap opera, *Eldorado*. Phil had a new Morris Minor that he'd give people rides in. One day, the sun came out, which was a big deal. Colin had been outside and he announced it, and everyone ran outside and took their shirts off.

"They were a very democratic band even then, although Thom would tend to get more hung up on stuff. Slade and I were like their driving instructors. When they started, they didn't know how to work in a studio. They were a baby band. We had to show them that you can't let your desire for being Pink Floyd bog you down. You have to *finish*.

"The main thing was just to get the whole band to mesh and jell and get into a groove. That was what they needed to work on the most. They already had songs—better than a lot of bands will ever write—and they already had Thom's voice. But they needed to get tight. A lot of old songs got aired and discarded because the tempo was never right for everybody. It was the next two years of touring that turned them into a tight band.

"Another thing that I can't forget about those sessions is that I gained about ten pounds during them because there was so much food around, and there was always some kind of heavy English dessert after dinner. For us at that time, it was not a cheap album. They must have spent upwards of a hundred thousand pounds."

With that much money invested in Radiohead, EMI wanted a decent return. A punchy mix would be crucial, and so once recording was complete, Slade and Kolderie were booked into a mixing studio in Farnham, near Surrey, well south of London. Unfortunately, the good vibes that had lasted through the Chipping Norton sessions soon dissipated in the new surroundings. "It wasn't a great studio," Kolderie says, "and it quickly became clear that mixing with the band in attendance was a problem. Nothing was right; everything sucked. So finally EMI realized this and said, 'It would probably be better to have you mix this back at Fort Apache, where you're comfortable, on home turf.'" Sean and Paul quickly agreed to this and brought the tapes back to Boston. The album's final mix was, Kolderie recalls, "pretty much rammed down the band's throat. EMI wanted it out, and that was that." Colin, for one, chose to remain sensibly balanced about the whole process: "It's just one of those things that it's best to file under 'experience' and move on."[18]

Following the *Pablo Honey* sessions, the band went back on the road for most of the fall, supporting Irish folk-rockers the Frank and Walters until mid-October and then backing up King-maker through the beginning of December. During the latter tour, they came on before a juggler (who, Yorke later quipped, "usually had a longer soundcheck than we did"[19]).

It wasn't long before at least one member of Radiohead began displaying telltale signs of rock 'n' roll road dementia. Perhaps not surprisingly, Thom was the most heavily affected by the band's change of lifestyle. Always prone to experimentation with his appearance, he now took to randomly hacking or shaving off clumps of his own hair. This do-it-yourself styling approach was often fueled by unwisely large combinations of chemicals, principally alcohol, in which Yorke indulged to such a degree that he sometimes became unable to perform. A handful of gigs were canceled around this time due to the singer's advanced state of intoxication. Thom later admitted that he felt the band "hadn't a clue what we were about," and that in reaction, "I hit the self-destruct button pretty quickly."[20]

Such behavior, though certainly understandable, would have made far more sense if it could have been attributed to the pressures of sudden fame. Yet as it was, the band could claim nothing of the sort; their struggle to gain a mere minimum of attention was still some way from being won. All that the rest of the band, their managers, and their rapidly growing organization (by now including their very own booker, Charlie Myatt of the ITB agency, and press officer Philip Hall) could do was hope for further success and, in the meantime, keep a considerate but watchful eye on Thom.*

Backed by "Lurgee," "Inside My Head," and "Million Dollar Question," "Creep" was released on September 21, 1992, as Radiohead's second single. But the excitement that EMI had felt about the song wasn't matched by U.K. sales figures. "Creep" only crept up to Number 78 on the charts, selling barely 6000 copies and getting hardly a mention in the press; the London *Evening Standard*'s description of it as "a gloomy anthem of self-loathing sprinkled with the F-word and a miserable refrain"[21] was probably the most notable. The BBC's Radio One played the song a grand total of three times before taking it off the playlist entirely, claiming it was too depressing. (Even for this pittance, Parlophone had to go to the trouble of issuing a "clean" version of "Creep," with Thom substituting "so very special" for "so fucking special.")

Although their management said they weren't disappointed—as Chris Hufford later put it, "Bryce and I have always tried to be realistic"[22]—the initial failure of "Creep" in England must have triggered some depression within the group's ranks. After all, they'd signed to the Beatles' label; they'd played over 100 shows in 1992, covering most of the U.K.; they'd even made a performance video to go along with the single, shot on the cheap (budget approximately £10,000) at the Venue in

---

*A major part of the Radiohead organization, of course, was their live crew, who had been largely picked up wholesale from the biggest sound reinforcement company in Oxford, run by Jim Parsons. People like live mixer Jim Warren and guitar techs Peter Clements and Duncan Swift were "the original Oxford punks," according to Ronan Munro, "hanging round the local monuments and making trouble. Once they grew up, they got into carting PA gear around. They'd been working at most of the local shows for years, and so it was only natural for Radiohead to bring them on."

Oxford.* But at year's end, they had little to show for the work they'd done. The capper to all this injustice came in the Christmas 1992 issue of *New Musical Express*. A review of one of the band's final gigs of the year, a headlining appearance at London's Smashed Club, was the harshest critique they had received so far. Author Keith Cameron concluded, "Radiohead are a pitiful, lily-livered excuse for a rock 'n' roll group."[23]

Oddly enough, the very same publication would soon name "Creep" one of the top ten singles of 1992 and, along with *Melody Maker,* would pick Radiohead as a band to watch in the coming year. True, the earlier write-off in *NME* was the product of a single reviewer's opinion, one not necessarily representative of the paper's entire editorial staff. But that review, coupled with the praise that soon followed it within the same pages, drove home a point that Radiohead needed to learn quickly, about the schizoid, overheated nature of their country's music press.

For a nation its size, the United Kingdom has an inordinately large number of music-related publications. Where, for example, America does not have a single national weekly music paper, Britain has two (and until fairly recently, there were three). The need to keep people reading every issue, and thus keep these papers financially afloat, leads to a constant, desperate search for the Next Big Thing, or at least something halfway promising enough to run with for next week and bill as the Next Big Thing until the *real* Next Big Thing comes along. Given such conditions, a band's rise to the top of the U.K. press heap can be stunningly rapid; groups have appeared on the weeklies' covers with no more than a couple of singles to their name. And their fall from favor

*The 250 people making up the audience in the video had paid a small fee for the privilege, but the money went not to the group or to their label but to the struggling local music newspaper *Curfew,* which had given the band its first press coverage. With help from the video shoot's proceeds, Ronan Munro was able to purchase his first personal computer.

can be swifter still, once the papers feel they've outlived their usefulness. In all cases, opinions both good and bad are expressed with the absolute maximum of hyperbole, the better to hold readers. The result is a veritable mountain range of hype, buzzwords, and regurgitated jargon, under which the actual music, the alleged source of all the verbiage, is overwhelmed and nearly forgotten.

Radiohead's early, wounding experiences at the hands of the whim-driven British press have led them to be wary of music journalism as a whole. They certainly haven't made themselves inaccessible; they give plenty of interviews, and they know how to play the media game. But they resolved long ago that they would never take that game too seriously (although, as it would with anyone, that resolve has been known to break down every once in a while). "*Melody Maker* and *NME* are frighteningly irrelevant articles of fiction for the most part," Thom would later say. "They're totally conscious of being the focus and the head of everything and they're really not. Their opinion is of no consequence [this line reappears almost verbatim in the lyrics of "Paranoid Android"]. It's very provincial. . . . The way we feel about it at the moment is, if people want to talk to us, then we'll talk to them, because why not? But the pettiness and the fighting are things we experienced enough at school."[24]

No matter what the weeklies said, one thing was becoming clear: Radiohead's first taste of big-time success would not be had in England. That the earliest appearance of "Creep" on a Top 10 chart occurred overseas was therefore not surprising. But surely no one at EMI or in Radiohead's organization could have predicted the country where the song would have its largest initial impact.

Carol Baxter, Radiohead's representative in EMI's international division, started receiving reports toward the end of 1992 from a very excited colleague in Israel named Uzi Preuss, who'd been working for the company as a local promotion man for about six months. Not only had Preuss taken a shine to "Creep" himself, but so had an old friend of his, Yoav Kutner, a DJ at the IDF (*Galei Zahal* in Hebrew) armed forces radio station in Tel Aviv. A 20-year broadcast veteran, Kutner was the most respected jockey in the country, the Israeli equivalent of the BBC's John Peel. "At that time," Preuss remembers, "there were only a couple of radio stations in Israel that played alternative music. It was a small market—it still is, of course, but that sometimes means you can make a big impression in a short time. When I first heard 'Creep,' I figured Yoav would like it, because I knew we had similar musical tastes. I also thought this band could become very big."

Preuss' instincts were correct on both counts. Kutner played the song several times on the air, and the listener response was stunning. "Creep" vaulted into the upper reaches of the country's pop charts. A brief Israeli tour by the band was soon deemed a necessity; dates were set for March. Dave Newton says, "I remember Chris Hufford calling me up in obvious disbelief saying, 'What do you know about Israel? The record's a huge hit down there, and we've gotta go do some shows.' I couldn't help him much, I'm afraid. I was almost as shocked as he was."

Before long, "Creep" was having similar success in New Zealand, Spain, and Scandinavia. But the biggest news was still to come.

In the fall of 1992, Aaron Axelsen was the music director at KCRH, a small college station in California's East Bay area. He was also an intern at the San Francisco FM station KITS (Live 105, one of the top "alternative" stations in the U.S.), and he worked behind the counter at a record store in Berkeley called Mod Lang, which carried a wide selection of foreign imports. Axelsen would frequently pick up discs from the U.K. at Mod Lang and play them on KCRH. One of those discs was the *Drill* EP, which had turned Axelsen into an early, perhaps the earliest, American Radiohead fan. When the band's next single arrived at the store, he was knocked out. "That was the unedited version of 'Creep,'" he remembers, "with the line 'You're so fuckin' special.' It was so potent."

Axelsen quickly added "Creep" to the KCRH playlist. "We created a little buzz in the East Bay," he says. "All these people were calling, saying, 'What is this record?'" At this point, Axelsen decided that he should try to make use of his connections at the bigger San Francisco station where he interned: "I used to bring a lot of imports into Live 105 and play them for Steve Masters, who was the music director there at the time. So I brought him the record, saying, 'Here's this band Radiohead, the record's getting huge on my college station, I'm starting to sell records at the store, check this out.' I gave him my own import copy of the single, the only copy I had, and he gave it a listen."

Masters was as taken with "Creep" as Axelsen, and he played it on the air. As had been the case at KCRH, the call-in response was overwhelming, and the song went into regular rotation. Within a month or so, Live 105 put together its annual year-end singles poll, and after the numbers had been tabulated, "Creep" was on top.* It wasn't long before several other West Coast stations had begun playing the song, most importantly Los Angeles' highly influential KROQ. As 1992 turned to 1993, Radiohead was slowly but surely winning attention in America. Now the only question was: Would this interest be enough to convince Parlophone's U.S. sister label Capitol to release "Creep" domestically?

In the meantime, the band set off on another series of U.K. gigs, commencing on January 13. At the beginning of February, Parlophone released their third single, the roaring anthem "Anyone Can Play Guitar," produced once again by Paul Q. Kolderie

---

*Due in part to his early recognition of Radiohead, KITS hired Aaron Axelsen as a full-time music assistant soon thereafter. He is now the station's music director.

and Sean Slade. The song was backed by "Faithless, the Wonder Boy" and "Coke Babies," two more Yorkean alienation specials. Of the two, "Faithless" (which featured, for the first time, Thom on acoustic guitar) is slower and catchier, its verse structure similar to "Prove Yourself," its lyrics dealing in part with the emptiness of teenage fashions, and its big rock chorus a repetition of the unsettling line "I can't put the needle in." The band has always insisted that this line is about getting revenge on someone, not doing drugs. As for "Coke Babies," its ruminative vocal and spacy guitar effects hint at the direction the band would take in later years, but the somewhat flimsy arrangement lacks the body of future efforts in this vein.

Though still far from a mega-seller, the single made it into the British Top 40, peaking at a respectable 32, and *Melody Maker* named it Single of the Week. Later that month, Radiohead undertook its first engagement outside Britain, traveling to Paris, where they played a national radio show called *The Black Sessions*. Among the selections in their set was a cover of Glen Campbell's "Rhinestone Cowboy," which hinted both at the band's love of slightly cheesy pop music and at their sense of humor.*

Finally, on February 22, Radiohead's first full-length album, *Pablo Honey*, was released in England. The album's name was taken from a recording that was at the time available only in underground circles, a poor-quality tape made by the notorious New York phone pranksters the Jerky Boys, who would later go on to have their fiber-optic gags sanctioned by a major record label. (The tape that the Radiohead boys heard had originally been acquired by another Thames Valley band, Chapterhouse.) On one part of the tape, a Jerky Boy calls someone and pretends to be

*Ronan Munro reports that Radiohead had previously played the Campbell chestnut at a special "covers-only" night at the Jericho Tavern featuring several other local bands, and that the entire jolly affair was videotaped.

his mother; he opens the conversation by moaning in a weak falsetto, "Pablo, honey." Thom later said that the title was appropriate because Radiohead were "all mother's boys."[25]

The rather juvenile source of the album's name didn't bode well for its contents, but in a *Melody Maker* interview around the time of its release, Thom Yorke made a claim that suggested quite the contrary. "With this LP," he said, "we're actually going to save pop music."[26] Thom was evidently in a joking mood when the interview was conducted, for in addition to that bold assertion, he responded to the question of whether he was interested in being a pop star with this pointed quip: "Nah. Look at us. We're a lily-livered excuse for a rock group. We might as well accept the truth and carry on."[27]

PABLO HONEY

5

It's fashionable these days for enthusiasts of Radiohead's more recent work to put down the music on their debut album. The general critical view, put forth mainly by writers who didn't latch on to the band until *The Bends or OK Computer,* is that *Pablo Honey* consists of a couple of decent tracks ("Creep" and "Anyone Can Play Guitar") padded out with

a lot of middling filler. Following this line of attack, it's only logical to further point out the dramatic contrast between Radiohead's initial amateurishness and the top-notch tunes that the
band would soon produce. Many critics have emphasized how
sudden and completely unexpected Radiohead's move into the
creative big leagues was, as if it had been impossible for anyone to
foresee what was to come on the basis of what they had already
done.

Though the members of Radiohead don't wholeheartedly
agree with this estimation of their early work, they have cemented
it to a degree with their frequently stated lack of regard for *Pablo
Honey*. Ed O'Brien has described the album, truthfully but also
rather condescendingly, as "a collection of our greatest hits as an
unsigned band,"[1] while Jonny Greenwood once claimed that "a
lot of those songs were arguably recorded better earlier."[2] (If they
were, those recordings certainly didn't appear on the *Drill* EP.)

All this is a little unfair. Of course, no one can argue that
Pablo Honey is an awe-inspiring work of art or that Radiohead's
music didn't evolve tremendously within a relatively short time
following its release. Yes, the album does suffer from a lack of
clear artistic direction. The influence of bands like the Pixies is
worn too obviously, and the band's inability to completely digest
such influences can leave some tracks sounding a tad lumpy. But
listening to *Pablo Honey* now, you can clearly hear the bewitching
traces of Radiohead future—in the unvarnished emotion of
Thom Yorke's voice on "Stop Whispering," in the delicacy of
"Lurgee," in the feverish energy of the album's climactic closer,
"Blow Out." More to the point, all these songs are eminently lis-
tenable, even enjoyable.

Much of the band's own critical attitude toward the album
can probably be put down to the rushed nature of its recording.
Jonny feels the album lacks "freedom. We were so frightened that
the stuff was a lot more regimented, I think, through our own

fear and lack of experience." To which Thom adds, "The sad thing was that it was so far removed from any other recording we'd ever done." Ed agrees: "We'd never been in a proper studio before, we were not very cohesive as a band, and we were desperately insecure. Sean Slade and Paul Kolderie did an amazing job, considering how we were pushing and pulling in so many different ways." Not surprisingly, Kolderie has a similar assessment. He remembered the *Pablo Honey* sessions as "a bit of a struggle. It was their first record and they wanted to be the Beatles, and the mix had to have no reverb, and they had all the ideas they'd ever come up with in twenty years of listening to records. But we managed to get it done."[3]

During the sessions, Slade and Kolderie quickly learned that the band played their best when they were least aware of their own playing. For example, Thom's singing was noticeably better when he wasn't able to hear himself. Once they'd realized this, the production duo made special monitor mixes for him to listen to while the band was tracking, mixes that buried his voice underneath the other instruments. "Letting them get unconscious was the key," Kolderie says. "They are a band of destiny, as long as you just get out of the way and let it happen."

One idea that seems to have been generated originally by the producers but certainly met with no resistance from the band was to pile the songs up with multiple layers of overdubbed guitars. "There was a need to put more and more guitar tracks on *Pablo Honey*," Thom says. "You know, four rhythm guitar tracks, and everyone had to play on a part." Already boasting at least one more guitar player than most rock bands, Radiohead were thrilled to travel even farther down the road of string-driven excess. As O'Brien recalls it, "Sean Slade would go, 'I want fucking eight walls of guitars here, eight overdubs,' and we were like, 'Yeah, yeah, yeah, let's do it, that's great.'"

The album's opening song, "You," was a clear beneficiary of

this approach, coming off far more powerfully in the Slade/Kolderie version than on the earlier *Drill* recording. Comparing the two, you can feel the extra guitaristic heft of the former as the quadrupled chords crash against each other. Jonny's cleanly picked, tremolo-enhanced intro line, which drops out of the *Drill* version when the rest of the band start playing, is more prominent on the album, lending the arrangement some needed depth. Thom's voice is mixed up front this time, where it belongs, and Phil's drumming is muscular but restrained, a far cry from his clattery, almost out-of-control performance on the earlier take.

Lyrically, "You" isn't one of Thom Yorke's greatest creations. Referring to a loved one as "the sun and moon and stars" doesn't win any prizes for originality, and later lines that hint at apocalypse—"You say the world is going to end so soon. . . . I can see me drowning, caught in the fire"—don't rise far enough out of vagueness to be affecting. But on the musical side, the song has several elements to recommend it. The frequent shifts between major and minor chords add a sense of tension that's heightened by corresponding shifts of meter. "You" is an early indicator of the band's affection for waltz (3/4) time, and for adding and/or skipping beats (every fourth bar of the verse section is only two beats instead of the usual three); both of these traits are developed further on *The Bends* and *OK Computer*. Finally, the song's sinuous melody is handled splendidly by Thom. Toward the end, the band stops for a moment and he bursts out in a daredevil yell that's a thrill to hear.

Contrary to some reports, "Creep," which follows "You," is not a completely live recording. Some touch-up work was done on Thom's vocal and Colin's bass following the band's initial first-take performance; Jonny's piano part was also a later addition.*

*During the song's final mix, Kolderie forgot to include the piano until near the end. "I was ready to do the mix over again," he says, "but when they heard it that way, everyone said, 'That's it.' I'd been worried that they'd notice the mistake." It wouldn't be the last time that a mixing flub would receive an enthusiastic thumbs-up from the band.

Still, most of that first take was kept on the finished release. "The recording of ['Creep'] taught us a lot," Thom later said. "We realized, 'Hang on, we actually sound quite good when we don't know the tape's rolling.' "[4]

After EMI had decided the song should be a single, a "clean" version (without the word *fucking*) was deemed necessary for radio play, and so Thom returned to the studio with Sean and Paul to recut the offending lines. Kolderie took advantage of the opportunity to mention something that had been bothering him for a while. "When we first did 'Creep,' " he says, "the first verse was different. I don't remember exactly what it was now, but it was not good lyrically, sort of stupid and funny—there was something in there about a leg of lamb. When we went back in [to do the *fuck*-less version] I told Thom I thought that verse could be better, and at first he said, 'It's already written, I can't change it.' I said, 'Of course you can. Look, we're here to change these other words, we're going to record some vocals anyway. Come on, you can do better than that.' And he did. He went away, and came back about 10 minutes later with another verse [the first verse you hear on the finished recording], which sets up the song much better. I mention this because Thom's one of the only people that I've ever been able to do that with. Ever since then, I've tried to do that with other artists—'Hey man, why don't you just go in right now and make that better?'—and I'll tell you, it's a rare person who can do it."

"Creep" was already an old song by the time Radiohead recorded it. Thom had written an early version while he was at Exeter, rewriting the words later. As for the song's inspiration, the most Thom has said publicly about it is that "the idea came from a rocky relationship I was having."[5] *Select*'s John Harris once posited that the "special" person referred to in the song was a girl Yorke knew in Oxford who hung with a crowd that fancied itself much hipper than the Jericho haunters who were Radiohead's nearest acquaintances: "You're either part of the Little Clarendon Street crowd or the Jericho crowd, and never the twain shall meet. I think 'Creep' was about some girl who used to frequent the Little Clarendon Street side of things and Thom thought he'd never have anything to do with that, hence 'What the hell am I doing here, I don't belong here.'"[6]*

In any case, it's clear from the lyrics' hyperbolic nature and from Thom's deadpan delivery that all is not completely serious. Both the singer's dismissal of himself as a creep and a weirdo and his high praise of the "angel" he's addressing seem laced with sarcasm. Later, Yorke would at least partly confirm this impression in an interview with the radio trade magazine *Hits*: "'Creep' is more the way people look at you. The guy in the song doesn't necessarily believe that he's a creep, but he's being told he is. But these things change."[7]

Besides Thom's lyrics, the most talked-about component of "Creep" was Jonny's rifle-cocking guitar hook. Explanations for its genesis abound. Some say it was an accident. "That nervous twitch he does, that's just his way of checking that the guitar is working, that it's loud enough," Thom once explained, "and he ended up doing it while we were recording. And whilst we were listening to it, it was like, 'Hey, what the fuck was that? Keep that! Do that!'"[8] Others say that Jonny wasn't too keen on "Creep" to begin with, and that his crunchy interjections were an attempt to punch up, maybe even sabotage, the song. Whatever the truth may be, by the time Radiohead laid down "Creep" at Chipping Norton, Jonny's *chu-chunk*s were part of the permanent arrangement.

---

*Little Clarendon Street turns off Walton Street at the southernmost edge of Jericho, about seven blocks from the Jericho Tavern. Only a couple of blocks long, it's the center of a small sector of *chi-chi* bars and restaurants, including Brown's, where Ed once worked as a waiter, and the Beat Café, at one time a regular Yorke watering hole, and one that some Radiohead watchers postulate was the setting for the story outlined in "Creep."

Once he'd heard a few dozen interviewers' questions about the "meaning" of "Creep," Thom began to distance himself from the topic. Not that it really mattered from the start what the song's author thought of it; just as had happened with Nirvana's "Smells Like Teen Spirit," "Creep" was taken to heart by a bunch of young listeners who heard something in it that spoke to them, and what each one heard didn't necessarily correspond to what any of the others heard. In 1995, Yorke would say, "I always took that song to be a bit of a joke. The one thing I regret about that song is people identifying me as the creep. Everyone sets me up to be the Mr. Serious of rock, which is ridiculous. I used to take myself very seriously, so I suppose I asked for it. Oh well, it could be worse. I could be a Mod, for example."[9]

Thom may not have been much enamored of Mods, but his attitude toward the punk movement was apparently less cut-and-dried, at least in 1993. The next track on *Pablo Honey,* "How Do You?" is the closest thing to punk rock Radiohead has ever recorded. In its frenetic, guitars-revved-to-the-max fashion, it's faintly reminiscent of Manchester's legendary Buzzcocks, although the brief atonal jam at the end puts it more in wanna-be Pere Ubu territory. Yorke delivers the lyrics in his snottiest Johnny Rotten voice, painting a sour-faced portrait of a character seemingly without any redeeming features. Strangely, the people who gather around this fellow, who's alternately called "a stupid baby" and "a dangerous bigot," overlook his faults, maybe because they understand that beneath his unpleasant exterior "he wants to be loved." Is the song about a particular person, a former classmate of Thom's perhaps, or maybe even Thom himself? The one-sidedness of the lyrics makes it difficult for us to care one way or the other. Still, the up-front aggression of the band's performance keeps things worthwhile. A section of the Jerky Boys' "Pablo, honey" sketch, from which the album takes its name, is briefly sampled here.

"Stop Whispering" is one of the oldest compositions in Radiohead's recorded repertoire, having featured prominently on the second On A Friday demo tape that John Butcher played for Chris Hufford. The only major differences between that demo and the *Pablo Honey* version occur late in the song; on the demo, Thom's line "Dear sir, I have a complaint" is repeated by Ed in a posh sing-speak voice, and the final buildup features what sounds like a Hammond organ played (probably by Jonny) through a wah-wah pedal.

Musically, "Stop Whispering" is a simple ditty, oriented around only two chords, driven by Phil's gently brushed drums and Colin's supple bassline. The lyrics also stick to one basic point, that in the face of various injustices (namely, being ignored, cursed, and/or spat upon by all around, including our own mothers), we should "stop whispering [and] start shouting." It's a point well made by Thom's emotive vocal, reminiscent of U2's Bono in his younger days. At more than five minutes—the longest track on *Pablo Honey*—the song gets plenty of time to breathe and to build. The semipsychedelic rotating-speaker effect that pops up on Jonny's guitar during the second verse is the first of several clever sonic touches. By the time Phil switches to sticks and the inevitable fuzzboxes kick in, the journey has become most rewarding.

From there, we move on to "Thinking About You," reportedly Colin and Jonny's mother's favorite song on the album, probably because it's the quietest. (The double-tracked acoustic guitars and delicate pump organ in the background fit the tune far better than the revved-up electric arrangement on *Drill*.) Mrs. Greenwood's affection for this song tickled her youngest son no end. "She had no idea it was about wanking," he once commented slyly.[10] To be honest, the song's not solely about wanking (a British slang term for masturbation); its principal focus seems to be lost or unrequited love, though the line about "brib[ing] the company to come and see you" is a little mysterious. The references to fame and an entourage of hangers-on suggest that this particular love object may be a pop star whom the singer has never actually met; it's also possible that she doesn't exist anywhere other than in his fantasies. When Yorke comes right out and sings, "I'm playing with myself," the explicit reference, while not exactly delicate, doesn't break the prevailing mood of wounded dignity.

Though onanism is a common obsession of most teenage boys, going to a single-sex school, as all the members of Radiohead did, can only enhance its importance. The legacy of the band's time at Abingdon, where their experience with girls was severely limited, was a certain awkwardness around members of the opposite sex. "I feel tremendous guilt for any sexual feelings I have," Thom once said, "so I end up spending my entire life feeling sorry for fancying somebody. Even in school I thought girls were so wonderful that I was scared to death of them. I masturbate a lot. That's how I deal with it."[11] Of course, repression on all social fronts, not just sexual, is a hallmark of British culture. As another early Yorke lyric, "Inside My Head," puts it, "I've got a disease, an English disease."

Pablo Honey's first half concludes with "Anyone Can Play Guitar," perhaps the album's most immediately catchy tune, cut with bursts of distorto noise from Ed and Jonny; the latter strokes his Telecaster's strings with a paintbrush at a few opportune moments, most notably during the brief aural-traffic-jam intro section. For that section, Kolderie explains, "we rounded up everyone in the studio—all five band members, Sean and I, the studio owner, the cook—and gave each person a guitar. Everyone got assigned their own track, and they could do whatever they wanted. The idea was to live up to the title: Anyone can play guitar. So they did, and we made it into a little sound collage at the beginning." According to Thom, the song's uplifting chorus was the first part to be written, and it hung around for a while before anything else came along: "We just hammered away at it for ages and got all these nice clever bits in it. The 'anyone can play guitar' thing, I was going to change it. I didn't like that title. But everyone else said, 'No, that's the best bit, keep it,' so we did."[12]

At first, the song appears to be a serious ode to the power of youth's rock dreams. "Anyone can play guitar and they won't be a nothing anymore" could be a capsule summary of the punk spirit. Yet Thom's opening exhortation, "Destiny protect me from the world," coupled with the way he bitterly spits out a later line about wanting to be Jim Morrison, suggests that his tongue is planted firmly in cheek. The members of Radiohead knew as well as anyone the schoolboy's desire to play in a famous rock band— they'd lived it. But they also understood the underlying silliness of that desire, and how it can blind one to more important matters in life. On "Anyone Can Play Guitar," they deftly tackle both sides of the issue.

The central image presented by the lyrics of "Ripcord" is that of being dropped from a plane with no hope of opening the parachute, an apparent reference to the band's sense of directionlessness after being signed. This cheery picture is abetted by suitably jet-propelled music; for further excitement, the verses employ an extra half-bar of two beats as a delaying tactic, making us feel the gratification all the more when Ed and Jonny finally slash in. But though Thom's melody is solid and the chorus, powered by Phil's pounding tom-toms, is arresting, the guitars are set to stun a little too often for complete comfort. By the end, the proceedings have gotten predictable; the song's central descending chord progression, ear-catching at first, has turned into sloppy garage rock.

Like "Stop Whispering," "Vegetable" adopts a stance of resistance against suffocating outside forces. "I'm not a vegetable," Thom shouts, "I will not control myself." And like "Ripcord," the song makes heavy use of extra beats; each line of lyric gets a measure of ten beats rather than the more usual eight. The brief bridge section at the end of the verses has definite Beatles connotations. But the most effective part of the song is its middle eight, which shifts to a minor key and is enhanced by Jonny's lovely feedback-laced single-note guitar line. Another part of "Vegetable" that's worth mentioning is Thom Yorke's guitar playing. Though Thom has been known to jokingly credit himself with playing "inaudible guitar," his rhythm work, both here and on much of the rest of *Pablo Honey*, is actually quite audible and absolutely essential, forming the foundation of the song and also ornamenting it with the occasional delicate filigree.

The remaining four songs of *Pablo Honey* combine to produce a mood of nearly unbroken misery. "Prove Yourself" starts the ball rolling with the bluntly stated observation "I'm better off dead." The contrast between soft, sensitive verse and loud, pulverizing chorus is the same as on the earlier *Drill* version of the song, but the Slade/Kolderie wall-of-guitars production lends both parts more power. Once again, Thom's voice is higher in the mix, the rhythm section seems more in control, and Jonny contributes an energetic guitar solo.

"I Can't" is one of two *Pablo Honey* tracks produced by Chris Hufford at Courtyard but mixed by Sean and Paul back at Fort Apache. Despite its different sonic origins, it fits well into the album's general scheme. As the title suggests, the song's lyrics deal with the singer's inability to do much of anything due to his doubt and insecurity, though he does find just enough strength to confess, "If you give up on me now, I'll be gutted like I've never been before." (Not necessarily the best argument to make someone stick around, but . . .) Following an initial flourish of ambient guitar effects from Ed and Jonny, the main body of "I Can't" takes on a dirty pop tone that's agreeably similar to the roughly contemporaneous work of Glasgow's Teenage Fanclub—who would, several years later, tour with Radiohead. The drums-and-bass breakdown toward the end of the song, however, is all U2.

The other Hufford-produced track on the album, "Lurgee," directly follows "I Can't." Over a lush, reverb-heavy backdrop, Thom sings a simple series of lyrics in his most angelic voice, starkly claiming that his lover's leaving has been a good thing for him. With quiet insistence, he asserts several times that he feels better, that nothing is wrong, that he's gotten his strength back. The way these lines are repeated clearly implies that they are the desperate efforts of someone trying to convince himself of something that is untrue; everything is wrong, and the singer is weaker than ever. Underneath Thom's vocal, the guitars pick their way through a very open-sounding chord progression, and Colin's bass swoops majestically. The band plays differently here than on the rest of the album; instead of anxiously rushing, they're taking their time, achieving a pace that's almost stately. The song's noisy outro doesn't really lead anywhere, but by that point it doesn't matter. A mood has been successfully created, a mood of beautiful sadness. More than any other song on *Pablo Honey*, "Lurgee" points to the road Radiohead would travel in the future.

Pablo Honey's final song, "Blow Out," begins with a light, breezy groove that bears a faint tinge of bossa nova. The chord progression is simple but striking, employing the same kind of major/minor clash that marked the album's opening track, "You." (A clever bookending device? Perhaps.) Sounding as if he's grappling with some deep inner pain, Thom proclaims, "Everything I touch turns to stone." The closing jam, in which everyone's amp is turned up to 10 and Jonny runs a coin down his guitar's fretboard for extra scratchiness, does its best to live up to the song's title, but one suspects that the overall effect might have been a lot more breathtaking if the band hadn't played similar sonic cards several times previously over the course of the album.

Of all the opinions about *Pablo Honey* that have been aired since its release, a quote from *Melody Maker*'s original 1993 review seems the most appropriate: "Promisingly imperfect."[13] Looking back on Radiohead's debut from the vantage point of 1998, Ed O'Brien says, "There was certainly a period, because we did play those songs so much live, that we didn't like them anymore, but now, with hindsight, we look at it differently. It's five years ago, and we're a different band now—that was a naïve, young, impressionable band. But I think it's important that a debut album should not have all the answers, it should just hint at things. And *Pablo Honey* hints at things, it hints at a more perverse approach to songs. 'Creep,' obviously, is fairly direct but different, it's quirky. And songs like 'You' kind of hint at stuff on *The Bends*. There were a lot of mistakes on *Pablo Honey*, but we've only learnt really from our mistakes.

"It's a very up album. It's not as dark as *The Bends* or *OK Computer*, it's quite hedonistic, kind of 'Let's turn those guitars up loud.' I think it's one of those albums you might put on in an open-top car on a Saturday night if you were going to a party and you have your initial little smoke or whatever." Ed pauses and adds with a chuckle, "But I could be wrong."

6

In March 1993, with their debut album having already reached its U.K. chart peak of Number 25, Radiohead traveled to Israel to play three shows that EMI hoped would capitalize on their sudden success there. When they arrived in Tel Aviv, they got the full star treatment for the first time. Keith Wozencroft later recalled that the customs officers at the airport recognized the band: "[T]hey had the whole lot of them, managers and band . . . everybody . . . sing 'Creep.' They said that they wouldn't let them through otherwise."[1] It didn't end there; the audiences at the Israeli concerts displayed a level of enthusiasm the band hadn't seen before. At one show, a group of overly excited fans pulled out a clump of Thom's hair, a move that was coincidentally not that far out of line with Yorke's own brand of coif management at the time.

One Israeli admirer who managed to connect with the band in a slightly more civilized manner asked Colin if he could play bass on "Creep" at one of the shows. He didn't get the gig, but they allowed him to play at the soundcheck. "That was fine," Colin said. "If someone in New Order had let me play bass on one of their songs, it would have been great fun. It's the ultimate fan thing, really."[2]

"They were mobbed in the street," EMI Israel's Uzi Preuss remembers. "One day they went to a flea market in Tel Aviv and all these people recognized them from the 'Creep' video. They hadn't expected anything like that—in the U.K., hardly anyone knew who Radiohead was. It was an exciting time for them, and also very emotional."

By this time, U.S. rock radio was latching on to "Creep" with a vengeance, giving Capitol all the incentive they needed to issue *Pablo Honey* domestically. The release was set for April 20. An American tour wasn't in the cards yet—further U.K. and European tours had already been arranged, lasting from the end of April through mid-June—but a whirlwind promotional trip to New York and Los Angeles was quickly booked for the band. EMI's Carol Baxter remembered the event with barely disguised horror four years later in *Mojo*: "Eight A.M. breakfast with this executive, one P.M. lunch with fifty-five retailers, solid press interviews in between, seven P.M. dinner with this many journalists and, by the way, can you do a live radio phone-in at two A.M.? It was a sixteen- to eighteen-hour day with no breaks. I couldn't handle that. But they managed it."[3] It was an early indication of Radiohead's willingness to take on as much work as their label requested, no matter how much they might rather be doing something else. Their drive to succeed had, at least temporarily, won out over their distaste for following orders.

Somewhere between their voyages to the Mideast, the U.S., and Europe, Radiohead found the time to record some new material with their live sound engineer Jim Warren behind the board. The results of these sessions weren't all immediately released; one of the tracks, "High and Dry," wouldn't come out for nearly two more years. But a snappy up-tempo number called "Pop Is Dead" made the cut as the band's new single, released in the U.K. on May 10. (That single also featured live versions of "Creep" and "Ripcord," plus one other new song, "Banana Co.," a mildly Beatlesque tune with lyrics that hinted at a general loathing of multinational corporations. Quirkily, the original release of "Banana Co." was all-acoustic; the full-band electric version would not appear until January 1996, on the B-side of "Street Spirit.")

As its title suggests, "Pop Is Dead" takes the sarcasm of "Anyone Can Play Guitar" several giant steps further. Opening with the lines "Oh no, pop is dead, long live pop/It died an ugly death by back catalog," Yorke goes on to personify pop music as a drug-bloated zombie, skin peeling off its face from countless unsuccessful attempts at plastic surgery. Driven by a nasty chromatic riff from Jonny (which unfolds over 10 beats, yet another example of the band's taste for subtle rhythmic play) and an ensemble performance that's the epitome of raunch, the song was a feisty up-yours to record company executives, radio programmers, the rock press, everyone in the music industry who deluded themselves into thinking they had their finger on pop's pulse.

That such a song might not be greeted with open arms shouldn't have been much of a surprise. In any event, reviews were decidedly mixed, airplay was practically nonexistent, and "Pop Is Dead" peaked at Number 42 on the U.K. charts, not a total flop but not an indication of the direction the band wished to go in either. The members of Radiohead quickly distanced themselves from their latest single; Thom described it as "corking"

(British slang for "fantastic") around the time of its release, but even then he sounded a little sarcastic.[4] Nearly five years later, Ed O'Brien called it "a hideous mistake . . . Thank God it was never released in America." But not everyone shares that opinion. Robin Bresnark, one of the editors at *Melody Maker*, said of "Pop Is Dead" after *The Bends* was released, "If they came out with it now, it would be a Top Five single."[5] In truth, it's one of the better early Radiohead songs, a pleasantly aggressive, if minor, addition to the canon.

For his part, Thom Yorke continued to hold true to the beliefs underpinning "Pop Is Dead," maintaining that pop music had lost its vitality in the last 10 years and that Radiohead's goal was to try to bring that missing spirit back. "Remember the last time pop was good, you know, in the early eighties?" he once said. "That's kind of a reference point for us, bands who just sounded like themselves—Talking Heads, Depeche Mode. You hear them and it's just them. You don't get that now."[6]

Continuing their attempts to win new listeners, the band embarked on another short tour, taking in more U.K. cities and also performing for the first time in the Netherlands, at the Bevrijdingspop Festival in Haarlem. The band was gradually becoming known for its high-energy performance style; they'd progressed from the mere breaking of strings and drum heads to stronger stuff. Guitarists' fingers were regularly cut open, and Thom even gashed his head once while getting a little too physical with his instrument. "Our guitar tech loves it, because there's always loads of blood on all the guitars at the end of the night," he joked. " 'Performance' for us means we don't know what we're going to do."[7]

Thom's distinct way with words continued to endear him to new acquaintances on the road. When I first spoke to Thom in March 1996, he, Ed, and Jonny recalled one friendly incident from around this time:

O'BRIEN: There was a great one about a couple of years ago when we were in some gig up in the north of England, and one of the P.A. guys accused us of nicking a D.I. [direct audio signal injection] box. This guy's huge, he's taller than me, about six foot seven, and twice as wide.

YORKE: Like a fucking psycho.

O'BRIEN: And basically, Thom says no. [The soundman]'s still giving us hassles, so Thom tells him to fuck off, and looks up at him with a mean stare. So this guy gets Thom by the neck . . .

YORKE: He pinned me against the wall.

O'BRIEN: . . . and Phil and I had to take one arm each of this guy and try to wrench them off.

YORKE: I didn't tell him to fuck off.

O'BRIEN: Yeah, you did. I think that was the problem, really.

GREENWOOD: It was.

YORKE: Well, all right.

O'BRIEN: [*Laughs*] Considering he was upset anyway.

Bringing good cheer wherever they traveled, Radiohead continued the *Pablo Honey* tour in June with further shows in Denmark, Sweden, Holland, and France. From there, it was on to America.

The signs coming from the States were encouraging. *Pablo Honey* had debuted on the *Billboard* album charts in late May at an undistinguished Number 184, but as "Creep" garnered more airplay, it began a slow upward climb. And by now, the band had won its most significant U.S. endorsement yet: from MTV's cartoon team of Beavis and Butt-head. During the course of their usual informed commentary on the videos of the day, Mike Judge's troubled adolescent duo responded to the crunchy chorus of "Creep" with a hearty shout of *"ROCK!"* For Thom Yorke, a professed *Beavis and Butt-head* fan, it was a great moment. Capitol wasted little time turning the animated twosome's acclaim into part of the *Pablo Honey* marketing campaign. As Paul Kolderie later characterized it, "They were doing I'M A CREEP contests and placing ads that said BEAVIS AND BUTT-HEAD SAY THEY DON'T SUCK."[8]

Yet all this attention, far from pleasing Radiohead's managers, made them extremely wary. "I remember running into Bryce in Boston when they were coming in to tour and 'Creep' was blowing up," Kolderie says. "I said something like, 'Hey, we're doing good, huh?' and he gave me this classic sour look and said, 'I don't know, mate, it feels like a problem.' I said, 'What do you mean? We're doing awesome.' And he goes, 'Nah. At Capitol, they think it's a one-hit wonder, and they're just gonna work it, goose it to platinum, and then drop us.' So they were already counterattacking and saying, 'Don't you dare think of us that way.' They had to fight some people at Capitol who were not thinking very long-term, I have to say." Winning the right to success on the band's own terms against severe record-company pressure wasn't going to be easy.*

Radiohead arrived in the United States on June 22, 1993, for their first American performance, at Bill's Bar in Boston. They had literally just come off the previous European tour. "My first memory of getting to America," Thom said, "was that we drove

---

*According to some observers, this pressure didn't just come from the U.S. branch of EMI. Ronan Munro says that around the time *Pablo Honey* was released in England, "I remember hearing via a very reliable source that Parlophone had given the band six months. If they didn't do it in six months, they were going to be dumped. It was only because they did so well in America that they were kept on the label. The attitude of total apathy was unbelievable." John Harris, however, doubts this was the case: "Keith Wozencroft doesn't work like that with groups. You might give a pop act six months, but when you've got a rock act, especially one of such quality, with such a clear idea of who they are, and who are obviously in it for the long haul, no way." Still, one should remember Wozencroft was still a new member of the EMI A&R team at this time; the band's fate wasn't completely his decision.

overnight from Paris, caught the ferry, drove to Heathrow, then flew to New York. So in twenty hours we covered Paris, New York, and London, and then we drove straight out to Boston. I woke up on a coach, walked into this hotel in Boston at seven o'clock in the morning, switched on MTV, and there was 'Creep.' It was like, 'Oh my God. . . .' "[9]

Over a nearly month-long headlining club tour that would also cover New York, Chicago, Detroit, Toronto, Seattle, Los Angeles, and Dallas, the situation would stay largely within the realm of the surreal. The band's first live TV performance was on *The Arsenio Hall Show*—"Thom was so nervous that he was actually shaking," Jonny later reported[10]—followed in short order by an appearance on MTV's *Beach Party,* for which "Creep" made a bizarre soundtrack to shots of frolicking suntanned, designer bathing suit–wearing girls and boys. Their show at L.A.'s legendary Whiskey A Go-Go sold out within 20 minutes, but the band remembered the gig as a disaster.

Unable to see much of the country due to their strict schedule, Radiohead had to make do with a series of disconnected snapshots—a cultural landmark here, a few homeless people there—all the while freely expressing their surprise. Thom likened the tour to "going to Mars"[11] or "joining the circus,"[12] while Jonny said he was dumbfounded, even scared, by America's enthusiastic response to the band. "I don't think we can explain what the Americans like about us," he confessed.[13] That this was all happening basically because of one song was something the band members couldn't get their heads around: "[W]e always thought we would be the type of band that would just put out an album and people would buy it, and we wouldn't have to hear anything from it," Jonny said.[14] Ed later described the mood within the band as "hysterical . . . One moment we'd be giggling, the next we'd be really down. Our reactions were extreme."[15]

After the gig in Dallas, Ed was approached by a fetching

groupie-in-waiting with a tempting proposition. "[She said], 'My parents are away,'" he remembered, "'do you want to come back with me and do loads of coke?' I didn't have a girlfriend at the time and we had a day off the next day, but I was just flabbergasted."[16] The gallant O'Brien politely declined. In so doing, he helped establish a reputation for Radiohead, at least in the media, as conscientious abstainers. In the coming years that reputation would solidify, as observers of the band would typically comment on their preference for a spot of tea and a round of bridge on the tour bus to any all-night party scene.

Of course, this characterization of the band was only partially based in reality. True, Radiohead's behavior on tour will never be confused with that of Led Zeppelin. They're not heavy boozers, at least not normally, and they don't go in for one-night stands. Yet the image of bridge-playing tea drinkers presented in so many early media depictions of Radiohead was an exaggerated one, created largely by the band for their own amusement. The members of Radiohead, especially Jonny, are known to get a kick out of playing the foppish Englishman abroad. (Ask the younger Greenwood how he's doing, and he's apt to reply, "Jolly well, and how about your good self?" It's all a big laugh.) And they certainly aren't opposed to chemical indulgences; as Jonny once put it, "Playing bridge goes very well with drugs."[17]

Radiohead's first U.S. tour may have been unmarked by sexual conquests, but it paid off in commercial terms. In August, "Creep" peaked at Number 34 in *Billboard*, and *Pablo Honey* reached Number 32. On September 1, the album was certified gold (for sales of 500,000 copies) in the States. (It has since reached platinum status, selling over a million copies in America alone.) However, this success abroad spawned unexpected results back home. The U.K. media were frankly mystified that a band who hadn't amounted to much so far on British soil could raise so much hay elsewhere, and along with that disbelief came suspicion. A headline in the London *Evening Standard,* "British Pop Unknowns Storm U.S.A.," pretty much told the story. The general British conception that Radiohead were "bigger" in America than in their homeland would linger for years, far past the point of its being disproven, and would foster a certain amount of mistrust in the nation's often xenophobic music press.

"There was a great deal of skepticism, particularly at the *NME,* as regards Radiohead," John Harris confirms. "Even after *The Bends* came out, you'd have been hard pressed to find a cover with them on. In fact, the features editor at the *NME* once told Philip Hall that over his dead body would Radiohead ever get in the *NME.* For them to have a hit in the States first was a great stigma, tying into that whole British snootiness about groups like the Fixx and Wang Chung—people don't like the idea of 'We should like this because it's big in America.'"

The band's return to England at the end of July was further clouded by Thom's receipt of a disturbing fan letter. As was the case with many such letters, the writer felt a sense of identification with "Creep." What made him different was that he was an inmate in a British prison, serving a life sentence for murder. As Yorke reported later, "He said, 'I'm the creep in that song. I killed this bloke. They made me do it. It wasn't me, it was the words in my head.' I felt like someone had walked over my grave."[18]

It wouldn't be the last such letter Radiohead would get, but at an already trying time it helped tip the band's emotional balance. The psychic discomforts of sudden fame were clearly getting to Thom. In August, he and his bandmates were scheduled to make the usual European summer festival rounds, and they held up their end of the bargain through two appearances in Belgium and one in Holland. But when it came time to play the high-profile Reading Festival back in the U.K., Radiohead pulled out. The reason given: Thom's voice was shot. It was true enough, but the source of Yorke's laryngitis sprang more from high stress than from any sort of virus or bacteria. He later explained that the cumulative effects of his own anxieties had turned his neck as hard as concrete. "Our so-called success in America . . . allowed us to do lots of things," he said, "but it also meant that somehow we *owed* somebody something. But I couldn't work out who and I couldn't work out how much."[19] Sensitive to a fault, Thom obsessed over questions like this to such a degree that he was liable to put himself out of commission.

Meanwhile, Parlophone was making plans to reissue "Creep" in Britain. With all the attention the song had belatedly gotten from Israel to America, it seemed only right to give it a second chance in the country of its original release. The band weren't fond of the idea—for them, "Creep" was rapidly becoming ancient history—but that made little difference. "We did all originally agree not to re-release 'Creep,'" Colin said, "but after doing so well in America, there was this tremendous pressure from radio people, the press, the record company, even our fans, to put it out."[20]

The second edition of the single was released on September 6. Backing "Creep" up this time were the simmering rocker "Yes I Am" (from the same sessions with Jim Warren that produced "Pop Is Dead"), a remix of "Blow Out," and a live, raging "Inside My Head" recorded at Chicago's Metro club during the summer U.S. tour. In a typical move to milk more cash out of rabid fans, EMI also issued a limited-edition vinyl 12-inch single combining a solo acoustic version of "Creep," recorded at L.A.'s KROQ, with three more Metro recordings: "You," "Vegetable," and "Killer Cars," another piece of automobile-related paranoia from Thom. (Like "Banana Co." before it, this was an acoustic performance; an electric studio version of "Killer Cars" wouldn't appear until '95.)

EMI's instincts were right. A year after its initial release, "Creep" rocketed up to Number 7 on the U.K. singles chart. Now Radiohead's services were requested on the national TV show *Top of the Pops.* It was, in a sense, a vindication of the band in their home country, yet it also doomed them to further repetition of a hit song that was growing all too familiar.

With Thom having recovered from his bout of laryngitis, it was time for Radiohead to return to the U.S. for a second tour. Capitol had wanted them to open for labelmates Duran Duran, the '80s heartthrobs who were then making a comeback with the smash hit "Ordinary World." But Chris Hufford was adamantly against this. He pushed instead for an opening slot with Belly, the new group fronted by ex–Throwing Muses guitarist Tanya Donelly; the bill was more low-key, more credible, and harmonized more with the tastes of the band, many of whom were ardent Throwing Muses fans.

In the end, Hufford got his way. Radiohead joined Belly on September 17 for a tour that would last over a month. The choice of act to support turned out to have been an inspired one, as the two bands got along famously. Tour highlights included another TV appearance, this time on NBC's brand new *Late Night with Conan O'Brien* (as the show's first-ever musical guests), and a gig at the famous 40 Watt club in Athens, Georgia, attended by none other than Athens natives Mike Mills and Bill Berry of R.E.M. Yorke described meeting his longtime idols as "a bit of a laugh."[21] It was also the beginning of a friendship that would prove to be highly important in the years ahead.

The Belly tour concluded on an unusual note, but one that typified Radiohead's ultracivilized demeanor. In celebration of their final gig together, the two bands decided to throw a book party. As Tanya Donelly remembered in 1995, "[E]veryone in our band bought books for everyone in their band, and they all bought books for us. Someone gave me *Geek Love*, which is a great book. [Belly guitarist] Tom [Gorman] and Ed [O'Brien] still mail books to each other."[22]

Perhaps the strangest gig of this American jaunt took place just after the Belly tour ended, a special show at the Aladdin Theatre in Las Vegas opening for Tears for Fears. The headliners' crew refused Radiohead a soundcheck and generally "treated us like pigs," in Ed's words.[23] Never ones to take such insults gladly, the Oxfordites trashed the stage during their set. "There were all these great lights down the front and they were eminently kickable," Thom recalled with glee.[24] Which made it all the more head-scratching when TFF encored that night with a cover of "Creep." "We thought he [lead Tear Roland Orzabal] was taking the piss," Ed said. "Apparently he loved the song and he didn't know anything about his crew being wankers to us."[25] Not that the band cared much for Orzabal's pompous reworking of the song—"He changed the lyrics, saying that he *was* special," Colin commented, "and there was no self-doubt in the tone of his voice"[26]—but the fact that TFF played "Creep" regularly for the rest of their tour did have its benefits: "He [Orzabal] has to pay money for it," Colin pointed out, "so that's cool."[27]

After covering the U.S., Radiohead ventured north to Canada, hitting Vancouver, Calgary, Montreal, and finishing up in Toronto on November 2. In just a little over a week, the band were scheduled to start another tour, this one in Europe supporting James, the arty English ensemble whose latest album, *Laid*, had been produced by Brian Eno. By this point, however, a deep confusion had set in within the band's ranks. The exhaustion of traveling, the endless rounds of press and radio interviews, the lack of inspiration on the road, had begun to make them suspicious that they were running on a treadmill from which they might not be able to escape. "There was a lot of soul-searching about why they were in a group at all," agent Charlie Myatt recalled.[28] As usual, Thom bore the effects most obviously. In some sort of attempt to turn himself into the rock star that he thought people expected him to be, he'd been inflicting more and more damage on his appearance. For some time, his hair had been an unbecoming peroxide blond. Now he'd taken to sporting an ungainly set of Medusa-like hair extensions. "I *was* rock," he later said with a laugh. "There were so many elements to that period, but the hair was the worst."[29]

Yorke's hair wasn't the only thing that had grown. With all the attention bestowed on the band in America, his ego had swollen to outrageous proportions. Not long after Radiohead returned from its preliminary transatlantic voyages, he admitted, "When I got back to Oxford I was unbearable. . . . [A]s soon as you get any success you disappear up your own arse and lose it forever. . . . You start to believe you're this sensitive artist who has to be alone . . . this melodramatic, tortured person, in order to create wonderful music. The absolute opposite is true."[30]

Asked in early 1995 whether the band had suffered from internal strife on the road during this time, Jonny responded, "Strife infers [*sic*] arguments and things being thrown, but it was *worse* than that. It was a very silent, cold thing, away from each other. No one was really talking to anyone, and we were just trying to get through the year, which was a mistake. . . . There were never rows or anything, which is worse in a way. Everyone withdrew. . . . [W]e thought we were trapped in one of those *Twilight Zone* slow time machines, and everything was drawn out. It was very strange: We could never play for fun anymore. We never got to rehearse. We weren't writing songs, which we had done for seven years."[31]

The band were bone-tired of playing the same old songs live every night. "Creep" was becoming a special strain. Thom said he was starting to feel as though he was playing a cover version of someone else's song, "except we just happened to have written it. It's very surreal."[32] Colin opined, "It's not that it's not fun playing it live, but it's a different mind game playing that song live compared to some other songs where you really feel you can let loose and take off with the music, like 'Blow Out.'"[33] According to some reports, Radiohead had renamed their biggest hit "Crap." What made things all the more disheartening was that, at so many of their recent gigs, a substantial portion of the audience didn't seem to care about any other song they played. The one-hit wonder status they'd all wanted to avoid was beckoning.

Still, the show had to go on, and the band joined the James tour in Europe as planned, traversing Germany, France, Switzerland, Spain, Portugal, and finally England again. According to Myatt, they "played like demons,"[34] but much of that energy grew from doubt and anger. Matters came to a head when they landed in Hamburg for the tour's first date; a group meeting was hastily called, during which Thom and his bandmates harangued each other on various points, the actual substance of which remains a mystery. Reportedly, no punches were thrown—these were still polite English boys, after all—but much alcohol was consumed, and both voices and emotions ran high. It wasn't long before the quintet realized they still had more in common than not, and accordingly, no shows were canceled. But feelings remained tender. At the end of the tour on December 13, the band dispersed for the holidays with relief.

Over the break, Thom turned his attention toward buying a house, a sign suggesting both that he'd come into some serious funds and that he was in need of shelter in more ways than one. After moving out of the Ridgefield Road Radiohead commune in 1992, Thom had found himself a small basement flat but had barely lived in it for any stretch of time since the band had been on the road so much. Now that he'd returned, he thought the place was too depressing. So Yorke invested in a three-bedroom detached house in the Oxford suburb of Headington, not far from Brookes University, for himself and his girlfriend Rachel Owen. He jokingly christened it "The House That 'Creep' Built," and although he could have made the down payment in cash, he chose not to, figuring that the royalties off his hit "might be the only money I ever make."[35]

Back in America, a follow-up single to "Creep" had been released in October: "Stop Whispering," in a new mix by Chris Sheldon, with most of the hard edges of the album version either removed or camouflaged under a gentle synthesizer pad. ("Pop Is Dead" appeared as one of the B-sides, coupled with reprises of the acoustic "Creep" and live "Inside My Head.") But any hopes that the song would build on the success of "Creep" were ill-founded. Instead, it quickly sank without a trace, dropping off the *Billboard* modern rock radio chart within three weeks after peaking at Number 23 and never denting the Hot 100. The effect this had on the band can best be conveyed by quoting at length from a subsequent highly charged interview with Thom and Jonny in *B-Side*:

> The single's destruction caused Thom pain. "It hurt." There's a brief pause until he adds, "It hurt *me* anyway."
>
> Jon quickly points out, "I was for releasing 'Blow Out.'"
>
> Thom isn't sparing any venom. "It was bloody stupid."
>
> In a charitable moment, Jonny begins a solid explanation. "Capitol came in and said radio will play this."
>
> An appallingly arch American accent emerges from Thom's mouth to kill off Jonny's attempt. "'Radio will play *this*. It will be great.' It *wasn't*. . . . We hadn't realized that the only way to create music is for the five of us to be sit-

ting in a room creating music rather than going, 'What should we be doing now, sir? OK, suck Satan's cock.' We hadn't learned yet, and now we have," he declares. . . .

Jonny again takes the more restrained tack. "I was upset, but they had been right about all those other things. You have to rely and trust them to an extent. So I think it's really foolish for bands to take the 'we hate our record company' line. It doesn't make much sense. You just have to be intelligent about it."

An epic sigh gusts from Thom's small frame, followed by a testy "Yeah, but the problem was we didn't *have* the distance from it to work out what the hell was going on, to work out that the song didn't sound any good, that the mix was *shocking* and we spent too much money on the video. It's the usual follow-up syndrome. We just wanted to move on, really. . . . We had done so many versions of 'Stop Whispering' that you wouldn't *believe* it. Now Radiohead have this rule: You never, *ever* record a song more than once."[36]

The new rule was a noble one, but they wouldn't stick to it.

There was a bright side to all this, sort of. The readers of *Melody Maker* and *NME*, as well as the staff of the latter, named "Creep" Single of the Year. It was the *Rolling Stone* writers' top choice for Best Song of 1993. And it made Number 2 in the Radio One year-end poll, beaten out just slightly by, of all songs, Take That's "Pray."

At the end of 1993, Radiohead had a dizzying number of achievements to look back on. In the year that had just passed, they had played 130 shows in 14 different countries, gathering acclaim and success that they could only have dreamed of previously. A strong organization had been established behind the band with Chris Hufford and Bryce Edge at the helm, and their record company had been incredibly supportive. And yet, even as they'd won more fame, they'd become less satisfied. Their original plan had been to release *Pablo Honey*, do a relatively brief tour in support of it, and then go back to the studio to work on new material. But as "Creep" grew to be a worldwide hit, the demand for public appearances by the band had put those plans on indefinite hold, and time had continued, irritatingly, to stretch on. "We joined this band to write songs and be musicians," Jonny said. "But we spent a year being jukeboxes instead."[37]

With no more tour dates scheduled for another five months and a new clutch of songs in the works from Thom and Jonny, it looked as though the band could finally get around to some serious recording. But things would get worse before they'd get better. The "usual follow-up syndrome," in Thom's words, hadn't been vanquished yet.

Nineteen ninety-four started off well, at least. Back in their apple shed/rehearsal space, Radiohead began to devise the arrangements for a large group of new songs. Actually, they weren't all that new, some having predated the release of *Pablo Honey* by nearly a year, but most of those older selections emphasized sides of the band that hadn't been heard before. Ed remembered those January rehearsals as "amazing"[38] and confessed that, when listening back to a tape of one of their practices, he was particularly struck by how connected the band's different musical parts were to Thom's words, a connection that had not been consciously planned: "It's not as clinical as 'He sang that, so we'll do something like that.' I think it's because we've been playing for a long time."[39]

The band were also encouraged by the news that the producer they'd wanted, John Leckie, had agreed to work with them on the new album. A well-regarded studio veteran, Leckie had started

The first press coverage of On A Friday, December 1991 . . .
(Courtesy of Ronan Munro)

. . . and their return to *Curfew*'s cover as Radiohead in February 1993. *(Courtesy of Ronan Munro)*

ABOVE: Abingdon School, where the members of Radiohead first met. *(Mac Randall)*

RIGHT: The Jericho Tavern, Oxford, as it was in the early '90s. *(Pat Loughnane)*

ABOVE: October 1993, San Francisco, with Thom deep into his Rock Hair phase. *(Jay Blakesberg)*

LEFT: An atomic performance at Glastonbury, 1994. *(Pat Loughnane)*

RIGHT: Colin (right) and Ed (left) get into the groove at an outdoor gig sponsored by early U.S. radio supporter KITS (Live 105), Justin Herman Plaza, San Francisco, April 1995.
(Jay Blakesberg)

BELOW: Thom in action, San Francisco, April 1995.
(Jay Blakesberg)

ABOVE: Thom and
Colin look thoughtful
for the camera in an
Oxford nightclub, 1996.
(Pat Loughnane)

RIGHT: Jonny in a
reflective moment
during a show for
Portland, OR radio
station KNRK,
August 1997.
(Danny Clinch)

ABOVE: Mr. Yorke and Mr. Stipe (and Mike Mills in the background) at the 1998 Tibetan Freedom Concert, Washington, D.C. *(Jay Blakesberg)*

LEFT: Thom tests P.A. capacity at the Troubadour in Los Angeles, June 1997. *(Danny Clinch)*

LEFT: Ed calls for the karma police, Radio City Music Hall, New York, April 1998. *(Ebet Roberts)*

BELOW: The brothers Greenwood (Jonny on transistor radio, Colin on bass synth) rehearse "Climbing Up The Walls" before their Radio City show, April 1998. *(Danny Clinch)*

Phil with eye-catching accessories, Portland, Oregon, August 1997.
(Danny Clinch)

out as an EMI engineer at Abbey Road assisting Phil Spector on George Harrison's *All Things Must Pass* in 1970 and had gone on to an illustrious career working with, among others, Pink Floyd, XTC, the Fall, and the Stone Roses (whom he'd patiently coached through the sessions of their influential first album). But it was his work on Magazine's 1978 debut, *Real Life,* that had most endeared him to Radiohead, especially to Colin, the band's most ardent fan of Howard Devoto and his art-punk cohorts. Adding value was Leckie's reputation as a calm, hands-off producer, something the band felt could be important in easing the way to a successful second album. "We haven't ever worked with a non-engineering producer who just sits there and tells an engineer what to do," Ed commented enthusiastically.[40] As Thom put it, "[H]e [Leckie] was the only one we were going to use."[41]

When Keith Wozencroft had first approached Leckie in the summer of 1993 to produce Radiohead, he'd sent along a copy of *Pablo Honey* and a tape of some of the demos under consideration for the next album. That fall, Leckie also saw the band play live in Gloucester on the James tour. He wasn't impressed with *Pablo Honey,* finding it "too noisy," but the new material was a different matter: "I liked the straight-aheadness of the demos . . . and I thought, 'This could be easy.'"[42] Unfortunately, circumstances quickly conspired to ensure that it wouldn't be. Sessions had originally been set to start in January at RAK studios in north London, but that schedule changed after Leckie, making an early exit from the laborious tracking of the Stone Roses' second album, was approached with an enticing short-term offer from another notable Oxford band, Ride. The group faced an emergency situation; their next album, to be titled *Carnival of Light,* had already undergone extensive pre-production work, but its intended producer, George Drakoulias, had bailed out of the project at the last minute. To come in under budget and on schedule, Ride needed to finish the album within a few weeks, and they wanted Leckie's help.

Even though the studio time that Ride requested overlapped with the beginning of Radiohead's proposed sessions with Leckie, the latter group, in a gesture of goodwill to their hometown compatriots, agreed to delay their own recording plans, pushing their start date back to February 24. (In the end, despite the two groups' best efforts to get out of each other's way, Leckie still spent a few days working on both albums simultaneously.) No one knew it at the time, but that simple postponement would end up wreaking a great deal of havoc. Given the dubious benefit of a few extra weeks in their rehearsal space, Radiohead proceeded to run their new songs into the ground. By the time they got to RAK, Yorke says, "We had all these songs and we really liked them, but we knew them almost too well . . . so we had to sort of learn to like them again before we could record them, which is odd."

To call the events of the next two months "odd" would be a severe understatement. The underlying problem wasn't with the producer, though. "The best part about working with John Leckie," Jonny recalls, "was that he didn't dictate anything to us. He allowed us to figure out what we wanted to do ourselves." Neither did anyone have any trouble dealing with the RAK house engineer, Nigel Godrich, a Leckie protégé who also became a good friend of Radiohead. Even so, the early sessions for what would become *The Bends* were exceedingly difficult. From the start, everyone in the band, but especially Thom, felt great pressure to make a follow-up album that would build on the success of *Pablo Honey*. And working under pressure was not Radiohead's forte.

From the point of view of the band's management and record company, most of the pressure was not imposed from without but from within the band. "Radiohead are infuriating sometimes because they hate anything that's second-best," Chris Hufford later said. "[M]ost of the problems were in their heads."[43] Colin seemed to second this opinion when he told the *Toronto Star,* "What we got bogged down on was finding a direction. Obviously we had to get as far away from 'Creep' as possible.* How to do that became this huge energy-sucking black hole."[44] Desperate not to repeat themselves but unsure of which way to turn, Radiohead could easily become overwhelmed by their own perfectionism.

Still, it wasn't the band that had come up with an October '94 release date for the album, thus imposing a production deadline that quickly proved unrealistic. Both Hufford and EMI's Keith Wozencroft have subsequently admitted that this decision was ill-made. "There were pressures on deadline," Wozencroft told *Mojo.* "But accidentally. We'd all sat around saying, 'In an ideal world, what would be good?' Setting a rough agenda. But being a young band, they took that seriously; they were very keen to achieve the best scenario."[45]

"The RAK sessions were fraught, to put it mildly," Hufford acknowledged. "There was a lot of mutual misunderstanding. We didn't understand the pressure Thom was under. We attempted to do it [push for autumn release] for the right reasons, but we fucked up majorly. We weren't as considerate as we should have been."[46]

EMI didn't help matters by making the foolish suggestion that the band should record the album's lead-off single first. Jonny later called this "a very bad idea because it set the album on a really wrong track."[47] The main problem was that nobody

---

*John Leckie says, "My impression was that they were being requested to do something *even better* than 'Creep,' and they felt like they were being asked to better something where they didn't know what was good about it in the first place."

agreed on what the lead-off single should be. Out of the two dozen songs under consideration for the album, four contenders had been chosen: "Sulk," "The Bends," "Nice Dream," and "Just." This being the case, the band was encouraged to concentrate on those four. However, it soon became apparent that starting a recording session trying to record four hit singles in succession was counterproductive. "Everyone was pulling their hair out saying, 'It's not good enough!'" Leckie remembered. "We were trying too hard."[48]

The recording process began to slow down. Whole days were spent in frantic search of the elusive tonal formula that would yield that magic mega-seller. Insisting that Jonny had to have "a really special sound" and ignoring Leckie's observation that he already had one, the band rented laughable numbers of guitars and amps to try out before coming to the conclusion that Radiohead's lead guitarist was better off with what he'd had to start with. "They felt like being exploratory," Leckie says with a chuckle. "Once you've got yourself a [rental] budget, you use it—you hire the '53 Les Paul and the electric sitar and all the fancy gadgets. But of course, the way Jonny plays is that the instrument becomes part of him. If the instrument takes over from him, he doesn't react in the same way and he doesn't play so well."

Weeks went by with barely a usable note committed to tape. "[E]very three or four days the record company or manager would turn up to hear these hit singles," Leckie said, "and all we'd done was get a drum sound or something."[49] The regular presence of these unwanted authorities only stalled the sessions further. "We were playing like paranoid little mice in cages," Jonny said. "We were scared of our instruments, scared of every note not being right."[50]

"I couldn't have been more freaked out," Yorke told *Select* after the fun was over. "If we hadn't pulled this record off I would have given it all up. It has got to be the hardest thing I've ever,

ever done. . . . We had days of painful self-analysis, a total fucking meltdown for two fucking months."[51] The RAK sessions were increasingly taken up by more and more directionless band meetings. At one point, Thom seriously considered scrapping all the songs they'd worked on so far and replacing them with an entirely new crop (as yet unwritten). Meanwhile, Leckie and Godrich did their best to remain encouraging. In answer to the band's continual question of how they should proceed, Leckie's response was reportedly: "It's up to you. Just do it rather than sit there thinking about it."[52] Leckie later admitted to being somewhat amused by the band's apparent disintegration. "Perhaps," he said, "they suddenly realized this is what they'd be doing with their lives: 'I didn't mean to be in the same room as you for the next ten years!' "[53]

Chris Hufford wasn't laughing, though. "That was certainly the lowest point I've had in my relationship with Thom and, I'm sure, vice versa," he remembered. "Thom became totally confused about what he wanted to do, what he was doing in a band and in his life, and that turned into a mistrust of everybody else. I came very close to saying, 'I can't be fucked with this any more. I can't be doing with all this hassle; it's just not worth it.' Thankfully, just prior to me—and Thom—really snapping, it suddenly turned around."[54]

In April, nearly two months into recording, and sensing that the ego conflict between Thom and his bandmates was once again coming to a head (the former wanted to keep working, the latter wanted a break), Leckie suggested that Thom should lay down some of the songs by himself on acoustic guitar. Free for the time being from having to consider anyone else's sound or part, free to concentrate solely on his own performance, Thom did as he was told. The first song he completed in this manner was "Fake Plastic Trees," a sort of antipower ballad that had previously eluded all the band's attempts to play it properly. This time, alone with his acoustic, Thom was finally pleased with the results. It was the breakthrough everyone had been waiting for.*

Unfortunately, the breakthrough had come too late for Radiohead to finish the album at RAK. Another concert tour was coming up in May, covering Spain, Italy, Switzerland, and Germany; returning to the U.K. for three dates at the end of the month; then jetting off for a first-time trip to Japan, Hong Kong, Australia, and New Zealand. The band wouldn't be able to record again until mid-June. EMI's original plan for an October release date was by now a lost cause, and a new single wouldn't be coming any time soon either. In the end, however, Radiohead left RAK far from empty-handed. They'd managed to nail definitive versions of several songs besides "Fake Plastic Trees," including "Just," "Planet Telex," "Black Star," "Street Spirit," and most of the tracks that would eventually make up the *My Iron Lung* EP (though at this time, all those songs were still viewed as contenders for the album).

Looking back on the RAK sessions, John Leckie is philosophical. "If you want to make a good record, you have to suffer a little, in theory anyway. That doesn't mean it has to be hell all the time, but I wouldn't say those sessions *were* hell. The main thing was that they went on for a long time—I think we were booked there for nine weeks straight. Now I've worked at RAK many times and it's a great studio, but it wasn't what I'd have chosen for two and a half months, working every day except Sundays. I'd

---

*Both Colin and John Leckie would later claim that Thom's performance on "Fake Plastic Trees" had been inspired by a gig that both band and producer had seen at the Garage club in Highbury the night before, one of the earliest appearances on British soil by a promising young American singer/songwriter named Jeff Buckley. Boasting a vocal range and sorrowful timbre similar to Thom's, Buckley stunned the crowd with just one voice and one guitar, reminding the band that simplicity had its virtues. Sadly, Buckley was not destined to live a long life; he drowned accidentally in the Mississippi River in 1997, having completed only one album, 1994's *Grace,* a recording that stands alongside Radiohead's *The Bends* as one of the most thrilling of the '90s.

rather spend two weeks, then have a couple of weeks off and come back to it. But because the band's schedule was tight, we couldn't work that way.

"Another thing about Radiohead is that they're very democratic. Usually when I go into the studio with a band, someone in the band becomes the central figure and steps into a production role with me. But what happens with Radiohead is that everyone's comment is valid. And when everyone has an opinion, the process gets lengthened. We'd talk about the tempo of a song, for instance, and I'd say, 'The last gig you did you played this a lot faster,' and it's like, 'Well, we want it slower now.' So then you'd have to record it again.

"What I remember most about those sessions, though—more than pressure from record company or management, people throwing wobblies [tantrums], people's insecurities or mistrust of each other—was that Thom would come in at nine o'clock in the morning and play piano for four hours. And that wasn't just once, it was every morning. He was *always* the first one in the studio. We'd get in around one o'clock and he'd be at the piano, and Nigel would say, 'You know, he's been there since nine.' It was inspiring."

Having supplanted their road weariness of the previous year with a newer studio weariness, the members of Radiohead soon found themselves surprisingly happy to be on tour again, playing in front of actual audiences—even if those audiences still did yell louder for "Creep" than for any other number. With each night's set containing a healthy amount of newer material, the band slowly began to regain a feel for the songs they'd been trying to record. By the time they arrived back in England for the opening U.K. gig at the Manchester Academy on May 25, they'd recovered a great deal of their confidence. Still, Thom, at least, was keenly aware of some lingering bad feelings, particularly in the British music press, about the band's abrupt pulling out of the previous year's Reading Festival. He greeted the Academy's 500-plus crowd with these words: "I was scared shitless about tonight. There are a lot of people out there who'd like to tear us to shreds. I hope you're not some of them."[55]

That night, Yorke definitely put his all into his performance. During "Anyone Can Play Guitar," his stage antics became so abandoned that he slipped and damaged his left ankle. What was at first regarded as just a nasty sprain was later discovered to be a hairline fracture. Yet the tour juggernaut missed nary a beat, and Radiohead appeared as scheduled for the next show in Wolverhampton, with Thom's foot snugly braced. The third and final U.K. engagement of the tour, a fiery show at London's Astoria on May 27, was filmed by MTV Europe, who quickly began airing clips from it; a video of the entire gig would be released the following year. The Astoria show was also caught on tape by John Leckie with a mobile recording unit and ended up yielding the final backing track of "My Iron Lung," a song that the band had labored in vain to get right during the RAK sessions.

It was also during this time that Jonny's aggressive, arm-snapping playing style began giving him serious pain. His doctor diagnosed a repetitive stress injury and advised Jonny to wear a brace on his right arm, which has since become something of a trademark. "It's conceited to deny there's any affectation, but having said that, I enjoy putting the arm brace on before I play," he admitted to *Q.* "It's like taping up your fingers before a boxing match. It's a ritual."[56]

From England, it was on to the Far East and Australasia. To everyone who was observing, it seemed that the band was finally back to something at least resembling normal. "Playing live again put the perspective back on what they'd lost in the studio," Chris Hufford said. "Suddenly there was a direction."[57] But direction or no, Radiohead hadn't lost its essential cynicism. Thom later recounted a telling incident during the New Zealand portion of that tour: "We were taken to one of the most beautiful places I've ever seen in my life, the place where they filmed *The Piano,* and there I was, thinking, 'This is wonderful. I don't think I've ever seen scenery so spectacular.' And suddenly it occurred to me that the only reason we were there was because . . . I can't put my finger on it, but something to do with the industry. A lot to do with MTV. And whenever you see MTV, there's a Coca-Cola machine right next to it. And I just felt like we were a part of it all. And all at once, the view lost all meaning."[58]

Perhaps Radiohead was turning into just another part of the entertainment media conglomerates' conspiracy to take over the world, but at least now they were showing that they could potentially make some worthwhile music while doing so. On June 16, back in England, the band began recording again, but this time the scene had shifted from RAK to Richard Branson's famous rural studio complex, the Manor. The difference in the band's attitude was striking, as songs that had caused endless trouble beforehand now went down on tape with barely a hitch. "We finished nearly everything at our time there," John Leckie said later. "I think it helped that they'd been on tour because they had confidence in a lot of the songs again, which I think they'd maybe lost during that lengthy recording period."[59] What little remained to be done after the Manor sessions would be accomplished at the legendary Abbey Road Studios in London, where Leckie would also mix several songs. One of those, "My Iron Lung," for which Thom had recorded a new vocal track on top of the band's live performance from the Astoria show, was now being earmarked as the next single.

As most musicians would be, Radiohead were excited to work at Abbey Road, particularly in Studio Two, which will be forever known as "the Beatles' room." Yet working in a typical studio environment, even one as well equipped and famous as Abbey Road, was already beginning to pale for the band. "It's an institution, first and foremost, like a hospital," Colin later said of EMI's flagship studio. "It's great, but it's not a farmhouse with a great kitchen, great food, and a big old space that you can record in [like the Manor]. The people there are fantastic, but you are in an EMI corporate thing."[60] Just as Radiohead's music was growing more refined, so was its taste in where to make that music.

Between recording sessions, Radiohead put in its time at the summer festivals. The first was Glastonbury, on June 26, by all accounts an incendiary set, and an experience that Thom remembered as "a bit of a shock to us. I've never really understood the appeal of standing in a field not being able to hear the band, but I could after that. There was just such an amazing atmosphere."[61] Their next festival appearance, at Roskilde in Denmark on July 2, was less pleasant; Jonny forgot his passport, severely delaying the band's arrival at the festival grounds. Once they did arrive, only minutes before they were due to go on, they found themselves playing to an audience that was mostly drunk and uninterested. Thom commented that "the entire crowd was made up of old people. I think everyone else had just passed out."[62]

The band's next big outdoor gig was on August 23 at the Sopot Festival in Poland, but that was just a warm-up for the main event: Radiohead's long-awaited debut at the Reading Festival on August 27. As Jonny later told *B-Side*, it wasn't just the press and the fans who regarded a Reading appearance as an event of high importance—the band did too. "[W]hen we were playing the Reading Festival," he said, "we were the most scared that we've ever been in our lives. We had went [*sic*] to Reading since we were fourteen and you have dreams about playing there, and . . . it all comes across as being surreal, what has happened to us. . . ."[63] The nerves didn't seem to inhibit the band too much, as they tore into a mix of old and new material and easily won over the crowd. They didn't win over Chris Hufford, though, who was reportedly miffed at the inclusion of so much unfamiliar new material in the set. Over time, Hufford would get a little more used to such tactics from his charges. He'd have to, because they weren't going to change their ways.

Following the Reading performance, Radiohead took a brief break from gigging and recording at Abbey Road. The time off was partly for Phil's benefit; he got married to his longtime girlfriend, Cait, and the couple honeymooned by the sea at Lyme Regis on England's south coast. On September 26, the first product of the long-running Leckie sessions, "My Iron Lung," was issued in Britain in four separate versions—two CDs, cassette, and 12-inch vinyl—each with a different track order of B-sides. This multiformat release was, like the re-release of "Creep" had been, a despicable ploy on the part of EMI to get Radiohead fans to buy the same song several times, thereby inflating its chart position.

Yet EMI was only following what was rapidly turning into standard U.K. music industry practice. In Britain during most of the '90s, it was common for major musical acts to release multiple versions of their singles in an attempt to gain higher chart positions for those singles; only toward the end of the decade did music-biz authorities step in and rewrite the rules on this issue, making it more difficult for singles with multiple B-sides to qualify for the U.K. singles charts and thus removing much of the incentive for the record companies' previous scheme. (The Australian version of "My Iron Lung" was the only one to feature all six B-sides on one disc, a sensible alternative that has since become widely available.)

"My Iron Lung" was greeted with puzzlement by fans and the press, but in retrospect, its jangly ring-modulated opening hook, smooth McCartney-esque vocal verse melody, and pulverizing guitar explosions in the bridge sections mark it as a prime example of the new, more refined Radiohead style. As for the other songs on the various single permutations, Thom noted, "You could say that they're outtakes, but they're a bit more than outtakes, really. They're songs that just didn't get on the album. So we said fuck it, we'll release it as a set of songs. . . . [W]e think they're good, otherwise we wouldn't have plugged them on."[64]

While most of these six songs would never make the Radiohead A-list—the band did the right thing in leaving them off the album—they are by no means throwaways. A rapidly growing sophistication is evident; though the "My Iron Lung" B-sides are, if anything, more stylistically diverse than the songs on *Pablo Honey*, the band's performances are far more assured here than on their debut, making what could have been a schizophrenic hodgepodge into a smooth, cohesive whole. And a distinctive one at that. Losing the obvious influence-peddling tendencies of their early years, Radiohead are gradually sounding more like themselves. The dominant strands that tie it all together, of course, are Yorke's singing, which sounds more wounded than ever—for the first (but certainly not the last) time, Thom mumbles and slurs words, forgoing clear enunciation in favor of a more direct conveyance of an emotional state—and the nearly unrelenting morbidity of the lyrics.

Of the six B-sides, the most developed compositionally are "The Trickster" and "Punchdrunk Lovesick Singalong." The former starts off with a grinding, ominous guitar riff and a propulsive but offbeat drum groove, both of which are highly reminiscent of Sonic Youth. But when the band launches into the song's next section, they enter grander territory; Thom sings about "talking out the world" over a stately descending chord pattern (in yet another irregular rhythm—this time, two bars of 4/4 followed by one of 3/4) that rings out like a choir. By song's end, Thom, Jonny, and Ed are engaged in a scintillating guitar conversation that veers close to the realm of classical counterpoint. A few arresting lyrical images ("Rust in the mountains, rust in the brain," "A can of brick dust worms") distract us briefly from what appears to be the main message: All things are doomed to fall apart, but "this is only halfway." Should we be reassured or disturbed by this cryptic observation? It's hard to know.

"Punchdrunk Lovesick Singalong," meanwhile, is a slow, bleak tale of seemingly life-negating adoration for another. (As the chorus puts it, "A beautiful girl can turn your world into dust.") Though the song sounds simple enough, its chord progression is actually fairly complex, moving in such unusual ways that it's often hard to determine just what key the song is in. Jonny's mournful lead guitar part, enhanced by judicious use of a delay effect, adds further poignance to the proceedings. The desolate ambience of the music, full of open spaces but underpinned by deep emotion, betrays a heavy Pink Floyd influence, a sign of things to come.

The other four B-sides are more minor but still interesting. "Lewis (Mistreated)" is the most balls-out rocker of the bunch, matching nasty skronk guitar with lyrics that seem to be urging a friend against some kind of fateful decision, perhaps suicide (although "Lewis, save yourself the pain, it never really mattered" might not necessarily be construed as the world's most life-affirming advice). "Permanent Daylight," produced by Nigel Godrich in John Leckie's absence (his first-ever production credit) and mixed by Jim Warren, is another one from the Sonic Youth school, more a mood than a song, with Thom's voice filtered to sound as though it were coming through a transistor radio. "Lozenge of Love," which takes its name from a line in the Philip Larkin poem "Sad Steps," is a delicate acoustic number based around a drone, with more despairing lyrics and some fine falsetto singing from Thom; the semi-Celtic atmosphere recalls the work of Brit folk-rockers like Fairport Convention and Pentangle. And "You Never Wash Up After Yourself" is a snippet of solo Yorke, recorded in the band's rehearsal space by Jim Warren. (If you listen closely, you can hear Phil clicking his drumsticks together in the background—he wasn't aware Thom was being recorded.) The song's words, a thumbnail sketch of slow domestic neglect and decay, are grim in the extreme.

Whatever hopes the Radiohead organization had for "My Iron Lung" were encouraged briefly when the single entered the U.K. charts at Number 24. But that initial position turned out to be its peak. Once again, the song received next to no radio play in Britain. On the other side of the Atlantic, Capitol's reaction was muted. No one at the company thought "My Iron Lung" was a worthy successor to "Creep." Marketing VP Clark Staub, using what might now be viewed as cynical reasoning, said they should release the song anyway. "I made the suggestion that we test out the band's U.S. fan base," he later said, "because my suspicion was that there was no fan base."[65]

Staub may have been cynical, but his suspicions seemed well founded. Though "My Iron Lung" topped the college radio charts, it sold barely 20,000 copies in the U.S. What many music-bizzers had long thought—that the hundreds of thousands of American listeners who'd snapped up *Pablo Honey* because of one song had no "brand loyalty" to the band—appeared to have been proven true.

Of course, one could make the counterargument that because Capitol invested only a minuscule amount of dollars and promotional muscle on the single—claiming that it was silly to do otherwise because the band, still busy recording the second album, couldn't actively promote the song themselves—Staub's prediction was preordained to become a self-fulfilling prophecy. (The members of Radiohead certainly made that argument, and didn't make any friends at Capitol by doing so.) "It was released to colleges," Jonny recounted, "and suddenly it was being played by some other stations, but there was no real release planned, but oh never mind, we'll just see what happens. . . . It's like, you don't have to play it, that's all right. *What?* This is *strange.* I don't think any harm would be done by people hearing it outside of colleges. People can hear it: I'm not *embarrassed* by it."[66]

And yet the very fact that the single didn't perform commercially in the U.S. was eventually turned to the band's advantage. The key in this case was the American nonmainstream-music press, the smaller magazines and fanzines who despise one-hit wonders but love an underdog. The success of "My Iron Lung" on the college charts coupled with its lack of recognition elsewhere put Radiohead in a position that would have been highly unlikely the year before. Whereas previously the band had been mostly ignored by "alternative" publications, who viewed them as corporate tools, now they were increasingly seen by those same publications as artistically worthy but unfortunate victims of the whims of fashion. Though it would be going too far to say that Capitol orchestrated the resulting boost in nonmainstream press coverage, to say they helped to encourage it would not be wildly inaccurate. Appearances in publications like *Alternative Press, B-Side,* and *The Big Takeover* might help build the grassroots music–junkie following that radio and MTV couldn't provide, and could boost sales of the next album on the basis of the band's own artistic virtues rather than that of a mega-hit single. It was a crafty strategy.*

The nonsuccess of "My Iron Lung" also prompted EMI to make another significant decision at around the same time: After John Leckie and the band were finished with the album tracks, those tracks were to be sent to Sean Slade and Paul Kolderie in Boston for a remix. The logic behind the decision was obvious—

---

*It's also worth pointing out here that Capitol probably never expected much success from "My Iron Lung" in the first place, for the simple reason that the U.S., unlike the U.K., isn't a big singles-buying market. For an American record company, issuing an EP almost always means a loss. Given that, the fact that "My Iron Lung" sold 20,000 copies could actually be seen as encouraging, a sign that the band *did* have a small but solid core audience in the States.

stick with a proven winner—and if anyone had an objection, it wasn't voiced loudly. However, no one broke any speed records telling the album's producer about this move. Noting that his Abbey Road mixing sessions were sparsely attended, Leckie got suspicious, but he didn't fully realize what was going on until EMI enigmatically asked for copies of the multitrack tapes.

Many a producer might have taken such an apparent snub badly, but if Leckie let it get him down, he's never shown it. In truth, EMI's decision wasn't a huge surprise. Leckie himself noted later that "the record company had been going on about trying to get an American sound for the record from the minute I got involved,"[67] and he has since acknowledged that the idea of having someone approach the music with a fresh ear was a solid one. Still, when he finally heard Slade and Kolderie's mixes, the studio vet was frequently surprised, and not always pleasantly: "The annoying thing for me a little bit was that there are things on there that they'd told me not to do originally—like using big reverbs on the voice or certain tones that were forbidden—that the Americans did. I found it quite funny."[68]

For his part, Kolderie insists that he and Slade never lobbied to remix the album. The decision, he says, was EMI's first and foremost, but it was seconded by the band after they heard *Pablo Honey* blasting through a massive sound system during an in-store promotional appearance in Scotland and realized that Sean and Paul had given their music a punch that they liked. "Having one team produce the record and another team mix it happens all the time these days," Kolderie observes. "That's the way the industry's going. It's getting harder and harder for a producer to see a whole project through. We rarely do it anymore—we either mix it or we produce it and hand it off. Most of the time, I'm happy to let it go and have someone else deal with it. That said, we had no hidden desire to take John Leckie's job away from him. I've never had a chance to go on record about this, but John Leckie did an amazing production job on *The Bends*. There's not much we could have done if the tracks were lousy, but the tracks were great, and that's a tribute to him."

In the end, despite Slade and Kolderie's hard work, three of *The Bends'* 12 songs would feature Leckie's mixes; the other nine went through multiple versions before the band were satisfied. "They just kept sending the tapes back saying, 'Well, not quite,' " Kolderie remembers. "We mixed 'Just' four or five times. It was an unusual process. I think it actually helped that they didn't come over [to Boston] and sit with us during the mixes, because it allowed them to be more detached."

Sean and Paul weren't singled out for this treatment; the band also asked Leckie to mix the same songs several different times. "I'd do a mix," he says, "and it would take a day or two, and then the following week Chris Hufford would phone up and say, 'Oh, we need to recall this bit because the bass isn't quite coming through,' so I'd go in for another day and recall it, at enormous expense. And they were doing the same with another crew of people in America . . . for the same song." Leckie laughs wryly. "It's absolutely crazy, that kind of indecision, insecurity, or whatever. The thing with *The Bends* is, if you put the multitrack tape on and just put the faders up, it would sound hardly any different from the finished record, because that's the way it was recorded, with very natural and organic sounds." If Leckie's contention is correct, then EMI wasted a whole lot of money.

In support of "My Iron Lung," Radiohead embarked on another short British tour from September 27 to October 8. The 10 dates included Thom's alma mater Exeter, the Shepherd's Bush Empire in London, and a benefit concert for the Oxfam Rwandan Relief Fund at the Old Gaol in Abingdon, a former detention ward that had been converted into a recreation center, located on the banks of the Thames just a few blocks away from the quintet's old school. These gigs were followed by time in slightly more exotic locales: two nights in Bangkok (October 14 and 15) and an eight-date tour of Mexico, including Mexico City and Guadalajara, from October 19 to October 29. It was on the Mexican portion of the tour that the intraband tensions long suppressed for the sake of group harmony during the recording sessions exploded. "Years and years of tension and not saying anything to each other, and basically all the things that had built up since we'd met each other, all came out in one day," Thom later reported. "We were spitting and fighting and crying."[69]

As with the harried band meeting that took place in Hamburg just before the start of the tour with James in late '93, it's difficult to determine exactly what took place during this Mexican showdown. But there was no doubt that Radiohead had had a rough year. Likewise, it was clear that the difficulties they'd experienced, both on the road and especially in the studio, had to be dealt with eventually in some way, or the band might disintegrate. "Things had been brewing and they basically came to a head," Ed recalled. "We were all completely knackered on this Mexican tour bus, twelve of us, with six bunks and they were about five foot six inches long, so you're getting no sleep. It was just ridiculous. It was something we'd been spending eight or nine years working towards, and it was like, we'd never been totally honest with each other. . . . We're not into bonding, we're friends and everything, but because of maybe our upbringing or the school that we went to, we don't tell each other our problems."[70]

"I think what happened within the band," John Leckie says, "is that they had this kind of paranoia about being polite, straight, from Oxford, never getting into any trouble or scandal, very clean, not rock 'n' roll at all. That's the way they are, and yet at the time they were worried about that, about taking on a rock 'n' roll career and not being rock 'n' rollers. They had to learn to be themselves, and to be comfortable with that. It was definitely a growing-up period."

The unusual venting session seemed to work, but although nerves soon died down, a refreshing change was needed. To that end, Thom and Jonny played a few acoustic shows by themselves in selected East and West Coast U.S. cities to conclude the tour, harking back briefly to those not-so-halcyon days when they busked on the streets of Oxford. The two later confessed to hating this type of performance, but these weren't the last ones they'd do, and with MTV's *Unplugged* attracting plenty of attention at the time, stripped-down gigs were all the rage.

From the States, it was back to England and Abbey Road, where the last song pegged for inclusion on the album, "Sulk," was finally finished. After the horrific experiences at RAK, the band had polished off the remainder of the album in a little over two weeks' worth of sessions (though those two weeks were actually spread over several months). "When we finished *The Bends*," Thom says, "it felt like going back and doing four-tracks again. That's what was so exciting—that we were in control of it, it was our thing. We were simply satisfying ourselves, and there was nothing about, 'Oh my God, this is a record,' or anything like that."

After we sent the band the first mix of 'Bones,' everyone was incredibly excited. Chris and Bryce said they were dancing around the office going 'Yes!' And when we met up in Boston after the mastering of *The Bends*, Thom was as happy as I've ever seen him. The combination of a great sequence and a fantastic mastering job had completed the album, unifying all the disparate mixes and songs: this was the first time we all felt a real sense of accomplishment and potential." For a time, at least, it felt as though the pressure was off.

Radiohead's first official engagement of 1995 was to fly back to America to shoot two videos. The first was for "Fake Plastic Trees," a surreal concept piece directed by Jake Scott (son of

Blade Runner director Ridley Scott) that featured the band being wheeled in shopping carts through a space-age supermarket, passing various disturbing, implicitly violent tableaus. Filming took place in a hangar at Los Angeles' Van Nuys Airport, just around the corner from where the final scene of *Casablanca* was shot. The second video, the U.K. version of "High and Dry," was a more standard performance-based clip, filmed by first-time director David Mould in Vasquez Canyon outside L.A. The band, playing in front of a large water tower, were doused with artificial rain during the shoot. Unfortunately, the crew hadn't realized that the water was close to freezing; Colin caught a severe cold as a result.

"High and Dry" was picked as the band's next British single, appearing on February 22, backed by another album track, "Planet Telex." Two different versions of the single were issued in the U.K. The first featured an alternate mix of "Telex" by Steve Osbourne and another crunchy guitar fest called "Maquiladora," its title taken from a Spanish slang term describing the elaborate fences put up by U.S.-based manufacturing corporations to protect their factories in Mexico and its dyspeptic lyrics incorporating a quip about "useless rockers from England." (Originally, the song was called "Interstate 5.") The second part of the single release featured another alternate mix of "Telex" and the electric version (recorded with John Leckie at RAK) of "Killer Cars," a song that had first popped up as an acoustic B-side on the British reissue of "Creep."

Just before the single was released, Thom and Jonny played another four acoustic duo shows in England. The full band played a surprise gig at the Lomax club in Liverpool before heading back home to Oxford and the lavish confines of the Apollo Theatre on George Street, where they performed on February 25 in front of approximately 70 international journalists and a large chunk of the EMI staff. Two other bands opened, both locally based: Supergrass, an exciting teenage pop trio who'd just been taken under the Hufford/Edge management wing, and the Candyskins, who almost exactly three years ago had played a show at the nearby Venue supported by a group called On A Friday. *Melody Maker*'s review of the proto-Radiohead back then had been lukewarm, but this time everything was different. "Gloriously good songs by thin English boys," the paper proclaimed.[71]

Another Oxford-oriented activity that Radiohead took part in around this time wasn't noticed so much by outsiders but was welcomed by the city's musicians and musicgoers. In early 1995, Oxford's local music scene was in a state of disarray. The number of area venues for live rock bands, never large to begin with, had shrunk dramatically. Within a single six-month period, three major clubs—the Jericho, the Hollybush, and the Venue—had closed down for various reasons, and *Curfew,* the local music paper, had ceased publication because there was nothing to write about. In the face of this grim situation, the Venue's former promoters, Nick Moorbath and Adrian Hicks, came up with a plan to reopen the club. The main obstacle was money; the club's previous owners had, through a series of shady financial dealings, run up considerable bills that no one on the staff could afford to pay. For this reason, Moorbath and Hicks approached several local bands who'd played the Venue at one time or another and who had since made good to lend their support. Chief among them was Radiohead, who readily agreed to invest in the new venture.

Working out the legal details among the various bands took some time, but the result was a success: The Venue was saved. Reopened under a new name, the Zodiac, it has since become the leading provider of live music in Oxford, and the members of Radiohead, who filmed their first video there back in the old days, still own shares in the place.*

*Not long after the opening of the Zodiac, the former talent booker at the Jericho Tavern opened a new club called the Point, and *Curfew* resumed publication. Though the latter has since been renamed *Nightshift,* both remain going concerns to this day.

At the beginning of March 1995, "High and Dry" reached its U.K. chart peak of Number 17. Within two weeks, Radiohead's second album, *The Bends,* would be released worldwide. On the eve of another round of touring and media duties, Thom Yorke professed uncertainty about his band's fate. "When we started this thing," he said, "I really did believe the good will out, the best rise to the top. But I no longer believe that. People are continuously overlooked and ignored. You only have to watch the news to know that. It's not just artists. It's everybody."[72] For better or worse, Radiohead wouldn't be able to count themselves among the ranks of the ignored for much longer.

THE BENDS

For their second album, Radiohead chose an extremely symbolic title. "The bends" is the colloquial name for a complaint suffered by deep-sea divers who rise to the surface too quickly. In deep water, high pressure causes the release of excess nitrogen into the bloodstream; if a diver re-enters a lower-pressure environment without giving the

7

nitrogen time to properly dissipate, bubbles temporarily form in the diver's blood. The result is severe discomfort, often making the diver bend over in agony (hence the name).

The parallels we are meant to draw here are obvious. Like a diver with the bends, Radiohead rose too high too soon (due to the huge success of "Creep," which they were hardly prepared for) and had to suffer the unpleasant consequences (critical backlash, record company pressure, general confusion and dismay about how to continue meaningfully). By calling the album *The Bends,* the band seemed to imply that the new music they were offering us was in effect the sound of their suffering. Not the most appealing prospect in the world, to be sure, but it mirrored the near-obsession with disease, injury, and abnormality present in the songs' lyrics.

"It's a really medical album for me," Jonny observed upon the album's release. "Thom went into a hospital to take pictures for the cover artwork, and it struck me the other day how much it's all about illness and doctors. It kind of makes sense, because we've all been on a cycle of illness. . . . There's also that feeling of revulsion about your own body; that resentment that you're so reliant on it. Just looking at your hands all the time and seeing all the bones. Urgh."[1] Seeing Thom onstage performing these songs, you'd sometimes think he was desperately trying to wriggle out of his body, to escape the pain-ridden flesh cage he was forced by fate to drag around with him.

Tellingly, one of the few albums Yorke cited as a major influence during the *Bends* sessions was John Lennon's *Plastic Ono Band,* a deeply personal collection recorded in 1970 in the aftermath of Lennon's primal scream therapy with psychologist Arthur Janov. This influence was at least partly the result of pure coincidence. At the beginning of Radiohead's first day of recording at RAK, John Leckie, who'd been the tape operator at Abbey Road during the *Plastic Ono* sessions, put the album on. The band hadn't requested that he do so, but Thom was struck by the choice, and the mood was set. (As they listened, Leckie couldn't stop himself from pointing out where all the tape edits in Lennon's songs were, a revelation that Yorke said shattered his illusions.) "Lyrically I really love that album," Thom once commented, "because it makes you feel really uncomfortable."[2] It was the same feeling for which Radiohead were striving.*

Of course, the band weren't trying to slavishly imitate Lennon's magnum opus. From both musical and production standpoints, *The Bends* is far more lush and complex than the deliberately stripped-down *Plastic Ono Band*. And though Yorke's lyrics may be based in personal experience, he never comes close to the brutal directness of, say, "My Mummy's Dead." He never intended to. In fact, Thom later claimed Lennon's cut-to-the-bone lyrical approach was "something I could rail against while we were doing *our* record: 'Well . . . I really love that, but I don't want to do it like that.' "[3] Yorke was mastering the art of meaningful concealment. "I know what's true and what's not," he said, "and nobody else does. . . . I took a step back from what I was writing in words. I just sort of treated that as another instrument rather than this is *me* personally giving you all, everything in my soul. You do that once, and you never ever want to do that again."[4]

At the same time, the similarities between the two albums, separated by 25 years, can be striking. One of the key tracks on *Plastic Ono Band* is called "Isolation," and that word goes a long way in summing up *The Bends* as well. Paul Kolderie, who mixed the album along with Sean Slade, told *Mojo*, "*The Bends* was neither an English album nor an American album. It's an album

---

*Another disc Leckie played during the *Bends* sessions that made a mark on the band was Tom Waits' *The Asylum Years* compilation. Leckie says Thom had never heard Waits' music before: "He was stunned by that voice."

made in the void of touring and traveling. It really had that feeling of 'We don't live anywhere and we don't belong anywhere.' "[5]

Judging by the highly accomplished soundscapes that the band creates on *The Bends,* light-years beyond anything on *Pablo Honey,* one could be forgiven for thinking that the one place they just *might* belong was in the recording studio. For the most part, the band attributes the album's sonic brilliance to the work of John Leckie. "He earned his money," Thom says with approval. Shortly after *The Bends* was completed, Yorke was frequently referring to Leckie as a genius: "He saw what he had to do, and what he had to do was to get rid of our phobia of studios."[6] Jonny seconded the opinion. "He didn't treat us like he had some kind of witchcraft that only he understands. There's no mystery to it, which is so refreshing."[7]

Still, much of the credit for *The Bends'* artistic success belongs to the band. Right from the opening chords of "Planet Telex," it was clear that Radiohead had taken a stunning leap forward. This was music of the arena-rock variety, no doubt, but with an intelligence and sensitivity that indicated something special. The growing intricacy of arrangements first evidenced on the "My Iron Lung" EP had developed even further, as the band continued to make better creative use of its three-guitar lineup. According to Ed O'Brien, the key to this development was that they had realized the virtues of playing less. "I think we were very aware of something that we weren't aware of on *Pablo Honey.* The approach to *The Bends* was, if it sounded really great with Thom playing acoustic with Phil and Coz [Colin], what was the point in trying to add something more? Everything that was added had to make the track better." Or, as Thom puts it, "Sometimes the nicest thing to do with a guitar is just look at it."

In general, it could be said that the division of guitar labor in Radiohead is that Thom plays rhythm, Jonny plays lead, and Ed makes weird noises. But that's an oversimplification, as any one is capable of doing anything at any time. Thom downgrades his fine guitaristic skills by saying, "I just keep time really," while Jonny bristles at being called a lead guitarist: "You could describe it like that, I suppose, but it's not really like that." To which Thom responds, "When I run out of melodies, there's usually something on Jonny's guitar that's a melody, like Mr. [George] Harrison used to do. You know, pick a melody up here [fingers upper reaches of imaginary fretboard], and so on, because it gets a bit boring listening to one voice all the time."

Another difference between *The Bends* and *Pablo Honey* is the greater amount of group contribution to the songwriting. Though all Radiohead's songs from the start have been credited to the entire band, most of the early ones were mainly Thom's babies. By the time of *The Bends*, this situation had changed. "I wasn't even responsible for all of the chords," Thom said approximately a year after the album was released. "Lots of bits and pieces on all the songs were either Jonny's or the others', which is brilliant for me 'cause it really takes the pressure off. There's no sort of, 'Ohmigod, I've got to come in with something,' none of that. There are songs that I've had virtually no part in at all, except we came up with it in rehearsals, you know. And it's a nice feeling—makes it much less of a job and much more of an enjoyable being-in-a-band thing." However, Yorke still claimed responsibility for the lion's share of the lyrics, although "the others help me with spelling, stationery, and basic grammar."

The Bends is also marked by a more prominent use of keyboards than *Pablo Honey*. The bulk of the keyboard parts are handled by Jonny, but Thom plays the huge, echoing piano chords that open and close the album's first song, "Planet Telex." According to Yorke, the sound created by those chords was something "I'd always wanted to try." Thom says he instructed John Leckie to put the piano through a noise gate and four vintage Roland Space Echo units in series. Leckie remembers this differently: "I don't think they had any Space Echoes at RAK, though that sound—a filtered delay—is similar to what a tape echo like that can do. We probably used the delay on a Yamaha SPX90 or something, whatever the easiest thing to plug in was, and put the delay return through the graphic EQs on the console. Then you just randomly flick the graphic so it makes a peak, and the EQ filters the delay as it repeats. It's a crude way of doing it, but it works." The result is a clipped, compressed echo that feeds back on itself, a suitably spooky way to open the album.

"Planet Telex" was the only song on *The Bends* that was written in the studio, during the RAK sessions. Originally titled "Planet Xerox" until the band was denied clearance for use of the Xerox name, it's primarily a Thom composition, although Jonny helped write the music for the verses. (Speaking of which, one of the most interesting features of the song, at least from a music-theory point of view, is the harmonic relationship between the verse and the chorus. Both parts revolve around chords that employ the same chromatic moving line—E to D-sharp to D and then back to D-sharp—but the verse gets through that line in half the time of the chorus, and the two parts also have different tonal centers: B for the verse, E for the chorus. This combination of surface harmonic change with underlying repetition reinforces the song's general message that we are trapped in an unbreakable cycle of disappointment, one whose essence remains the same despite any outer alterations of appearance.) In a sign of things to come, Phil's relentless drum groove is actually a loop cannibalized from another Radiohead song, the electric version of "Killer Cars." Despite its synthetic nature, it coaxed a remarkably warm performance from Colin, whose spacious, funky bassline is simple yet indispensable.

"We did 'Planet Telex' one night after coming back from a restaurant," Leckie remembers. "Going to a restaurant was a rare thing for us, because RAK usually supplied food. But this one night they came to us and said, 'The chef has to have a day off, here's a hundred pounds, go spend it at a restaurant.' So we said, 'Oh, okay.' And out of that, on the way back to the studio, came this creative moment: 'Hey, let's put these drum loops together.' It was three different fragments of the drum track from 'Killer Cars' that we looped and edited together in a quick arrangement. Then we got the piano going through the delay. We had the whole thing down within a couple of hours, which was really refreshing and really fun to do."

Thom recorded the vocal to "Telex" drunk, slumped in a corner. "It was four o'clock in the morning and John Leckie said, 'We've got to do the vocal now.'* Ed remembers it more, but apparently I sang it all with my head on the floor because I couldn't stand up. I was bent double and I hadn't a clue what I was singing."[8] To add further sonic distress symptoms, the vocal signal was distorted by overloading the recording console.

Under the circumstances, some slurring of words on Thom's part was probably inevitable, but in fact this is only the first of many instances on *The Bends* when consultation of the lyric sheet is necessary, and not all of these can be blamed on alcohol or electronic enhancements. Some critics have charged that the growing dodginess of Yorke's enunciation stems from self-consciousness about his lyrics; there may be some truth to this, but it's also likely that he simply enjoys singing the words in an odd way. "I've never been able to write a song if I just go straight in and write it and I know what I want to write," he says. "That never works. Usually, you just end up getting off on the sounds of the words. The songs I like most are the ones where I'm not into the words, but the sounds the words are making. I'll spend fucking weeks on something and then just choose the one that sounds nice when I go *wharrraeioughhh*, just the vowel sounds."

*Leckie says it was two o'clock and recalls commenting that it was past Thom's bedtime.

In any case, the lyrics to "Planet Telex" make an appropriate introduction to the album and its concern with all manner of dysfunction. The first words Thom sings are "You can force it but it will not come/You can taste it but it will not form." On this particular planet, any kind of effort that an individual makes is doomed to failure from the outset. The only thing that one can achieve is to be reminded that, as Yorke brays in the chorus, everything and everyone is broken. If read by themselves, the words can seem unrelentingly miserable. But coupled with the music and the psychedelic, effects-laden production, they take on an air of exhilaration. It's a combination that Radiohead performs with expert skill.

"Planet Telex" is followed by the album's title track. "The Bends" was an old song, dating from before *Pablo Honey*, and it was often played live by the band before the sessions for the new album began. The album version was recorded in one take at the Manor. Phil was reportedly in a hurry to go look at a house for rent that day and so wanted to get through the session quickly; the rest of the band were pleased to oblige. The new sense of guitaristic restraint that marks much of the album is pleasantly missing here, as Thom, Ed, and Jonny indulge in the splendor of three guitars loudly clanging against one another, particularly on the choruses (which, in what was rapidly becoming a Radiohead trademark, are divided into irregular numbers of measures, the better to disorient the listener with). John Leckie found this version of the song a little too lacking in subtlety. The band thought otherwise.

Yet from a songwriting standpoint, "The Bends" is far from a primitive noisefest. In fact, it's one of the most structurally complex songs on the album, composed of five distinct sections. (Compare that to "Creep," which is nothing more than one endlessly revolving four-chord sequence played at different volumes.) Jonny's imposing countermelody during the second verse doffs its hat ever so briefly to the Smiths' "How Soon Is Now" before fading into the ether. The younger Greenwood also steps out on recorder here, for the first time on record, though his multi-tracked piping is submerged in the final mix.

The muffled yelling and crackling noises that open "The Bends" were taped by Thom from a hotel room window while the band were on one of their U.S. tours. (Documentation of the group's travels was becoming a general obsession.) "There was this guy training these eight-year-old kids, who were parading up and down with all these different instruments [outside the hotel]," Yorke remembered. "The guy had this little microphone on his sweater and was going, 'Yeah, keep it up, keep it up!' "[9] What element of the song this "found" snippet is supposed to reflect isn't entirely clear, but it's possible that the drill instructor might in some way represent all the authorities the band felt pressing upon them, baying for another hit, leading them on a forced march. The rest of the song explores the themes of insecurity, loss of identity, and general malaise brought on by near-constant travel; the protagonist is "lying in a bar with my drip feed on/Talking to my girlfriend, waiting for something to happen." In his weakened state, he makes a series of pointless observations, including the at least half-sarcastic wish that it was still the '60s. ("Levi's jeans wish it was the Sixties," Thom would later clarify, "I certainly fucking don't."[10]) By the end of the song, the music has swelled to heroic proportions, and the tone of Yorke's voice has moved from a wish to a demand, but it's one of the more pitiful demands in the history of pop music: "I want to be part of the human race."

One particular line in the song, "We don't have any real friends," was meant to be taken literally. "That represents how we felt, yes," Jonny said. "There is a sense of isolation being in Radiohead."[11] For all its poor-little-me overtones, the line was grounded in reality; the band's contact with their old friends from

Oxford and elsewhere had decreased as they spent more of their time away from home, and keeping any sort of meaningful relationship going with anyone outside the group had grown increasingly hard. "You go away for two, two and a half months at a time," Colin would observe later, "then come back, then go away again, and meanwhile your friends have gone on with their lives. . . . What was magical at first—being in a band, touring—becomes commonplace, but it's still removed from their experience. You can drift out of touch with people, but they don't hold it against you, and that's kind of bad in a way. It's like, 'Well, Colin's going to be doing this and this, so I won't write to him for another two months.' It's very difficult."[12]

In contrast to "The Bends," the song that follows it, "High and Dry," is probably the least complex on the album: three chords, two distinct melodic sections, plus an intro. It's also the oldest recording on *The Bends,* put down in early 1993, almost a year before the RAK sessions. Along with the likes of "Yes I Am" and "Pop Is Dead," "High and Dry" had been recorded at Courtyard with the band's live sound engineer, Jim Warren, behind the board. It was already an old song at that point, having been written while Thom was at Exeter and originally performed by his college band, Headless. Jonny didn't like it; he thought it sounded like Paul McCartney's "Mull of Kintyre" (a comparison that most listeners would find unlikely, to say the least). Thom, Colin, and Phil, on the other hand, thought it sounded like Rod Stewart (much more reasonable, especially when you consider Thom's quasi–"Maggie May" acoustic guitar riff at the beginning).

Though no one was particularly enthusiastic about the song, the band recorded it anyway. Colin and Phil laid down their parts with Thom, but Ed and Jonny couldn't be bothered to come in until later. "The whole funny thing about 'High and Dry,' " Ed says with a laugh, "is that it's one of the very few tracks where we haven't actually all been in the studio [at the same time]. We weren't really into doing the song."

After the song was recorded, Thom says, "we didn't even listen to it back. I remember finishing it and being like, 'We don't need to listen to this, this is fucking dreadful.'" As Ed observes, "It made no sense at the time when we did it. It didn't fit into what we were doing around that time." It would take nearly two years before Radiohead would give the song another chance, coaxed by someone else in their organization—probably Chris Hufford— who'd heard it and smelled a potential hit, an opinion seconded by Keith Wozencroft, who put it on the first band demo tape that he sent to John Leckie. Though Leckie says now that Wozencroft told him the song was "to be 'kept for the next album' and so was never really on the list to be recorded," upon listening to it again, the band were pleasantly surprised. "It's one of those things where you record something and you can't even remember doing it," Thom commented. "We had to relearn it all 'cause we couldn't remember any of it." In the end, the band elected not to try to re-record it, going with the original '93 version as remixed by Sean Slade and Paul Kolderie.

"One of the main reasons we wanted to include it [on *The Bends*] was because it precursored what was going to happen later," Yorke says, "and the lyrics sort of touched a nerve. It was also really loose. The rest of the album's quite polished, and we wanted something that was fairly random." Having a gorgeous melody didn't hurt either; the sheer beauty of Thom's falsetto part on the chorus makes one wonder why the song only barely stumbled into the British Top 20. Other musical highlights of the song include a very live drum sound—"I think they'd just put a new skin on the kick drum," Thom recalls, "'cause Phil was sitting there going, 'That sounds great, don't bother putting any stuff inside it'"—and the spine-tingling high notes in the background on the verses, produced by Jonny lightly brushing his guitar's strings with a nail file. (Jonny is also responsible for the guitar solo, but the part he plays was actually written by Thom.)

Though Thom says the lyrics of "High and Dry" touched a nerve, he claims not to remember what the inspiration for those lyrics was. Still, they fit well with the album's general pattern, sketching out a character whose daring actions—he appears to be an Evel Knievel–esque motorcycle jumper—are little more than a cover for inner insufficiencies. Yorke cautions that the person he's addressing is becoming a stranger to himself, and then implies that the real problem is a sexual one: "All your insides fall to pieces/You just sit there wishing you could still make love." The song's concluding line, "The best thing that you've had has gone away," though certainly not optimistic, perfectly suits the yearning nature of the music behind it.*

Probably the best-known song on *The Bends* is the slow-building "Fake Plastic Trees," which it would be tempting to call a "power ballad" if that term weren't so frequently connected with histrionic displays of (usually false) emotion, just the type of fakery that the song decries, albeit cryptically. As Thom describes it, "Fake Plastic Trees" started out as "a very nice melody which I had absolutely no idea what to do with, and then . . . well, the thing when you have a melody, you go to sleep and you wake up, and you find your head singing some words to it. What I tend to do is I just keep notes of whatever my head's singing at that particular moment. Or if that doesn't work, I'll get some nifty phrases and just force them on. Som times I just force it on for the sake of it, 'cause you're not supposed to. But that song was

---

*Thom's original demo for "High and Dry" was based around a groove lifted off a 12-inch single by hip-hoppers Soul II Soul, but the groove proved difficult to replicate. "That's why we buried the song," Thom says, " 'cause we couldn't do a convincing Soul II Soul rhythm. We didn't really want to. And so we did a dodgy Rod Stewart version of it and then ditched it." Jonny adds with a broad grin, "So we're proud of it."

very much the opposite. That was not forced at all, it was just recording whatever was going on in my head, really. I mean, I wrote those words and laughed. I thought they were really funny, especially that bit about polystyrene."

Indeed, the entire second verse of "Fake Plastic Trees," about the "cracked polystyrene man," is quite droll. After depicting an environment in which everything—consumer goods, plants, the earth itself—is fake and made out of plastic, the focus shifts to a plastic man, who, logically enough, performs plastic surgery on women (a brief harking back to the lyrics of "Pop Is Dead"). Actually, correct that: He *used* to perform plastic surgery in the '80s, but he's since retired due to the lack of success he's had with his patients. As Thom sings sweetly, "Gravity always wins." Things get more serious toward the song's end. Faced with the prospect of a "fake plastic love," the singer is left to muse on what things would be like "if I could be who you wanted all the time," if he could successfully become fake himself. The "you" Yorke is addressing here could be an actual lover, but it could just as easily be any number of people, including Radiohead's own listeners. (Later, Thom would often single "Fake Plastic Trees" out in interviews as the first song in which he felt he'd found his own lyric-writing voice.)

Thom remembers the recording of "Fake Plastic Trees" as "a fucking nightmare." Ed says, "There was one stage, at the first session in RAK, when it sounded like Guns N' Roses' 'November Rain.' It was so pompous and bombastic, just the worst." Hearing the band's performance of the song from the May '94 Astoria show, it's clear that they hadn't quite figured out how to do it justice. The ensemble playing becomes too aggressive too early (Phil is a prime culprit here) and stays that way for too long; an appropriate sense of dynamics is sorely lacking.

Eventually, as detailed earlier, Thom recorded the basic track of "Fake Plastic Trees" by himself on acoustic guitar and vocal in a single take. One of the microphones Leckie used to record

Thom's guitar, a Neumann U67, began to crackle as Yorke was playing, but the performance was so outstanding that it was decided not to redo the part. The rest of the band were left with the challenge of building a song around that performance, a process that Ed says took "three to four months of coming back to it, and it wasn't until the final mix that they [Sean Slade and Paul Kolderie] actually pulled all these different things together."[13] Leckie says that most of the tracking work on the song was done within a few days of Thom's basic; the months of work consisted of "not adding stuff, but taking stuff away." The day after the acoustic guitar and vocal were recorded, two string players—Thom's old friend from Exeter John Matthias on violin and viola and sessioneer Caroline Lavelle on cello—put down several multitracked parts written by Jonny. Indeed, the main impetus for getting Thom to nail a definitive version of "Fake Plastic Trees" was the fact that the strings were scheduled to come in the next day.

"They knew they wanted a string quartet kind of thing," Leckie remembers, "but the day before the players came in, they still hadn't decided what songs they should play on—Jonny was still writing the parts. For 'Fake Plastic Trees,' I think he was inspired by [twentieth-century American composer] Samuel Barber. The strings originally went all over the verses, very sustained, with changes in mood and texture. What we did in the end was take almost all of that away, except for a couple of parts."

Besides coming up with the subtle string arrangement for "Fake Plastic Trees" (the writing of which he later described as "my studio highlight, in a megalomaniac kind of way"),[14] Jonny also contributed a magisterial series of chords on Hammond organ.* For his part, Phil lays out completely on the first verse and

*In later interviews, the band said this track was recorded at Abbey Road, on the same organ once used by—yes, you guessed it—John Lennon, but John Leckie thinks it was laid down at RAK on a rented Hammond.

gamely restrains himself on the second, only playing at full volume when the distorted guitars come in on the final verse.

Speaking of distorted guitars, one more development that helped save the song from the realm of rock clichés actually came about through a mixing error on that final verse. "Paul [Kolderie] missed a cue," Thom says, "so the guitars don't come in at the right place. They were supposed to come in at the beginning of the bar. It was a mistake, but we kept it." You have to listen back carefully to hear what he's talking about; though one rather distant electric guitar does come in at the very beginning of the third verse, it's not until more than halfway through the second bar of that verse that another, much louder guitar enters at an unpredictable moment, the result of Kolderie's flub. If you're not listening for it, though, you'd swear it had been planned that way. To which Yorke responds sarcastically, "Oh, it was planned that way." Jonny adds, "We recorded forty minutes of accidents and we put it out and called it *The Bends*." This particular accident, however, does nothing to diminish the song's strange poignance and may even enhance it.

The next song, "Bones," had also been tough for Radiohead to get on tape satisfactorily. The original version from RAK, Thom said, "had the ending going on for about a minute and a half, which was something Jonny got from the Fall."[15] When the band returned from their Far East tour in June '94, the song had been shortened to its final length. Playing "Bones" regularly live had made it substantially easier to record; having attempted unsuccessfully to record it earlier also helped in a strange way. "A lot of the time," Thom says, "we'll completely change a song once we listen to it on tape, just sort of go, 'Oh my God, that sounds dreadful,' 'cause while we're playing, we're all thinking how wonderful it sounds but not actually listening back. You get off on it in another way when you listen back to it, 'cause you're not making the effort to play the chords at the same time. Which is why recording stuff is like having an audience. You know, you have to do one or the other. You can't just record the song and say, 'That's wonderful.' Audiences are better, though, 'cause you're face to face with people and you have to make up your mind." The finished album version of "Bones" was laid down in very little time at the Manor, on the same day as "The Bends." "Easily the best day of recording," Jonny later commented.[16]

Like "The Bends," "Bones" explores the louder side of Radiohead, keeping the three guitars crunchy and raucous most of the time. Also like "The Bends," it employs a clever rhythmic device (in this case, consecutively alternating a measure of six beats with a measure of eight). The most distinctive sonic feature of the song is the rippling effect that starts things off and recurs frequently from there on in, which is produced by Jonny turning the rate knob on his homemade tremolo pedal. Yorke once again sings about someone who is falling to pieces; he delivers the verses in little more than a mumble, but when it comes time to sing briefly about the past, when "I used to fly like Peter Pan," his voice, appropriately, soars into the stratosphere.

"Nice Dream," another fairly old song (written in 1992), was originally a simple four-chord Thom composition in waltz time. Jonny later added several choice bits, including the ominous arpeggiated intro—which makes use of the tritone interval between A and E-flat, the so-called devil's interval—and an extra chord in the chorus: "It used to be F-sharp minor," Jonny explains, "and we just made it F-sharp with a second-inversion B major at the top. It sounds like a song from a show, a kind of Cole Porter chord." (Jonny's explanation amuses Ed no end. "I don't know what a second-inversion B major is," he chuckles.)

Thom didn't immediately welcome Jonny's alterations of the song. "You know, it's boring and it's one note and everything," he says, "and it's very anal to talk about it, but for about two weeks, I couldn't stand that intro chord. Which is the best bit of the whole song. But I hated it when he wrote it. I could not get my head round it. For me this song was just these four chords going round and round and I was quite happy with that. But things like putting these extra bits in take the song from being just going round and round without pushing it in other directions that I would have never thought of. And that's the whole point of Radiohead, I think, really."

Those of you who have made it this far probably won't be very surprised to learn that the title "Nice Dream" is a trifle misleading. The dream recounted here, apparently inspired by an actual dream that Thom had, doesn't sound all that nice. Even the song's first verse seems full of foreboding, despite its pleasant images of gardens and sunshine. In the next verse, we are informed that "the good angel" is unfortunately unable to help us because "the sea would electrocute us all," a non sequitur that's deeply disturbing. Shortly thereafter, the hushed music (enhanced once again by the violin, viola, and cello of John Matthias and Caroline Lavelle) gives way to a turbulent middle section. Jonny mercilessly attacks his guitar, which spews forth violent bent notes. But the spell soon passes, and we're back where we started, roughly. Thom's singing here is exquisitely sad; his delicate, drawn-out falsetto note introducing the final chorus is one of the album's vocal highlights. The whale sounds in the background as the song closes are courtesy of John Leckie's tape collection. "My stupid idea," he says humbly.*

The music to the propulsive "Just" was largely written by Jonny, who Thom says "was trying to get as many chords as he could into a song. It was like writing a medley." Ed revealed the song had been even more involved in preliminary rehearsals, stretching to "about seven minutes long."[17] (The intro—solo guitar banging out a stop-and-start rhythm for two bars before the

*An early demo of "Nice Dream," with different lyrics, appeared in February '95 on the monthly compilation CD/magazine *Volume*.

full band bursts in—sounds like a more or less conscious nod to the opening of Nirvana's "Smells Like Teen Spirit.") Thom's words describe someone caught in a degrading relationship, but they are far from sympathetic. According to the song, the blame for the continuation of the relationship falls squarely on the shoulders of the person whom the singer's addressing. The chorus rails, "You do it to yourself, you do/And that's what really hurts." Thom's malicious vocal vibrato on the last line is worthy of cabaret legend Anthony Newley.

"Just" was the first successful recording Radiohead made at RAK. Getting the song's demanding dynamic changes down couldn't have been easy but with Phil and Colin's powerful support the guitarists tackle them perfectly. Particularly thrilling is the transition between the overdriven, frantically picked monster-movie guitar break after the second chorus and the cool, chiming chordal part that immediately follows it (played by Thom and Jonny in harmony). Jonny's scorching solo at the end of the song, played on the upper reaches of his Telecaster's fretboard, was recorded while Thom was taking a break. Upon his return, he gave it high marks: "I thought it was the most exciting thing I've ever heard us come up with on tape."[18] The gloriously ugly note at the beginning of the solo, which starts out at a frequency so high it's almost in dogs-only range and then lurches down into subsonic territory, was produced with the help of a new favorite Radiohead toy, the pitch-shifting DigiTech Whammy pedal.

"My Iron Lung," the first product of the *Bends* sessions to be heard by the public, follows "Just" in the album's final running order. It was written in late 1993 during the increasingly miserable tour, backing first Belly and then James, that followed Radiohead's pullout from the Reading Festival. A bitter response to those who'd castigated them as one-hit wonders and a thumb in the eye of the casual listeners who'd bought that one hit, the song was, according to Thom, meant to be "the final nail in the coffin

. . . of the previous song that shall remain nameless."[19] An iron lung is an antiquated medical contraption designed to assist those who have difficulty breathing; as Yorke's darkly ironic lyric would have it, "Creep" is Radiohead's iron lung, a life support system without which they'd be too weak to survive on their own. "We are losing it, can't you tell?" he sings, sarcastically echoing the band's critics. (The notion that the singer is suffering from a lack of oxygen also connects "My Iron Lung" thematically with "The Bends," a neat tying together of the album's lyrical imagery.)

In the song's aggressive midsection, paranoia rears its head as Thom rants behind a cloud of distortion about a rapacious bunch of "headshrinkers." (Oddly, these lines are not reproduced in the CD lyric sheet.) Are the nameless villains armchair psychologists, picking through Yorke's songs for personality clues, or are they hostile critics, wanting to cut the band down to size? Whoever they may be, it's clear the singer doesn't like them. Finally, any remaining doubt about "My Iron Lung" being in some way inspired by "Creep" and the reaction to it is dispelled in the last verse, when Thom sings, "This is our new song/Just like the last one/A total waste of time." In fact, this new song isn't like "the last one" at all; though the abrupt, jarring transitions between loud and soft are similar to those of "Creep," in most other respects "My Iron Lung" is far more complex. "A friend said he didn't like this song because it sounds like two songs stuck together," Ed reported. "Yeah, great!"[20]

Radiohead had attempted to record "My Iron Lung" during the RAK sessions, but nobody was happy with the results. Yet the version the band recorded during their May 27, 1994 gig at the Astoria in London met with everyone's approval, except for Thom's vocal, which was replaced later in the studio. "It was essentially a live recording tidied up, the audience taken out," Thom told *B-Side*. "We didn't want to release it sounding live and having the audience cheering. . . . That would be really crap."[21] Only a minimal amount of ambient hall noise gives any clue as to the track's origins. John Leckie says, "Considering that it was recorded in the back of a truck outside the hall—not the best sound to get something from—we did quite well."

"Bullet Proof (I Wish I Was)" is another pretty, acoustic-based number of the type Radiohead were quickly becoming expert at devising. As with "High and Dry," Thom, Colin, and Phil recorded the basic track together without Ed and Jonny. The other two guitarists were uncertain what they could add to the song; Jonny had figured out a combination rhythm/lead part to sweeten the chorus, but that was all. "It needed something," Thom says, "and we hadn't got a clue what." Eventually they arrived at a plan: Jonny and Ed would simply make random sounds, running their guitars through a pile of effects ("the old Floyd trick," Jonny wryly called it)[22]—and they'd do it without hearing the track they were playing over.

"We just said 'Go,' and they made weird noises," Yorke recalls. "We taped that a few times. [The final version was a composite of several different overdubs.] You know, sometimes the best stuff happens when you're not even listening at all. I think once you get to a studio, you either do it together live at the same time so you can hear what you're doing, or do the exact opposite so you don't know what's going on at all. A lot of the time, you have to either make it really, really random or really, really calculated. There's no middle ground. That's one of the most exciting things about recording for us, the fact that sometimes you'll just put stuff down and you won't have a clue what you're doing until a few days afterwards, when your brain finally makes the connection."

Ed wasn't initially so thrilled about this recording tactic. As he later recounted, "I remember thinking at the time, 'Bastards. I've never recorded like this before. How are you supposed to do it?'"[23] But the eerie atmosphere created by the new tracks won him over, as it did everyone. Jonny and Ed's distant space calls blend beautifully with Thom's fragile singing and fragile lyrics to match: Yorke depicts himself, among other things, as a doll to stick pins in and a target to be shot at.

The next song, "Black Star," was recorded at RAK very quickly, in an afternoon, with Nigel Godrich producing while John Leckie was off at a wedding. The almost competitive sense of "let's get this done before he gets back," felt by both band and surrogate producer, led to one of the few pleasurable experiences during the early *Bends* sessions. "There was a real 'teacher's away' larkiness to that day," Jonny commented, "hence the ace raggedness of the playing."[24] As with "Just" earlier on the album, the subject is a failing relationship, but in this song the situation seems to hit closer to home, and Yorke is less judgmental, his words a verbal equivalent of throwing up one's hands in despair: "What are we coming to?/What are we gonna do?/Blame it on the black star/Blame it on the falling sky."

"My favorite thing about this song," Thom told *Vox*, "is Jonny's guitar when it comes in on the chorus. It was completely crazy afterwards because everyone was saying, 'We've got to do the guitar again because it sounds such a mess.' Me and Jonny were going, 'No no no.'"[25] They were right to stick to their guns, for the gritty, nearly out-of-control tone Jonny musters here best befits the song's raw emotion. Besides Jonny's "mess," the most musically notable aspects of the song are the rather grand intro and outro sections (organized in groups of three measures rather than the more usual four) and the fact that for much of the final verse, Thom sings over a simple backdrop of Colin's bass and Phil's drums, an achievement that the younger Radiohead, with its love of thick guitar camouflage, couldn't have abided.

"Sulk," the penultimate track on *The Bends*, was written by Thom in the summer of 1987 as a response to a bloody incident in Hungerford, Berkshire, that shocked the entire United

Kingdom: 27-year-old Michael Ryan's senseless shooting spree on August 19 of that year, which left 17 people dead, including Ryan himself. Originally, the song ended with the line "Just shoot your gun," but Thom changed this later to "You'll never change," not wishing anyone to think that he'd been writing about Nirvana's Kurt Cobain, who shot himself in 1994.

Of the 12 songs on *The Bends*, "Sulk" took the longest to get on tape satisfactorily. An up-tempo number in 6/8 time, it was one of the first songs Radiohead tried at RAK in February '94, and it was the last song recorded for the album at Abbey Road after the band's return from America in November. When the sessions started, it had been one of the four contenders for a leadoff single; by the end of the sessions, it was said to be the band's least favorite song on the album. Certainly the circumstances of its recording couldn't be remembered pleasantly by Jonny, who played his part sprawled on the studio floor with a bad case of stomach flu: "Mexico's revenge," he termed it.[26]

Still, "Sulk" has much to recommend it. The music is exceptional, especially Jonny's guitar harmonies and Colin's clever descending bassline on the second verse. In interviews following *The Bends'* release, Thom rarely tired of mentioning the song's multiple tambourine overdubs, which are barely audible in the finished mix but help push the track along. However, the focal point of "Sulk" is Yorke's superlative vocal performance, which first justifies all the comparisons to Bono that he'd been lumbered with over the years and then goes several steps beyond them—the high note he hits on the song's final chorus is positively operatic.

The Bends comes to a close with a more subdued song, "Street Spirit (Fade Out)." (For those who are curious, it's Jonny's favorite track on the album.) Written in 1993 around the same time as "My Iron Lung," the song emerged from a repetitive but insinuating rhythm guitar pattern devised by Thom and played by him in unison with Ed. The harmony that Jonny plays over this pattern is one of the tastiest guitar parts on an album loaded with delectable six-string moments. Although "Street Spirit" can't be called optimistic, it distinguishes itself from the rest of *The Bends'* songs with its veiled implication that all our efforts in this world may not be wasted after all: "Be a world child, form a circle/Before we all go under," Thom sings. The song's last verse, dominated by the arresting image of birds trapped in partially cracked eggs struggling to hang on to existence, seems to address the ephemeral nature of all things, the life and the death force alike. Its closing line, "Immerse your soul in love," is lyrically the most positive note on the album, although the music remains in a resolutely minor key to the end.

With *The Bends,* Radiohead accomplished what most outside observers would have thought impossible. Not only did they beat the dreaded sophomore jinx and cast off their reputation as mere makers of novelty songs, but in the process they also created one of the most original and compelling rock albums of the '90s. From this point on, the band would be taken seriously—sometimes maybe too seriously. Later in the year, Thom would offer this comment on Radiohead's artistic breakthrough: "*The Bends* was an incredibly personal album, which is why when it came out I spent most of my time denying it was personal at all. Since then people have regularly accused us of being miserable fucks. I don't really mind that."[27] As long as the music backing up the misery maintained the same power that had distinguished *The Bends,* there was no need for him to be concerned.

8

For Radiohead, all the struggle and strain that had gone into making *The Bends* proved to have been worth it in the end; they had created a masterpiece. At the same time, the band were well aware that such a drastic departure from their earlier music might not necessarily lead to inspiring sales figures. In an interview with the respected U.S. fanzine *The Big Takeover*, Thom noted that the new album was "a leap for us in terms of who we are as a band" and confessed that even he didn't fully understand the genesis of that leap. But he added pointedly, "It's not a leap commercially. We have to swallow *that*."[1]

The band's U.S. label, Capitol, was particularly perplexed by the new material. There was no obvious single here, no successor to "Creep." Rumors spread that the album might not even be released in America. Eventually, it was decided that "Fake Plastic Trees" should be the first single; Clark Staub called it "a left turn" that would "dismiss the perceptions of Radiohead as one-hit wonders."[2] To help dismiss those perceptions, the label hired the well-respected producer/engineer Bob Clearmountain to remix the song for radio and video play. When the band heard Clearmountain's work, they were shocked. "All the ghost-like keyboard sounds and weird strings were completely gutted out of his mix," Yorke remembered, "like he'd gone in with a razor blade and chopped it all up. It was horrible."[3]

Capitol pushed hard to issue the remixed "Fake Plastic Trees" as a single, but the band would have none of it. Memories of the "Stop Whispering" remix debacle were still fresh in their minds, and they weren't interested in a repeat performance. "If it doesn't get on the radio the way it is now, then I don't think it's going to get on the radio at all," Thom commented. "There's nothing anyone can do to it. . . . People say it won't work on the radio, but I have no fucking idea what they mean."[4] With the band putting up such formidable resistance, Capitol was forced to release the original mix, only slightly edited, to radio (backed by an acoustic version of the song, plus the electric "Killer Cars" and a remix of "Planet Telex"). It got a substantial amount of airplay on commercial "alternative" stations, and the video—whose image of Thom in a supermarket shopping cart played on the frontman's bitter sense that he and his music were just another commodity to be bought and sold—made MTV's Buzz Bin, but that wasn't enough to even make a dent on the *Billboard* singles chart.

In Britain, the news was better. *The Bends* debuted on the U.K. charts at Number 6, higher than *Pablo Honey* had ever gotten. And the reviews were overwhelmingly positive. *Q* called it "a powerful, bruised, majestically desperate record of frighteningly good songs,"[5] while *Select* noted, "*The Bends* is set to be a monster album simply because it deserves to be."[6] *Melody Maker* praised "its uniform strength, its intelligent timelessness, the fierce uplift of its attack,"[7] and the stalwart London *Times* proclaimed, "Radiohead have suddenly bloomed into one of this country's most magnificent bands."[8]

Next to what else was happening on the British music scene in 1995, *The Bends* stuck out a mile. This, after all, was the year when the movement dubbed "Britpop" by the London press reached its apotheosis.* In truth, it wasn't much of a movement, just a bunch of bands who all reveled equally in music that celebrated the pop styles of Britain's past. Of course, the '60s wave of Beatles, Stones, Kinks, and Who came in for the most attention, but '70s icons like Bowie and T. Rex weren't far behind, and neither were new-wave acts like Squeeze, XTC, and Madness. Led by Sheffield native, former St. Martin's College film student, and perennial wit Jarvis Cocker, Pulp tipped their hat to Roxy Music and the New Romantics, while Justine Frischmann's punky outfit, Elastica, owed a major debt to Wire and the Stranglers (the publishing representatives of both bands certainly thought so—they sued Elastica for copyright infringement). By the summer, old-fashioned good-time youth anthems like the Boo Radleys' "Wake Up Boo!" and Supergrass' "Alright" were riding the charts, and the biggest question was whether Oasis' "Roll with It" or Blur's "Country House" would take the top spot on their first joint week of release. (Blur won that battle, but Oasis won the war, selling over four million copies of their next album in America alone.)

In the midst of this retro style–obsessed scene, Radiohead just didn't fit in very well. They too had been influenced by the Beatles and the Smiths, but their music didn't glance backward lov-

---

*One can argue for eons about when Britpop actually began, but the general view is that Suede's 1992 David Bowie–centric single "The Drowners" started things off and Blur's 1994 masterwork *Parklife* kicked it into high gear.

ingly as so many of the Britpoppers' did. And their attitude—toward making music, toward playing in a band, toward life in general—was also far more sincere than that of bands like Sleeper or Menswear, who assiduously cultivated the art of the pose. "The Britpop movement was wrong for us because it was so awash with this knowing irony," Jonny said later. "In some ways, it wasn't about . . . being serious about being in a band."[9] Thom wrote the movement off in typically acidic shorthand: "It was a convenient marketing ploy at the time. Marketing ploys come and go and that one's gone now. We did it for a while and then got off."[10] Actually, if Radiohead benefited from anything to do with this particular "marketing ploy," it was from their careful avoidance of any direct connection with it, a tactic which would only help them in the long run, after the Britpop wave had run aground.

From the evidence presented by the band's first U.K. tour in support of *The Bends,* British audiences seemed to appreciate their difference. The tour, which ran through March 24, concluding at the Forum in London, was a great success, with a string of sellout dates. The band sounded more confident than ever, and Thom had transformed himself once again—the ill-advised blond hair extensions of '93 were relegated to the distant past, replaced by a spiky orange-ish mop that resembled John Lydon's 'do during his Sex Pistols days. The only major hitch was the last-minute cancellation of the band's Sheffield appearance due to Thom's developing stomach flu; management narrowly avoided a melee at the venue by handing out free T-shirts and declaring an open bar. Otherwise, perhaps the most notable feature of the tour was that Phil, now the owner of his own house in Oxford, got into the habit of driving back home to his wife, Cait, after nearly every gig, further distancing himself from any semblance of the stereotypical rock 'n' roll lifestyle. "I clock on and clock off," the genial drummer commented dryly.[11]

Driving home wasn't an option for Phil on the next few legs

of the tour, which included stints in America, Europe, and Japan. But Radiohead's skinsman would eventually receive a kind of compensation in return for this relative inconvenience. Upon the band's arrival in Osaka for a show on June 20, they quickly learned that a bunch of local Radiohead enthusiasts, including several female employees of EMI Japan, had formed a Phil Selway fan club. Phil was the only member of the band ever to have received such flattering attention, and he took it with characteristic good humor. "It was strange . . . going to play a show and then spot[ting] someone wearing a 'Phil Is Great' T-shirt," Selway later recalled with a smile. "Only in Japan, I suppose."[12] (The Phil Is Great club eventually ceased operations, after some of its members began to suspect they might have offended the rest of the band.)

Radiohead bookended their Japanese jaunt with two North American tours; in service of *The Bends,* they'd end up crossing the continent no fewer than six times. The band had already played some shows on the East and West coasts in April, preceded by a handful of Thom-and-Jonny acoustic dates, mainly in Canada. Toward the end of May, Yorke and Greenwood took on a few more unplugged duo engagements, most of which were purely industry-based promotional affairs, including the annual National Association of Record Merchants (NARM) convention. They hated every minute of it. "The way I play the guitar, it depends on everyone else to keep things moving, and if I do something too extreme, no one will notice," Jonny said at the time. "Now [playing acoustic] I'm more exposed and it's harder. We do hate this acoustic thing. It's *evil,* the idea. We don't have barstools and we don't just play acoustic guitars. But it's horrible, the power that MTV has to make these changes. Yuck!"[13] Still, they did what they were told, and Capitol loved them for it.

The unfortunate result of all this jetting around America was that by the time the first U.S. *Bends* tour officially started, at the

Paradise in Boston on May 26, Thom was suffering. Too much time spent in and out of airplanes, pressurizing and depressurizing, had caused fluid to settle in his ears. Worried that he was going deaf, uncertain whether he could sing in key, Yorke was forced to wear earplugs for the first part of the tour, which didn't ease his agitation. During the Boston show, he snapped at the moshers in front of the stage, hitting one with his guitar and yelling, "Stop all this fucking moshing!" In support of Thom's actions, though, it must be said that the crowd was in a stagediving frenzy that night. Ed said later, "It seems the people who are into moshing are those people from college who you detested, the sports jocks. The ones who normally stayed away from so-called alternative shows, and who were seen at a Van Halen or Bon Jovi show, and now think alternative music is their thing. And that's fine, I'm very much for winning those people over, but don't bring your fucking bullying instincts to one of our gigs, where there are young girls and blokes out there. It's become an ego thing, so they get to be a hero with their friends. Maybe we should have a cage at stage right, like Metallica. We could throw them meat during the show."[14]

He may have had good cause for his outburst in Boston, but all the same, Thom's advanced state of stress didn't bode well for the rest of the tour. By May 29, when the band arrived in New York for a show at Tramps, Yorke was begging tour manager Tim Greaves to book him on a flight back home immediately. "I had a complete breakdown that night," he confessed to *Alternative Press*. "What brought me back was just talking to the others, 'cause they're my best friends and if there's something wrong, they need to know about it."[15]

It quickly became apparent that what the band needed more than anything was time to work on new material. Touring for months on end without a chance to concentrate on writing or rehearsing had nearly done Radiohead in after *Pablo Honey*, and that cycle couldn't be repeated. "It's the only thing that keeps us going," Thom said. "I can't write at home because home is home, and when I try to pick up a guitar, it's like, 'Oh, he wants to write something,' and suddenly all these ghouls come up and start looking at you saying, 'Oh, go ahead, write something good.' On tour, your whole existence is music anyway. . . . The band is my life, like ninety-nine point nine percent. That sounds horrible, it sounds really crap, but it is true. What a sad twat I am. I obviously need help."[16]

Thom would get help soon, though not necessarily the kind he needed most. From this point on, the band regularly rented rehearsal space wherever they were on a day off. New songs soon found their way onto the set lists, most notably a plaintive ditty called "Subterranean Homesick Alien." As the tour moved into its final stretch, concluding at the Palace in Los Angeles on June 15, the general mood had improved substantially. Still, road exhaustion was growing. Around this time, Ed noted, "We had two weeks off last year, and we've been together every single day since January this year. I remember I'd been ill, I think it was about three or four weeks ago, I'd just had the flu, and I sat at this meal, half joking but sort of crying into my soup, going, 'Oh my God, I've spent all my time with you guys!' "[17]

After the show at the Palace and the brief trip to Japan that followed, Radiohead returned to America yet again, this time to play club gigs in more out-of-the-way locations; cities in Arizona, Kansas, and North Carolina featured prominently. The band's U.S. touring helped *The Bends'* cause a little, but not much. The album staggered to a June 24 peak of Number 147 in *Billboard* and proceeded to thrash around the lower reaches of the chart for the next month and a half before vanishing entirely. To all concerned, it now seemed a certainty that *Pablo Honey*'s follow-up wouldn't come close to matching its predecessor's success.

Meanwhile, back in England, the album had slid out of the Top Ten. "Fake Plastic Trees" was released as the next Radiohead U.K. single on May 15 in two separate versions. One backed the song up with live recordings from one of Thom and Jonny's acoustic shows earlier in the year: "Street Spirit," "Bullet Proof," and another "Fake Plastic Trees." The other included the B-sides "India Rubber" and "How Can You Be Sure?" Both were melodic but minor numbers sketching details of obsessive relationships (yet again), the former a slightly techno-accented groove piece, the latter an acoustic ballad featuring, for the first and so far only time in Radiohead history, female backing vocals (by Dianne Swann). On June 3, the single reached its chart peak of Number 20, not even matching the performance of "High and Dry." It was another commercial disappointment for the band.

Yet these setbacks faded into the background when it was announced that R.E.M. had picked Radiohead as their support act for the upcoming European leg of their *Monster* tour. To share a stage with the band that had been perhaps their most important influence in their formative years was a high honor for Radiohead, one that took awhile to fully process. The experience began in England on July 30 with a performance in front of approximately 130,000 people at the National Bowl in Milton Keynes, part of a two-day festival that also featured the Cranberries and Blur. Before the band were due to go on, R.E.M.'s frontman Michael Stipe visited Radiohead's dressing room to wish them well. "Hi, I'm Michael," he said. "I'm really glad you could do this. I'm a very big fan." Thom would later confess that this down-to-earth statement by one of his all-time musical heroes had him "fighting for breath."[18]

The rest of the tour was a thrill, as the two groups forged what would prove to be a lasting bond. R.E.M. guitarist Peter Buck revealed that the reason they'd picked Radiohead to open for them was simply because *The Bends* was their favorite album of the year but they hadn't had a chance to see the band play live. "The one thing that I'm kind of proud of," Buck said, "is that we were like the older guys in that relationship. You know, that tour we did, we were writing these songs at the soundcheck and then playing them that night at the show, and I remember the Radiohead guys were really impressed with the fact that we had enough nerve to go out and put the songs that we'd only played once out in front of twenty thousand people who'd never heard them. And I think that was maybe a little influential to them, I hope so, because next time I saw them they had like five new songs in their set!"[19]

Yorke confirmed that R.E.M.'s way of conducting themselves on the road had a major impact on Radiohead: "Everything that we've come to expect was turned completely on its head, like the idea that you get to a certain level and you lose it and that's it—you're lost—and for everything to be amicable and there be no bitchiness or pettiness about it. Onstage, R.E.M. were playing with songs they've written, mucking around with the idea of being who they are and having no illusions about it—or seemingly so. And you compare that with a lot of what we feel when we are at home and it was just so different. It's such a headfuck."[20]

Perhaps the most important aspect of the R.E.M./Radiohead tour was the development of a close friendship between Thom and Michael Stipe, which continues to the present day. Over the course of the tour, the two spent a great deal of time together, during which Stipe counseled Yorke on, among other things, how to remain a sane, creative person amid the demands of growing fame, soul-sapping travel, and the pressures of the marketplace. Though Thom was nervous at first about even being in the presence of the man he regularly referred to as "Mr. Stipe," his anxiety lessened when Stipe told him about the similar feelings he'd had when he first met one of his greatest inspirations, Patti Smith.

Neither Yorke nor Stipe has ever volunteered much about the nature of their relationship, but the little that Thom has let slip over the years suggests that Stipe's confidences have demonstrably helped Radiohead's frontman come to terms with what he does for a living. "If you don't have any semblance of a normal life, then you won't be able to write, and if you can't write, then you won't be there," Yorke told Q two years later, echoing some of Stipe's advice to him. "He's helped me to deal with most things I couldn't deal with. The rest is not anyone else's business and that's what's great about it."[21]*

Through Berlin, Oslo, Stockholm, and Sicily, the two bands electrified audiences. When the tour hit Tel Aviv, scene of Radiohead's first success back in early '93, Thom suffered the ultimate embarrassment of being asked for only *his* autograph while seated directly across from Stipe at a restaurant. Luckily, this was soon followed by the ultimate elation of hearing Stipe say these words onstage at the next show: "There aren't many things that scare me, but Radiohead are so good they scare me." Moving in R.E.M.'s circle, it wasn't long before the band found themselves rubbing shoulders with some even scarier company. Colin later reported with mild amazement, "I met [Pearl Jam's] Stone Gossard. I had Neil Young standing behind me whilst we were playing, which was a bit unnerving. And they're like fans of our record."[23] Since things had gone so swimmingly on this part of the tour, R.E.M. invited Radiohead to open for them on select shows back in the States in September, an offer that the band happily accepted.

*Yorke also confessed that Stipe's ability to handle the glare of the media had altered his way of thinking. "I really admire the way he dealt with that whole period of his life around *Automatic for the People*, with the AIDS rumors. [It was widely believed in the early '90s that Stipe had contracted that disease; such rumors were unfounded.] He just wasn't gonna answer and they did give up eventually. Elvis Costello was the same. He just walked away from it all. If you love [the attention] so much, then you're asking for trouble."[22]

On August 21, another single off *The Bends* was released in England. This time it was "Just," once again in two versions; the first sported remixes of "Planet Telex" and "Killer Cars," the second, live recordings of "Bones," "Planet Telex," and "Anyone Can Play Guitar." The song itself—which didn't get beyond Number 19 on the charts—attracted far less attention than the accompanying video, directed by Jamie Thraves, which had been shot just after the band's first show with R.E.M. at Milton Keynes. In the video, a man lies down on the sidewalk of a busy London street for no apparent reason. Another man trips over him and offers to get some help, but the man insists he doesn't need any help. (Though we can see the characters' lips move, we can't hear what they're saying above the music; their dialogue is rendered in subtitles at the bottom of the screen.) Soon the man draws a large crowd around him, all inquiring why he's lying down. For a time, he refuses to answer the question, but finally he breaks down and tells them. (This is the one line of dialogue in the video without a subtitle.) In response to his words, the entire crowd lies down with him. The video's last sequence is a series of pan shots over the sidewalk strewn with bodies, a gripping image suggesting some horrific disaster. The members of Radiohead, playing in an adjacent building, are mere onlookers, barely figuring in the action (or inaction, as the case may be). Probably the most distinctive pop video of the year, "Just" picked up major airplay on MTV.

Though "Just" wasn't officially released as a single in America, the response garnered by the video altered the promotional game plan for the next "real" U.S. single, "High and Dry." Though a video already existed for that song, Capitol deemed it not nearly as interesting as the "Just" video, and so a new clip of the song was shot strictly for the American market under the guidance of director Paul Cunningham. With an obvious nod to Quentin Tarantino's *Pulp Fiction,* the new "High and Dry" takes place in a roadside diner and follows the comings and goings of a few shady-looking criminal types and a mysterious briefcase. (Thom plays a peripheral role as an observer; the rest of the band are featured even less than in the "Just" video.) After all the work was done, MTV complicated matters by objecting to the video's climactic closing sequence, which featured a car exploding in flames. With the offending shot excised, "High and Dry" was eventually allowed to air on the channel, a boon to sales of the single, which peaked at Number 78 in *Billboard* early in 1996—not a "Creep"-type success, but a lot better than "Fake Plastic Trees" had done.

Late in August, while Radiohead were occupied with more European gigs—including festival slots in Denmark, Holland, and Switzerland—the band were approached by representatives of a charity organization called War Child. With the help of sympathetic producer Brian Eno, they were putting together an all-star benefit compilation album to aid the children of war-torn Bosnia. All the artists involved in the project (the final total was 20, including Oasis, Blur, the Stone Roses, the Boo Radleys, Suede, Orbital, Massive Attack, and Paul Weller) would record their songs on the same day, September 4, and the album would be in the stores as soon as possible thereafter. Radiohead immediately agreed to take part. Jonny suggested that the band record "Lucky," a new, deeply Floydian song that they'd recently been playing live and that had gotten warm audience response. At first, Thom wasn't sold on the idea, principally because everyone else seemed to think it was a good call and because the song had been so easy to write and to play. The torturous *Bends* sessions had made Yorke expect everything to be difficult, but when the band entered the studio on the fourth (again with Nigel Godrich) to record "Lucky," the situation couldn't have been more different.

"There wasn't that sense of screaming and fighting and being on the phone to people for ages and spitting and swearing anymore," Thom said to *NME*. "But that was never any help to anybody, I don't think. . . . 'Lucky' is a song of complete release. It just happened, writing and recording it, there was no time, no conscious effort."[24] When asked later in the year what his personal highlight of 1995 had been, Ed automatically answered, "Recording 'Lucky.'"[25] The band completed the song in five hours. As the fourth track on the War Child compilation (officially titled *Help*), it was released five days later, on September 9. The album sold 71,000 copies on its first day in the stores, and *Melody Maker*'s review claimed that "Lucky" gave "further weight to the theory that [Radiohead] are no longer capable of anything but brilliance."[26]

Only four days after recording "Lucky," Radiohead were back in America, opening for R.E.M. at the Miami Arena. Given the luxury of an hour's soundcheck every night (a rare thing for a support act), the band continued to praise their American friends to the stars. "The music business is quite a bitchy and competitive thing," Thom commented, "and then after all that to meet people you really admire, and suddenly that whole competitive thing is gone, just not important—I found that helpful. . . . [It's] a shock when you discover that there are other people who have gone through that, are a few years ahead in the time machine, and have come back and said, you know, it's all right, I'm still alive."[27] The mutual lovefest continued for another few weeks, ending at the Meadows Arena in Hartford, Connecticut, on October 1; the band's plan to usurp R.E.M.'s set on the last night wearing giant lampshades on their heads was called off at the last minute, and the two groups settled for taking souvenir photos together after the show.

The next evening, Radiohead played an unannounced show in front of a tiny crowd at the intimate Mercury Lounge in New York. Spirits high, the band turned in a stellar performance. But Thom also got the opportunity to show off a little of his nasty side. During the set, the band was heckled mercilessly by a fellow just a few feet away from the stage. As they finished up and Yorke turned to the exit, he flipped the heckler a look of such withering contempt that it would have left a religious man praying for his life. Because the band had to walk through the crowd to get to their dressing room, a brawl seemed imminent. Yet as luck would have it, the heckler's unfortunate girlfriend apologized profusely to Thom right after the band left the stage, avoiding any further unpleasantness.

Within days of the R.E.M. tour, yet another American tour began, this time supporting the Minneapolis rockers Soul Asylum, whose newest album, *Let Your Dim Light Shine*, wasn't doing anywhere near the business of its multiplatinum predecessor, *Grave Dancers Union*. Despite the seeming stylistic discrepancy between the two bands, they got along well with one another. In a sense, they were in similar positions, following up a tremendously successful album with one that hadn't gained as wide an audience. But leader Dave Pirner and his cohorts had had a much longer, more arduous history in the music business than Radiohead. They'd spent years working on shoestring budgets for the Twin-Tone label before signing to A&M in 1988. Each one of their major-label releases was less noticed than its predecessor, and after three such outings, they were dropped. While the rest of the band went back to their day jobs, Pirner became convinced (erroneously) that he was going deaf* and wound up in a psychiatric hospital. It was only after his recovery from this disturbing episode that he and his band were re-signed, this time to Columbia, and Soul Asylum finally achieved the success toward which they'd been striving for nearly a decade. Their experiences and insights, like those of R.E.M., helped the young Oxfordites keep things in perspective.

*An obsession with incipient deafness is a trait Pirner shares with Thom Yorke.

Road-induced maladies continued to dog the band on the Soul Asylum tour. This time it was Jonny's turn. "My ear was ringing and bleeding for two weeks," he reminisced. "There was this terrifying gig in Cleveland, where I was nearly fainting. I was taken to the hospital at three in the morning and the doctor said the situation was really grim."[28] Jonny was advised that his ear would only heal if it was properly protected from loud noise. For that purpose, the doctor suggested that he wear a set of industrial ear shields at shows, the same type that road workers use when operating a jackhammer or other heavy machinery. Over the next few months, Jonny quickly grew accustomed to questions like "Why the headphones?" and "What are you listening to onstage?"

To top matters off, on the first night of the tour in Denver, all the band's musical equipment was stolen from their hotel. None of it was ever retrieved. Several shows had to be canceled, and the quintet had to invest in all new gear, which was purchased in L.A. on Thom's birthday, October 7. The band's guitar tech, Peter Clements—*aka* Plank, who built one of Ed's regular stage guitars—tried to put a good face on this unfortunate occurrence: "At least we know how long we've had everything." (Knowing this is useful both for insurance purposes and for talking to gear hounds in the music press.)

In spite of the weariness and even physical damage that repeated U.S. touring inflicted on them, Radiohead never stopped coming back. In this, they were unlike nearly all of their British contemporaries, who desired nothing more than massive American success yet turned up their noses at the prospect of actually having to play most U.S. cities. "Because they became so huge in Britain very quickly, bands like Happy Mondays and Stone Roses came to America with completely the wrong attitude," Ed O'Brien stated. "You have to keep touring."[29] Many British groups underestimate the vastness of the United States, but Radiohead were lucky to have managers who understood that the country consisted of much more than just New York and Los Angeles. In Paul Kolderie's words, "Radiohead have displayed a dogged determination to come and tour America and tour America and tour America. And not only that, but do all the stuff you have to do, go to those retail dinners and so on. Thom would sometimes make a bit of a scene, and he wouldn't always be there, but they've really made the effort to make friends in the industry. And that reflects a conscious strategy on the part of Chris Hufford and Bryce Edge."[30]

The implementation of that strategy continued with another British tour, beginning at the Barrowlands in Glasgow and ending at the Guildhall in Southampton on November 7. Once again, Phil commuted to the gigs from Oxford whenever possible. During this time, "Lucky" was released as a single off the *Help* album in the U.K., but it only reached Number 51 on the charts. It seemed a sad fate for such a fine song, but "Lucky" would end up getting a second chance soon enough.

Following the British sojourn, Radiohead traveled to Europe for a series of live dates. By the time they reached Munich on November 25, the intense touring schedule of the last few months had taken its toll on Thom; he was losing his voice. He'd already had a brief run-in with laryngitis during the last American visit, and as he later explained to *Q,* "It got bad again in Germany because we were sleeping on a cold damp tour bus in the middle of winter. The doctor turns up—usual thing, paid by the promoter—with this huge bag of steroids, which I refused. I didn't take anything because I thought I could get through it. We did the soundcheck [for the Munich show] and I was like, 'Oh shit, this is really bad.' My voice was not there at all. By that point, it's too late, you can't cancel. I go on and third song in, I lost it. I remember hitting the floor and then I wasn't there."[31]

Given a one-two punch by a combination of illness and

anxiety, Thom blacked out and collapsed onstage. Though the singer soon came to his senses, the show was stopped for good. Oddly, certain representatives of the British music press, perhaps unaware of the preceding events, wrote up the gig as just another example of pop prima donna–ism. The *NME* reported that Yorke had stormed off stage in tears, and made cutting references to "Thom's temper tantrum,"[32] as if blacking out in the middle of a performance was nothing to get too concerned about. "I did freak out," Thom later admitted, "but everyone was really supportive. I don't think people have any interest in me personally burning myself up."[33] (Radiohead rewarded the *NME* for its perceived slight by refusing to grant any interviews to the weekly from that point on.)

In any case, the tour continued, and the band even followed it up by going back to North America once more, this time concentrating on Canada. The Radiohead road show came to a temporary end on December 17, with the KROQ Almost Acoustic Christmas concert at the Universal Amphitheatre in L.A., where the band played alongside Oasis, Alanis Morissette, No Doubt, and Porno for Pyros. Capitol's Clark Staub recalled that the band "came out and completely blew people's minds. I was standing in about the eighth row and there was this row of fourteen-year-old girls and they were pulling their faces and screaming for Thom. . . . I think that was a really key stepping stone in the States."[34]

Another pleasant surprise came at the end of the year, as critics' and readers' polls began appearing in all the British and American music publications. The verdict was nearly unanimous: *The Bends* was one of 1995's best albums. In the U.S., critics at industry heavyweights like *Billboard* and *CMJ* ranked it near the top of the heap; in Britain, the readers of *Melody Maker* named it the Number 2 album of the year (second to Oasis' *[What's the Story] Morning Glory?*). Jonny later described this as a significant time for Radiohead: "[I]t started to feel like we made the right choice about being a band."[35]

Still, Thom remained sensitive about two things pertaining to *The Bends*: the general perception that the band's songs were all doom and gloom, and the inherent sadness of his voice. "It's sort of like a curse that people listen to my voice and think that everything I sing is important," he said.[36] Yorke told several journalists toward year's end that he wanted nothing more than to counteract this impression on the next album. "[W]e could really fall back on just doing another moribund, miserable, morbid and negative record . . . but I really don't want to, at all. And I'm deliberately just writing down all the positive things that I hear or see. But," he confessed, "I'm not able to put them into the music yet."[37]

As the holidays approached, the members of Radiohead dispersed and tried to catch up with their home lives. Thom went on a Christmas buying spree, loading up his girlfriend with household appliances. He later admitted that this compulsive shopping was at least partly an attempt to build an existence for himself beyond the bubbles of recording and touring: "[T]he most important thing in my life at the moment is establishing something outside of this. . . . The house is scattered with stuff, in boxes mostly, that I bought to try and claim my life back."[38]

January 1996 was the band's first full month off in a long while. Thom traveled around Europe, while Ed flew to India; the others remained in England. It was at this point that EMI released the fifth and final British single from *The Bends*, "Street Spirit." Like its predecessors, the single was issued in two different versions. On one, the B-sides were a studio-recorded full electric band rendition of that old chestnut "Banana Co." (at last) and a jaunty throwaway called "Molasses." (The former was tackled during the June '95 sessions at the Manor.) On the other, the extra tracks were far more intriguing, offering tantalizing glimpses of Radiohead's future.

Both "Bishop's Robes" and "Talk Show Host" were produced, once again, with help from Nigel Godrich. The former is a slow, moody meditation, with Jonny providing somber keyboard backing for the acidic lyrics about the band's old headmaster at Abingdon. The latter is another excursion into quasi-techno stylings, based around a distorted stop-and-start drum pattern by Phil, a simple but biting guitar riff, and more Yorkean lyrical desperation ("I want to be someone else or I'll explode"). Toward the end of the song the beat picks up, and Ed launches into some ace white-funk rhythm guitar, making expert use of his Lovetone Meatball envelope filter pedal. In their sparse power, both these songs stand proudly beside "Lucky" (which was recorded during the same three-day period just before the American tour with R.E.M.), pointing the way toward the emotional atmospheres of *OK Computer.*

Even with such outstanding B-sides, the decidedly downbeat "Street Spirit" was an odd choice for a single. Which made it all the more surprising when, without the benefit of radio play and with no tour or promotional activities to support it, the song immediately vaulted into the upper reaches of the British singles chart. (Jonathan Glazer's striking black-and-white video, shot in a trailer park and featuring various examples of film vari-speeding trickery, may have helped the cause some.) In February, it peaked at Number 5, Radiohead's highest placement ever. Now no one in England could continue to claim that "Creep" was the band's biggest hit. The hard work was finally paying off.

With the first month of 1996 coming to a close, Radiohead reconvened to work on new material at their rehearsal space in the apple shed, now wittily dubbed "Canned Applause." They'd come to a major decision: The next album would be produced by the band. According to Thom, *The Bends* had succeeded because "we had to put ourselves into an environment where we felt free to work. And that's why we want to produce the next one ourselves, because the times we most got off on making the last record were when we were just completely communicating with ourselves and John Leckie wasn't really saying much and it was just all happening. I don't know if it'll work again, but I hope it does." The refreshing experience they'd had recording "Lucky" and "Talk Show Host" with Nigel Godrich also played a part in this decision. As Jonny says, "It was like, 'We do B-sides very quickly and they're very good and they sound amazing, so let's just do the album like this. This can work.'"

Jonny insists that this move had nothing to do with their attitudes toward their last producer, whom they still highly respect: "I think it would have been more meaningful if we'd chosen a different producer. But the fact that we chose none at all is no reflection on John Leckie. It's a reflection on producers generally, I suppose. But then we keep meeting them and they say, 'I'd love to produce you, but you patently don't need me.' Scott Litt [producer of R.E.M. and many others] said this to us, which was a very pure compliment. But you know, he's a little sweetie, isn't he?"

Not only were the band planning to produce the next album themselves, but they'd also decided to buy all their own recording equipment for that purpose and set that equipment up wherever they liked. The idea came originally from Chris Hufford. "Our manager dropped this bombshell," Thom remembers. "He said, 'Look, you should just buy all your own gear.' We'd talked about producing on our own anyway. But this whole trip of actually getting your own gear, being responsible for it, and it's in cases, you take it where you want, it's your shit, was just the most exciting idea." The fact that Thom had recently been listening a lot to so-called Krautrock bands—'70s German progressive ensembles like Faust and Can, who took a similar do-it-yourself approach to recording—only added to the excitement. "Can, they always used to do their own stuff, and they were in a big room with bits of blankets and beds and shit, and Holger Czukay would endlessly, endlessly tape, tape, tape, and then splice it together. It just sounded such an amazingly cool thing to do. Basically four-track gone berserk."

To speed up the process of buying the new gear, the band got in touch with their pal Nigel Godrich for advice. "We knew that we wanted to get a plate [reverb]," Thom says. "That was Jonny's thing. We'd been listening to lots of stuff that had used plates, you know, early '70s, late '60s. It was the sound that we were looking for. Other than that, we basically just got whatever Nigel told us to get. I mean, we wouldn't know. I don't know what microphone to get." From his initial capacity as equipment adviser, Godrich quickly turned into co-producer of the project. Though the expense of purchasing all the machinery he recommended was high (nearly $150,000), Thom justified it as follows: "Next time we go to make a record, it's gonna cost us fuck-all."

While plans for establishing their own mobile recording studio continued to develop, the band kept polishing the new songs in their rehearsal space. On February 19, Thom took a break from the work at hand just long enough to accept, along with Brian Eno, the Freddie Mercury Award for the *Help* benefit album at the annual Brit Awards at Earls Court in London. Radiohead had also been nominated for Band, Album, and Video of the Year awards at the Brits, but came away empty-handed, as England's cultural heroes of the day, Oasis, took the honors in all three categories.

In mid-March, it was time to hit the road again. Back in the U.S. for yet another go-round, Radiohead made a couple of major TV appearances. First was a performance of "High and Dry" on *The Tonight Show,* which Ed describes in his best deadpan as "an opportunity we couldn't turn down," to which Thom responds with explosive laughter. "Yeah, we followed the contortionist in the box!" he cries. "It was the highlight of our entire fucking year!" A few days later, on MTV's *120 Minutes,* they played "Street Spirit," "High and Dry," and "The Bends." Ed said of the experience, "They record the bands from like ten- thirty in the morning till midday. I mean, those really aren't band hours, are they?" And Thom snorted, "Meeting VJs is the highlight of our existence."

With these two career peaks, the band's fifth American tour since the release of *The Bends* began. Many of the new songs they'd been working on over the last month and a half of rehearsals started appearing regularly on the set lists. Along with "Subterranean Homesick Alien," which had already been making the live rounds for a while, there was the winningly melodic but lyrically bleak "No Surprises," the pensive "Let Down," and the raucous "Electioneering."* Other selections that the band occasionally treated listeners to on this tour were by turns somber, cranky, and euphoric: "Motion Picture Soundtrack," "I Promise," "Man O'War," and a frankly gorgeous piece of songwriting called "Lift," driven by Thom's relentless rhythm guitar and featuring sweeping keyboard lines by Jonny, spine-tingling backing vocals by Ed, and lyrics in which Yorke refers to himself directly by name ("You've been stuck in a lift/We've been trying to reach you, Thom"), concluding with the gently posed admonition, "So lighten up, squirt."

*When I interviewed Thom, Jonny, and Ed in March '96, Thom offered, among other things, this remark: "I think every song is a phase, for all of us. So we're going through our 'Electioneering' phase now, aren't we?" I completely misinterpreted this at the time; unaware that it was the actual title of a new song, I thought Thom was just making another barbed quip.

Radiohead weren't just indulging their taste for the new by playing previously unaired material. Even their old songs were changing to some degree. The change was particularly apparent in Jonny's guitar parts, which could sometimes sound drastically different from the recorded versions. On the road, Radiohead's nominal lead guitarist never tired of improvising and tinkering. "None of the stuff I play on tape is especially precious and the best thing I could have done," he says, "so I carry on looking for something else even after the song is released. I mean, I won't start doing Van Halen hammer-ons and sliding across the stage on my knees or kissing the sax player or whatever, but . . . you know, I think we *will* do that to an extent." (Prospective Radiohead sax players, wherever you are, you have been warned.)

"The time to work out guitar parts is not in the studio," Thom adds. "It's almost impossible to do that, because unless you're all actually playing at the same time, you're always trying to calculate what else is going to happen, and it's just impossible. You second-guess everything. Playing the songs live helps a lot."

By and large, it was a more restrained Thom Yorke that took the stage on this latest five-week jaunt, a frontman less interested in frantic attempts to excite the audience through stage antics and more willing to simply let the music speak for itself. "What really pisses me off more than anything," he says, "is singers who *evoke,* and do shit with their arms, and get all melodramatic. You can learn all the moves; they don't take long. It takes about a year to learn all the moves to get people into a certain frame of mind to do all these things. And it's bollocks, really. So now if I find myself doing that, I just stop. Playing the song until you're into it, it could take a whole gig. But if you're not into it, just stand there and do nothing. That's what I do, 'cause there seems no point in trying to evoke anything." (At least one other member of the band feels pressure, of a sort, to put on a convincing live performance—according to Jonny, "Colin keeps coming over to me and saying, 'Jonathan, I want you to rock out tonight.'")

A few lucky audiences on Radiohead's March/April tour also got the chance to hear one of the few cover songs the band has attempted in concert since signing to EMI: Carly Simon's "Nobody Does It Better," the theme to the James Bond film *The Spy Who Loved Me*. Before performing the tune, Thom would often introduce it as "the sexiest song ever written." Though that statement is debatable, it would be hard for anyone who's heard the Radiohead version to argue that the song wasn't tailor-made for Thom Yorke to sing. Investing the lyrics with an over-the-top yearning that narrowly avoided edging into pure camp, he quickly made one forget the drabness of the original version. It was reported at the time that the band actually recorded "Nobody Does It Better" for a prospective album compiling new takes on James Bond theme songs, but so far, such an album has not materialized.

Now eight-time veterans of American tours, Radiohead were growing used to bizarre occurrences, like the fan in Vancouver who'd asked Jonny to autograph his arm and then, at the band's next gig several hundred miles away, turned up again with the signature permanently tattooed on. "Spending two years playing the same record and visiting so many places . . . a very strange experience," said Colin. "And the novelty can carry it over for so long, until the novelty itself becomes everyday—which is really weird."[39]

Despite *The Bends'* lack of initial American success, Capitol had never stopped working the album. Its high placement in so many year-end magazine polls had added to the label's enthusiasm and become the center of a whole new promotional campaign, while the band's willingness to keep coming back to the States also helped gain them new converts. The results were impressive. *The Bends* re-entered the *Billboard* charts almost a year after it had been released, climbing this time to Number 88, still no blockbuster but far higher than the album's previous chart peak. On April 4, the album was certified gold (signifying U.S. sales of 500,000 copies) by the Recording Industry Association of America. In Britain, following the surprise success of the "Street Spirit" single, the pattern was repeated, as the album reached a new peak of Number 4 and was certified platinum (signifying U.K. sales of 500,000 copies).

Soon after their return to England, the band checked back in with Nigel Godrich and finalized the purchase of the last necessary pieces of equipment for their mobile studio. They decided, for the time being at least, to install the gear in Canned Applause. A "normal" studio environment was to be avoided at all costs. "We have a peculiar horror of professional studios," Jonny said. "It doesn't feel very healthy to be part of that production line."[40] Between periods of aiding Godrich with the studio setup, they made several festival appearances, including the Pinkpop Festival in Holland on May 27, the Tourhout Wechter Festival in Belgium on July 6, and T in the Park at Strathclyde, near Glasgow, on July 13. The *NME* review of the latter show dubbed Radiohead "The Last Great Sincere Rock Band."[41]

By June, Canned Applause was ready for recording. To their credit, EMI made it clear that they had no desire to repeat the angst that had nearly wrecked the *Bends* sessions. Keith Wozencroft deliberately refrained from imposing a production deadline on the band; in fact, he told them they could take as long as they wanted to finish the album. "We didn't believe [him]," Yorke said at the time, "but apparently they meant it. So we'll probably finish it in a couple of months, and then not give it to anybody for six." What with the lack of label pressure and the band's calculated avoidance of traditional studios with their inherent bad vibes, it seemed that this time the proceedings should run smoothly. They didn't.

"When we went into doing *OK Computer*," Ed recalls, "we didn't think the tension could get as bad as it did on *The Bends*. The idea was for it to be as relaxed as it had been recording the B-sides." He pauses for a mirthless chuckle. "That was soon scuppered."

"I think one of the big things that contributed [to the tension] was that we'd decided to produce it ourselves," Phil says. "Certainly that's quite a big responsibility to take on. And it's also an awful lot to learn in a very short space of time." Of course, Nigel Godrich was there to lend a hand, but there was only so much he could do to resolve what was essentially a power dispute within the band. Making an album on which all five members shared equal production roles was certainly unwieldy, maybe even impossible; little would get done if all concerned had to sign off on every decision. So who would be in charge? The obvious answer was Thom, but it turned out that this wasn't necessarily the best choice for the band.

As Ed says, very diplomatically, "Thom has amazing energy and he's got lots of ideas—as we all have ideas, but he has the loudest voice. [Yorke himself put it this way in an earlier interview: "We operate like the UN; *you* can get the veto, but *I*'m definitely America."[42]] But that at the same time is not always the right thing. He had very set ideas when we went into [recording], and some of them were great and some of them weren't. It kind of works itself out after a while." But not without a little pain.

For his part, Thom says he came to the eventual realization that recording at Canned Applause wasn't such a good idea after all. "The problem was we could go home when we wanted. It was just around the corner. So it was really impossible to commit yourself to it mentally when you knew you had to go home and do the washing up." Jonny seconded this notion for even more practical reasons: "There was nowhere [at Canned Applause] to eat or defecate, which are two fairly basic human drives."[43] The search was on for a new location. "We had to go and find somewhere else," Thom says, "and it had to be a big place too."

The answer came in the form of St. Catherine's Court, a fifteenth-century mansion in a secluded valley near Bath, owned by actress Jane Seymour. Thom and Colin had heard about the place through the grapevine and learned that it was no stranger to musicians; it had previously been rented by such disparate players as the Cure and Johnny Cash. Excited by the prospect of recording in such grand surroundings, Radiohead booked St. Catherine's Court for the entire month of September. In the end, the nearly two months they'd spent working at Canned Applause had been far from a total loss. A grand total of four songs—"Subterranean Homesick Alien," "Electioneering," "The Tourist," and "No Surprises"—were more or less finished in the apple shed.

Before recording could continue, however, the band had more road duties to perform. From August 12 to August 29, they played 13 U.S. dates, mainly in arenas, sheds, and stadiums across the Northeast, in support of Alanis Morissette, whose 1995 album *Jagged Little Pill* had transformed her image from bubbly Canadian teen-pop queen to brazen spokeswoman for female empowerment. In front of large audiences that were decidedly different from those for R.E.M. or Soul Asylum and that contained a sizable portion of people who had only the vaguest idea who Radiohead was, the band continued to focus on new material, including an ambitious number called "Paranoid Android," which stretched on for over ten minutes and was made up of three distinct and completely unrelated musical sections.

The response was tremendous. "I was [at the final show] in Detroit," Capitol's Clark Staub remembered, "and Radiohead played all new songs with the exception of 'High and Dry.'. . . [T]his was an Alanis Morissette crowd at an amphitheater that held seventeen thousand people, and if they'd been allowed an encore, Radiohead would have got an encore."[44] Under the circumstances, it wasn't surprising that Staub and his Capitol colleagues began to believe the new album, once finished, would be a multiplatinum singles bonanza.

The tour's headliner made no bones about the way she felt regarding her opening act. Alanis regularly wore a Radiohead T-shirt during her set and took to covering "Creep" and "Fake Plastic Trees" as encores. Of the latter, Jonny remarked with jocularity, "It had a very American slant. The drummer got his hand about a meter higher than Phil does when he's playing it."[45] Of Morissette herself, Ed laid it out straight: "Her music's pretty terrible but she's a lovely person."[46]

All the same, many hard-core Radiohead followers had trouble with the idea of their heroes sharing the stage with such a blatantly commercial act. Yet for the band, the challenges of breaking in new songs and playing for a completely new audience were well worth taking. Of course, the financial aspects of touring with Alanis were also a considerable factor; Colin later admitted to *Select* that they'd gotten "silly money" for the privilege.[47]

Having temporarily appeased the ravenous road monster, the band returned to England and ensconced themselves at St. Catherine's Court. Nigel Godrich set the recording gear up in the library, and the band laid down most of the basic tracks in the house's vast ballroom. "It was wonderful going somewhere that wasn't designed for recording," Jonny said. "Recording studios now tend to be quite scientific and clinical. You can't really impose yourself without getting over the fact that there are fag burns in the carpet and gold discs all around. It's good to go and decide that we'll turn this beautifully furnished sitting room into whatever."[48]

"The fact that it was a big country house was a source of acute embarrassment," Thom admits, "but it's like, fuck it, we love private rooms. We didn't want to be lab rats in the studio, so it was the logical thing to do, and it had the most fantastic sounds. All this stone everywhere, fucking amazing. And the weird thing about it is, when we started recording, we were taking tapes home and we'd play them for our friends, and they'd go, 'It just sounds like a house.' Which was really exciting. Blows away every studio in London."

By now, the creative tension between Thom and the rest of the band had dissolved to some degree, as everyone had realized that working together wasn't always going to be easy and that minor disagreements were nothing to get freaked out over. "I think we know now that there are always going to be clashing moods whenever we make anything worthwhile," Phil says. "We've developed our coping mechanisms."

Still, it wouldn't have been a Radiohead session without something for the more sensitive members of the band to obsess about, and this time it was the very age of the house in which they were recording. "It was weird playing there," Thom says. "I spent my whole time terrified because it was fifteenth-century and you were just continually reminded of your own mortality. There was a church attached to it with ancient, ancient [grave]stones in it, and the place was badly haunted."

"One of the beds had '1612' carved into the side," Jonny reports. "Think how many babies had been born and how many people had died in that room, or had sex."

"Everywhere you go," Thom continues, "it's just lives in the walls coming out at you. Even if you *haven't* been taking drugs."

Partly to escape the spirits, partly to fine-tune the new songs even further, Radiohead took a break from recording at St. Catherine's Court after that first month, returning to Canned Applause for more rehearsals in October. On the 10th, Thom and Jonny played a secret duo gig at the Tramshed in London, organized by the magazine *Dazed and Confused* to celebrate the publication of their twenty-fifth issue. According to some who were in attendance, the moniker of the magazine was also an apt description of Yorke's demeanor that evening. "From the second he came on," *Melody Maker*'s Robin Bresnark told Nick Johnstone, "he was agitated and tense and he didn't really seem to want to be there."[49] Frazzled though he may have been, Thom did manage to make it through seven songs, accompanying himself on acoustic guitar while Jonny switched between guitar and keyboards. In addition to "My Iron Lung," "Fake Plastic Trees," and "Street Spirit," the twosome aired the newer numbers "Lift," "Let Down," "No Surprises," and "Exit Music (For a Film)."

Not long after this gig, the band made the difficult choice to jettison from final consideration for the album some of the material that had initially seemed the most promising, including "Lift," which many at EMI had already been counting on as a single. They defended their decision by saying that those songs simply didn't sound right and that there was no point in wasting any more time on them, at least not this time. Ed even went so far as to say that "Lift" was "a bogshite B-side and we were very happy to leave it off the album."[50] That Radiohead were unafraid to dash the expectations of others showed that they'd gained confidence in themselves, profiting from the harsh lessons about record company interference that they'd learned during the *Bends* sessions. Yet at least one band member professed he was sorry about the unused tunes. "The only regrets about this album," Jonny would say after *OK Computer* was completed, "are the songs we left off because we didn't record them well enough or soon enough."[51]

In November, Radiohead returned to St. Catherine's Court for another month of recording, during which the album was mostly completed. By Christmas, they'd narrowed the track order down to 14 songs. Two of those, "Polyethylene" and "A Reminder," were eventually selected as single B-sides. In January of

'97, string parts, orchestrated by Nick Ingman, were recorded at Abbey Road, where the album was also mastered; mixing took place over the next two months at several different London studios. Once again, perhaps because of a wish to maintain some sort of tradition, Sean Slade and Paul Kolderie were asked to mix a couple of tracks. This time, however, their "American" sound wasn't what the band were looking for, and the duo's work was never used. Besides the regrets they had about the songs that were left off, everyone in the band seemed pleased with the final results—even Thom, in his strange way. "When we finished it and were putting it together," he said, "I was pretty convinced that we'd sort of blown it, but I was kind of happy about that, because we'd gotten a real kick out of making the record."[52]

The first taste the general public got of the new music arrived by way of the movies. Australian director Baz Luhrmann, who'd previously manned the cameras for the film *Strictly Ballroom,* was working on a modernized L.A. gangland version of *Romeo and Juliet* starring Leonardo DiCaprio and Claire Danes and had asked Radiohead, among many other artists, to submit songs for the soundtrack. Along with "Talk Show Host," which would feature prominently in the action, the band gave Luhrmann "Exit Music (For a Film)." Appropriately enough, the song played during the film's closing credits (although it wasn't included on the soundtrack album).

Once *OK Computer* was finished, the band laid low for a month or so. During this time, Thom and Jonny helped out their old friend Michael Stipe, who was supervising the soundtrack of Todd Haynes' '70s glam-rock film *Velvet Goldmine.* (Stipe was also one of the movie's executive producers.) Under the mock-band name the Venus in Furs, Yorke and Greenwood collaborated on covers of three early Roxy Music tunes—"2HB," "Ladytron," and "Bitter-Sweet"—with the likes of Suede's

Bernard Butler and Roxy's own Andy Mackay. Though they weren't released until the film's premiere in late 1998, they demonstrated that Thom Yorke could do a spot-on Bryan Ferry impersonation if necessary.

The only major public appearance Radiohead made in February 1997 took place on the 20th, when the quintet traveled to Dublin to accept the honor of being named Best International Live Act of 1996 by the Irish music magazine *Hot Press*. Sharing a table with U2, the boys may have indulged in just a little too much of the evening's free light refreshment, for they later distinguished themselves by mislaying their award not once but twice—first leaving it behind on the podium after the presentation, then losing it again not long afterward, prompting a building-wide search after the ceremony.

At the end of April, Radiohead appeared on the BBC Radio One program *Evening Session* to announce upcoming tour dates and to premiere their new single, nearly a month before its release date of May 26. The single was "Paranoid Android," in all its six-and-a-half-minute glory, practically ensuring a dearth of radio play. It was an audacious choice, but one that could have been expected. After all, the first single to come out of the *Bends* sessions had been "My Iron Lung," not the most cuddly and approachable number to introduce a new album with. When the single was finally issued in the U.K., it came out, once again, in two different versions. The first bore the B-sides "A Reminder" and "Melatonin," both ambient and reflective, pretty but a tad underdeveloped; the other boasted the more satisfying "Polyethylene" and "Pearly," both aggressive rockers. "Polyethylene" is especially notable for being the most complex example of time-signature skipping the band had mustered so far (exploring the joys of six-, eight-, and nine-beat measures) and for making a song lyric out of the line "There is no significant risk to your health." "Pearly" features some kick-ass drumming by Phil and a densely layered outro, courtesy of Messrs. Yorke, Greenwood, and O'Brien.

Long before the single was released, advance copies of the new album were distributed to EMI and its various subsidiaries worldwide. Though the overall response was positive, especially in the U.K., the band's U.S. label was mystified. "When [Capitol] heard the album," Ed told *Option*, "they downgraded their expectations. Down from two million to five hundred thousand."[53]

"They thought, 'This album is going to be chock-a-block with radiotastic singles and we'll just have it away majorly,'" Chris Hufford said. "But when the record was finished, 'Electioneering' ended up being this very abrasive, garagey thing and the other songs [the label] had liked didn't even make it to the album. There was lots of 'Ooh dear, this isn't quite what we thought the record was going to be, I have to say we're a bit disappointed. . . .' So we steamed in and said to America, 'Get your industry heads off, forget the bloody singles, just listen to it like a punter for a few weeks and you'll realize what an amazing piece of work it is.' Thankfully, that's what happened. They started saying, 'You're right, this is amazing, but now what the fuck do we do with it?'"[54]

Clearly, after four years of glumly following the rules of show-biz (more or less), Radiohead had had enough of doing what their record company told them to do. They'd hardly forgotten what had happened during the *Bends* sessions; EMI's request to record a leadoff single first had put the band through months of needless angst. By following *The Bends* with an album that was widely perceived as noncommercial, the Oxford fivesome were, in some sense, thumbing their noses at all those who'd tried to dictate how the band should make their music.

OK Computer, as it was now called, was scheduled for release in Britain on June 16 and in the U.S. on July 1. Prior to the album's release, in mid-May, Radiohead would play a preview gig in Lisbon, Portugal. A few days later, the "official" European launch of the album would take place in Barcelona, Spain. Two concerts were scheduled there, on May 22 and 24, for which EMI were flying in label and media representatives from around the world. It was a big fiesta for what the company hoped would be one of their biggest releases of the year. Whether it actually would be was anyone's guess.

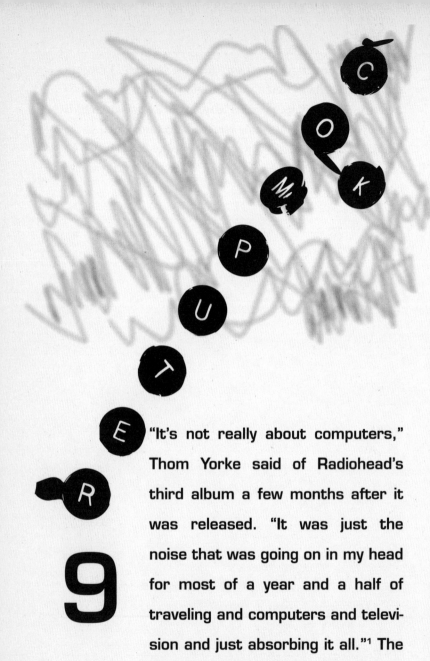

COMPUTER

9

"It's not really about computers," Thom Yorke said of Radiohead's third album a few months after it was released. "It was just the noise that was going on in my head for most of a year and a half of traveling and computers and television and just absorbing it all."[1] The key word here is "noise." Both musically and lyrically, *OK Computer* conveys a sense of humanity being nearly overwhelmed by audio-visual stimuli, endlessly bombarded with random sounds and images to the point that comprehension is impossible.

Thought of in this way, the album's title makes perfect sense. Does it directly address a computer? Is it a reflection on technology? A sarcastic depiction of the human brain (more emotional than rational, just an okay computer)? Or any number of other possibilities? There's no way to know, and that's the whole idea. "OK computer" is just another fragment of speech in the constant noise barrage. Taken out of context, it's suggestive but fundamentally meaningless, like a sentence badly translated from another language. As Jonny Greenwood aptly put it, "I think this album is too much of a mess to sum up. It's too garbled and disjointed, and the title is only supposed to introduce you to the record."[2] It may seem strange to refer to such a finely crafted piece of modern music as a mess, but in terms of what the album's overall point is, what it's supposed to "mean," Jonny's right. The mess is the message.

This doesn't mean that there aren't still some identifiable themes sticking out of the muck. Principal among them is the de-humanization of the modern world. As the power of technology grows, it becomes easier for humans to be ruled and potentially destroyed by what they have created. Every day's pace grows more rapid, leaving us exhausted and increasingly disconnected, both from others and from ourselves. *OK Computer* is heavy with the presence of machines, all of which pose at least one of two dangers: physical (injury to individuals, contamination of the environment) or spiritual (adding to the perpetual buzz that drowns out life). Cars and planes crash, radio signals cross, and eerie computer voices speak without a trace of emotion. The song titles alone, even the ones that were meant to be humorous, clearly evoke the rootlessness, confusion, and dysfunctionality of late–twentieth-century society: "Paranoid Android," "Climbing Up the Walls," "Subterranean Homesick Alien," "The Tourist," "Let Down."

Radiohead probably didn't plan this album to be a Big State-ment about the deleterious effects of technology on our lives. At least one hopes they didn't; that would have been a little pompous. But the fact remains that those suggestions, those evo-cations, are there in the music. It wasn't just critics who picked up on them either. According to Thom, "A friend of mine found this essay on a Web site that Thomas Pynchon wrote about Luddites, which is hilarious. Luddites were that lot in the last century that went around and smashed up all the weaving looms or whatever it was. And that was a reaction against the dehumanization of production and the fact that people were only becoming their hands or their feet . . . and not whole people anymore. My friend gave me this thing he found and said, 'There you are; that's what I think of this record.' "[3]

Are Radiohead modern-day Luddites? If so, they cut an odd figure, decrying the current state of affairs while continuing to use computers, samplers, and state-of-the-art digital recording equipment. It's a paradox of which the band are no doubt aware. And the way they wriggle out of its snares is to approach the tech-nology innocently, with no preconceptions and little formal know-how. If, in the course of their work, the technology is abused, stretched to its breaking point, all the better: Humanity triumphs.

The members of Radiohead have frequently asserted that they produced *OK Computer* knowing next to nothing about what they were doing. Of course, they had help on the technical side. "We didn't walk around going, 'Oh, need a bit more 4k,' " Yorke says as he mimes turning a console fader up. "Nigel Godrich is the one physically doing that." Still, the band's lack of detailed gear knowledge didn't diminish their tendency to run rampant in the control room. "We were coming at it from complete igno-rance," Thom told *Mojo*, "standing in front of some beautiful digital delay going [makes manic knob-twiddling motion and accompanying noise] and Nigel's going, 'Oh, fucking hell,' until suddenly everyone says, 'That sounds great!' And that's what we'd use. It's children with toys. You don't really know what's going on but you're digging all the lights. And usually, when it sounds good, something's broken."[4]

Yorke described the recording of *OK Computer* as being "like a workshop, and that was how we wanted to do it. We didn't want to be in the studio with A&R men coming around, nice air conditioning, staring at the same walls and the same microphones. That was madness. We wanted to get to another state of mind—one that we understood and could deal with. The only way to do it was to do it ourselves. That way we wouldn't have to explain it."[5] But no one would claim that the self-production process had been easy, even with Godrich's assistance. Thom estimated that out of the year it had taken to make the album, only about three months had been spent recording: "The rest was agonizing about it, trying to forget about it, rehearsing it or rewriting it."[6] The acknowledgment of this difficulty was right there in the CD booklet. "We didn't even put 'produced' on the album," Yorke points out. "We put 'committed to tape,' because that's what it was."

That commitment to tape did have a distinctive sound, however, and the man who mastered the album, Chris Blair, one of England's foremost mastering engineers, classified it best. As Colin recalled, "He'd mastered *The Bends* [as well] . . . and I asked him on the second day we were mastering *OK Computer* at Abbey Road what were the big differences for him between the two records sonically. He said to me that he'd been working at Abbey Road now for over twenty years, and *OK Computer* reminded him a lot of records that were recorded in Abbey Road, or brought to him to be mastered, in the '70s. They were albums that were recorded by a band like [Pink] Floyd, with an engineer as opposed to a producer, and had a more open, spacious sound, less compressed, more delicate-sounding and more extreme at the same time, less just one sort of sonic level. And that was what he was going to try and bring out, that return to that kind of '70s sound . . . and I thought that was really interesting."[7]

Indeed, the album's "'70s sound" led a lot of listeners to link Radiohead's new music with the progressive rock that so defined that decade. The epic sweep of the songs didn't hurt, and neither did the frequent appearance of that stereotypical prog implement, the Mellotron, a pre-synthesizer, pre-sampler, tape-based keyboard instrument used by bands like Yes, Genesis, and King Crimson to simulate the sounds of orchestras and choirs. Jonny was a recent convert to the Mellotron, and he admitted that he'd been listening to a lot of records that incorporated it, but with little pleasure. "I've been trying to find lots of good prog rock," he said at the time, "but unfortunately it's all awful. Every last record is terrible. All I've come away with, really, is the Mellotron as an instrument. But musically, there's nothing. I quite like *Meddle* by Floyd, but that's not really prog rock. I mean, that's just rock 'n' roll, isn't it? So it was a bit disappointing. I just got suspicious of [people saying], 'Punk came along and killed [prog],' and I was like, 'Well, what did it kill?' I was curious. But it is better off dead."

Those pundits who didn't say that Radiohead had gone prog took a listen to techno-accented tracks like "Airbag" and declared that the band was forging a new hybrid of electronic and guitar-based music, making the latter in the spirit of the former. Ed O'Brien downplays this idea, though. "I think that's more a critics' interpretation. What we try and do is be diverse. The guitar sound on 'No Surprises' was supposed to hark back to [the Beach Boys'] *Pet Sounds,* 'Let Down' was a nod to Phil Spector, 'Exit Music' had a [composer Ennio] Morricone atmosphere, 'Airbag' was an attempt to do something like [San Francisco techno artist] DJ Shadow—but because we haven't paid the dues, if you like, to play those types of music, we fail to get what we hope to achieve. But by going down that route, we find our own thing."

At least two other notable artists have been acknowledged by the band as major influences on *OK Computer*. The first is Miles Davis, and in particular his murky, ominous, jazz-rock masterpiece *Bitches Brew*. The most prominently featured instrument on that album, the Fender Rhodes electric piano, is all over *OK Computer* as well. "We're just obsessed by *Bitches Brew*," Thom says, "or by anything even vaguely like it. That's a record for the end of the world." The other influence is the Beatles, especially John Lennon and especially the White Album. Thom claims that the tripartite nature of "Paranoid Android" was inspired by "Happiness Is a Warm Gun," while the chord progression and piano line on the chorus of "Karma Police" owe a distinct debt to "Sexy Sadie."

Of course, it's the way Radiohead absorb these influences and turn them into something very different that's most interesting. They may be shooting for a certain familiar sound at first, but what they come up with is invariably new and quite their own. "I think our ears get bored very quickly," Jonny says. "Sometimes a guitar plugged into an amplifier isn't really enough. So you hear sounds in your head or you hear sounds on a record and you say, 'I want it to sound like this,' and sometimes it won't, for whatever reason. I can't play the trumpet so it's not going to sound like *Bitches Brew*. We don't have access to an orchestra, so it's not going to sound like Morricone. But at least you can try and emulate the atmosphere. You aim for these things and end up with your own garbled version." As Thom puts it, "Aiming and missing is the whole premise, really."

Besides experimenting with the sounds of their own instruments, Radiohead also played with studio technology on *OK Computer* to a degree that they never had previously. While on tour in 1996, Thom had bought a tiny MiniDisc recorder, and he'd entertained himself for long periods by recording anything that caught his attention—street noises, bits of conversation, TV shows—and constructing repeating loops out of those "found" sounds, some of which made it onto the finished album. "It loops seamlessly," Thom says approvingly of the MiniDisc, "with no jump, nothing, because it's digital and it's obviously memorizing it beforehand. You set it up once, it goes back and forth exactly. And it sounds so amazing."

With Godrich's help, the band also tried more than its fair share of digital cut-and-paste sampling and editing, plus traditional tape loops and tape editing. Many of the hard-to-classify background noises on tracks like "Exit Music," "Paranoid Android," and "Climbing Up the Walls" were produced by loops of one sort or another. "We got so into that," Yorke remembers. "We were making loops link up, you'd be watching the tape going around, and you were just touching it, just to slow it up enough every time. The beautiful thing about it is the way that the tape stretches. In theory, it's in time with itself, but actually it's going in and out. And there [in the studio], you have an [Akai] S3000 [digital sampler] in the corner, you can do [loops] in five minutes. But it's not as much fun doing that. I always thought we were doing well when there was loads of tape on the floor," he adds with a guffaw. "Something was happening."

As on *The Bends,* much of *OK Computer*'s music was contributed by members of the band other than Thom, especially Jonny, who wrote part of "Paranoid Android" and all the music to the album-closing "The Tourist." With the passing of the years, the younger Greenwood was becoming more confident about presenting his ideas to the band. "It's quite hard," he says, "or used to be anyway, to say, 'Listen to this. I know I can't sing a note, but what do you think?' But then there are some things like the 'rain down' section of 'Paranoid Android'—it needed a context, it needed a song, it needed words, et cetera, et cetera, but it was worth doing somehow."

Of collaborating with Jonny, Thom says, "It's brilliant for me, because I always get to a point with a song when I can't go any further. Or the other way round—he's got something and can't take it any further. We've always done it like that, actually. But now we have the confidence to do it with every song. A lot of it is down to the fact that I'm not the world's most interesting or interested guitar player. It always has been a totally functional thing for me. It's like Lou Reed, three chords, here we go, you know. So to respond to something that someone else has put forward is, I find, far more exciting."

Even on the songs that were essentially written by Thom, the input of the other two guitarists affected the music's direction more than ever. "We go for weeks [in rehearsal] when I can't hear what either of them are doing," Thom says. "Ed and Jonny will be sitting there and they'll have their amps really fucking quiet, working out what they're gonna do, and then suddenly, we get DADADADA [imitating loud guitar roar]. And then it's like, 'Wow, that's great.'" Jonny observes, "It's a combination of randomness and working on it for a long time." And Ed adds with a grin, "As a guitarist, I'm fortunate in that I've got lots of [effects] pedals to work with."

The music wasn't the only element that had changed. In a conscious shift away from the overtly personal nature of *The Bends'* songs, Thom adopted a different approach to lyrics on much of *OK Computer*, taking on characters and writing in a more detached, reportorial style. "The voices on 'Karma Police,' on 'Paranoid Android' and on 'Climbing Up the Walls' are all different personas," he commented, "though actually it's not blatantly obvious. But it was something I was acutely aware of. I didn't feel any need to exorcise things within myself this time. It wasn't digging deep inside, it was more of a journey outside and assuming the personalities of other people."[8]

Just what sort of personality the singer assumes on "Airbag," *OK Computer*'s opening song, is hard to determine. In any case, the lyrics seem to be preoccupied with the connections between near-death experiences and rebirth, although the type of rebirth that's postulated here—"In the next world war/In a jackknifed juggernaut"—isn't necessarily reassuring. Thom explained to *Q* that the words to "Airbag" had been inspired by reading Sogyal Rinpoche's *The Tibetan Book of Living and Dying* and applying its language to an age of fast cars and grisly road accidents. "Every age has its crazy idiosyncrasies, crazy double-think," he said. "To me, for our era it's cars. I always get told off for being obsessed about it, but every time I get in my car I have to say to myself that I might never get out again. Or I might get out but I won't be able to walk. . . . I suppose it just comes from being a worrier. But 'Airbag' is also about how, the way I've been brought up and most of us are brought up, we are never given time to think about our own death."[9]

The song opens with an appropriately doom-laden riff played in unison by Jonny on guitar and Mellotron, which is soon countered by a jangly guitar line, played by Ed; the vocal melody is another Yorke special, alternately soaring and somber. The most distinctive feature of "Airbag," however, is its drum track, which sounds like it's being broadcast, with occasional interference, from a shortwave radio transmitter somewhere in the Crab Nebula. Gritty, harsh, and trippily processed, it moves the band several steps further in the electronic direction that previous songs like "Planet Telex" and "Talk Show Host" had indicated. But Thom insists that its initial sonic reference point came from much earlier in the band's history. "Jonny wanted to put [the track] through his Moog [synthesizer]. When we were very young, we did a track like that. We'd done a loop and sat around and fiddled with the EQ. We were trying to imitate a very, very old demo that we'd done.

"It was my favorite song on the record," he continues, "but we had no way of playing it live that was satisfying. We had all the parts, except the drums never worked." The solution to this dilemma was only reached after much intense labor, which involved sampling Phil's original drum track with the Akai S3000 and then cutting, pasting, and otherwise manipulating the audio on the band's Macintosh. "We took inspiration from DJ Shadow, and the way that he would cut up drum tracks and then reassemble them," Phil recalls. "I went in and drummed for a quarter of an hour, and we got about the three seconds' worth of any value out of it, and put that back together and formed this really angular rhythm track for it, which you don't generally get from normal drum programming."

The resulting track is indeed notable for its surprising number of variations; it bears little resemblance to the mechanistic repetition of a traditional loop. "Breaking it down into little parts and then jumbling it all back up again just changes your approach to arranging," Phil observes. "I'd forced myself how to learn computers and programming," Thom says, "and it was really frustrating me because there was no life about it, the way it played was meaningless. I couldn't work out what [the problem] was, but I think basically my favorite records that have been programmed are ones that either totally repeat themselves like a machine every damn bar, or it's so organic you can't follow it, 'cause things are changing so fast. And then I was like, 'This isn't going to be a loop.' So me and Phil worked on it for two days solid, with Nigel."

"The rest of us couldn't be bothered," Colin cracks. "I'm not hanging around in the studio so they could mess about."

No studio hijinks went into the creation of Colin's idiosyncratic bassline on "Airbag," which slyly drops in and out at unexpected points throughout the song. The part you hear is as he played it and is not a product of the recording console's mute button. "I thought I'd probably think of something to put in the gaps later," Colin claims, "but I never got around to it." (Not just here, but throughout *OK Computer*, Colin's playing boasts a new fluidity and imagination, which may have something to do with the private bass lessons that he took during breaks between the many tours supporting *The Bends*.) Another interesting technical note about "Airbag" is that the band had originally planned to take Thom's rhythm guitar track, which had been recorded solely as a guide, out of the finished mix, but found that the music suffered without it. "You can't take something that has an organic acoustic base and, relatively quickly, try and make it into something that's a piece of programmed music," Colin observed.[10]

" 'Airbag' is great," Ed says, "but it's full of approximations, because we can't program." Still, an argument could be made that such approximation is actually a more creative approach to making music. In this case, the finished product backs up that argument splendidly.

The next track, the lengthy "Paranoid Android," was written, Thom says, "in three different sections at different times in different states of mind, and then put together. Our working model for it was 'Happiness Is a Warm Gun.' Walked into the rehearsal room one day, 'Well, you know "Happiness Is a Warm Gun," you know how that's like three songs put together? Let's do that.' And I didn't obviously think it was going to work, until we put it together finally, which was a fucking shock." In its earliest incarnation, as heard on the Alanis Morissette tour, the song ended with a long instrumental section featuring Jonny on Hammond organ. But since that part stretched the song out to nearly eleven minutes, it didn't make the final cut in the studio.

Colin explained that the band had become intensely interested in "brutal editing, where you just splice bits of music together, like the Beatles on *Magical Mystery Tour* or whatever. We really wanted to try that, just to see if we could make musical sense out of disparate elements. . . . ['Paranoid Android'] was one of the first things we finished in the sessions, and we'd listen to it and we'd just giggle. We felt like irresponsible schoolboys who were doing this . . . naughty thing, 'cause nobody does a six-and-a-half-minute song with all these changes. It's ridiculous."[11]

In a sense, you have to agree with his assessment. The whole notion of a song like "Paranoid Android" *is* ridiculous, and the title's nod to the malaise-stricken robot Marvin in Douglas Adams' *Hitchhiker's Guide to the Galaxy* only adds to the feeling that Radiohead are playing this one at least partly for laughs. Yet the very audaciousness of the song is thrilling in itself, and after a few listens, the separate pieces begin to make sense together, adding up to an emotional statement that covers the range from bitterness to yearning and, yes, even a little paranoia.

The song's opening section features Thom finger-picking his way through a tricky chord progression on acoustic guitar, while Ed demonstrates his skill on the clave. Paired with the delicate rise-and-fall melody, which makes excellent use of Thom's falsetto, is the first of several lyrical references on the album to an all-pervading, unstoppable noise ("all the unborn chicken voices in my head"), along with a caustic swipe at certain unnamed persons meeting with the singer's displeasure. After some spacy guitar interpolations by Jonny, we're on to the second section, during which more parts are gradually added—a deliciously busy Colin bassline, some Fender Rhodes chord stabs, and finally the whole band abruptly crashing in at full volume. Rhythmic play comes to the fore once again; the first section employs an odd number of measures and the second is partly in 7/8 time. Jonny denies that this was the product of conscious thought. "I think our ears are naturally bored with fours," he says. "But then the Pixies were the same in the '80s. And they never sounded like they were being clever when they did it. It was just like, 'Well, you know, you don't really need to hear the fourth time around on this riff. We think your life can be better without it.'"

In a 1997 interview with *Q*, Thom revealed that the "kicking screaming Gucci little piggy" mentioned in the second part of the song was a real person, a woman that he'd seen in an L.A. bar who erupted in fury when someone accidentally spilled a drink on her. "There was a look in this woman's eyes that I'd never seen before anywhere," he said. "Whether that was down to me being exhausted and hallucinating . . . no, I know what I saw in her face. I couldn't sleep that night because of it. . . . I mean, everyone was out of their minds on coke and I'm sure it was that. But it seems to be happening to me a lot. Seeing a look in someone's eye and [thinking], 'Fucking hell, what was that?'"[12] At the time of this unpleasant incident, the musical basis of "Paranoid Android" had already been in the works for months, but the lyrics came later that night as Thom's attempts to sleep were thwarted by the voices of the bar's inhabitants echoing in his head, "like demons from another planet," or so he said.

After the growing frenzy of the second section, the noise subsides and we're transported into a slow, brooding, almost classical succession of descending chords backing wordless, cathedral-sized harmonies. Eventually, Thom sings, in his most plaintive voice, a request to be rained down upon from a great height, a wish for cleansing (or further humiliation) that's repeated several times before a clever countermelody emerges. There are words to go along with that too, some twisted conflation of yuppies, pigskin, and vomit, concluding with a statement that drips sarcasm: "God loves his children, yeah!"

"To my ears," says Jonny, who wrote the music to this third part, "['Paranoid Android'] is a very tense song, until the slow section, which it needs to have. Otherwise it would just be unlistenable." The fact that the second section's central metalloid riff—which, if slowed down, might have made it onto a Black Sabbath album—returns at the end of the song also helps make the proceedings more comprehensible. Back at peak loudness, the band rips into the last few seconds, coaxing some nasty, unhinged playing from Jonny, who's very much in the "Just" bag here. The song ends like "Just" as well, all of a sudden, as if everyone's plug had been maliciously yanked out of the wall.

"Subterranean Homesick Alien" follows directly behind. The song's title may be an obvious reference to Bob Dylan's "Subterranean Homesick Blues," but musically it owes little to the bard from Hibbing, Minnesota, being instead the most blatantly Miles-influenced track on *OK Computer*. The prominence of the Fender Rhodes (played by Thom) in the mix isn't the only aspect of the song that's been touched by *Bitches Brew*: Jonny's high, whistling guitar line, produced with the assistance of his trusty Whammy pedal and some delay effects, also takes some sonic cues from the great trumpeter's '70s work. "When [Miles] is putting all those really trippy delays on his trumpet," Thom says, "that's exactly what Jonny was trying to do with the guitar."

Written during the sessions for *The Bends*, "Subterranean" is the oldest *OK Computer* selection. "We used to do that song acoustically, just with me and Thom, for ages," Jonny recalls. "And I didn't really know how to do it on record until the electric piano idea reared its head, and that became the center for the song." Between the hallucinogenic tremolo of the Rhodes and the spacy swells of Jonny's guitar, there's more than enough interstellar atmosphere to fit the lyrics, which deal in part with the phenomenon of UFOs. Thom, or the character he's representing, who lives in a dreary town "where you can't smell a thing," pictures aliens constantly filming the human activities on Earth, sending the video back to their own world. Our behavior puzzles them: "They're all uptight" goes the chorus (sung over a cascading unison line played by Thom on piano and Ed on Rickenbacker electric 12-string). The singer hopes to be abducted by the aliens and thus in some way transcend his mundane existence. He realizes that if this ever does really happen to him, no one will believe his story, but that doesn't matter; he'll be content knowing that he's seen "the stars and the meaning of life."

Thom originally categorized this tune as a joke song, "as much as my jokes are ever funny."[13] The lyrics were inspired by memories of an essay assignment he'd had to write back in his early days at Abingdon, which ran approximately along these lines: "You are an alien from another planet. You've landed and you're standing in the middle of Oxford. What do you see?"[14]* Yorke recalled that "[w]hen I was a kid I was always very confused about the difference between angels and aliens. I couldn't see that there was any difference. I had a very proud theory when I was a child that they were the same people. I just loved the idea of someone observing how we live from the outside . . . sitting there pissing themselves laughing at how humans go about their daily business."[15]

Both Thom and Jonny have explained in interviews that, to them, the true subject of "Subterranean" is the misplaced spirituality that so many people have invested in the mystery of UFOs and the search for alien presence on Earth. "Before UFOs it was the Virgin Mary," Jonny once said, "and before that it was something else. People flock to the same places with their cameras and hope to see the same things. And it's just about hope and faith, I think, more than aliens."[16]

The echoing final chord of "Subterranean" fades into Thom's distant acoustic guitar strumming the introduction to "Exit Music (For a Film)," a song that Yorke, its principal author, has called "the first performance we'd ever recorded where every note of it made my head spin—something I was proud of, something I

*One could argue that Yorke and his bandmates perceive their hometown in just such an "alien" fashion.

could turn up really, really loud and not wince at any moment."[17] As previously mentioned by Ed, the band had intended "Exit Music" to sound like the more stark, foreboding work of film score composer Ennio Morricone, but at least at the beginning, where Yorke is singing and playing by himself, the mood is closer to that of a haunted folk song. (Thom once remarked that it reminded him of something off Johnny Cash's famous live album, *At Folsom Prison*.) The cavernous reverb heard on Thom's voice is all-natural, courtesy of the stone hallway in St. Catherine's Court.

Although the lyrics of "Exit Music" are somewhat oblique, the basic storyline seems clear enough: In early morning, under cover of darkness, a young couple are furtively preparing to escape the clutches of their forbidding parents and make a new life for themselves. It's a Romeo and Juliet scenario, in other words, and not so surprising when you consider that the song was first publicly heard accompanying the closing credits of Baz Luhrmann's film version of that Shakespeare classic. Indeed, the song was written on commission, so to speak, after Luhrmann sent the band a 10-minute clip of the film and asked them to contribute music. Despite its written-to-order beginnings, Thom later would regard "Exit Music" as one of his most personal compositions, one more reason for Radiohead to request that it not be included on the film's soundtrack album. "It was about more than the film," Jonny said, "which is a bit arrogant to say—'It's bigger than Shakespeare.'"[18]

Two verses into the song, at the point when the singer urges his anxious love object to keep breathing and not lose her nerve, the music breaks into another, completely unexpected key. Jonny's Mellotron choir starts up, and the sense of vastness, of being on the brink of a terrifying new experience, is nearly overwhelming; the Morricone comparison fits here. (This was the first Mellotron track laid down for the album, recorded the day Jonny received the instrument.) For a brief period, we return to the tune of the previous verses, though the music is now backed by disturbing noises of whirring machinery (more tape loop experimentation).

With a burst of heavily compressed, Ringo Starr–like drumming from Phil, the rest of the band finally joins in. Colin's bass is obscenely loud, coated in a thick layer of gravel 'n' grit distortion. As the focus of the lyrics turns from the lovers' fears to their defiance in the face of their elders, the melody climbs ever higher and Thom's singing grows ever more dramatic, until he reaches the climactic peak: "Now we are one in everlasting peace." This line strongly suggests that the lovers, like Romeo and Juliet, have already met their deaths; it may be that the escape they've been planning was actually an escape from life, a joint suicide. If so, their contempt for the adults who have ruined their lives continues beyond the grave. The song's final line is "We hope that you choke." Its final chord is a cheery B major, a subtle stroke of irony given that most of the song has lingered in a decidedly minor key.*

Another clever segue takes us from the whir and hum of the traffic-noise loop that closes "Exit Music" to the chiming arpeggio (played in unison by Jonny on guitar and Fender Rhodes) that introduces "Let Down." This song, the highlight of *OK Computer*'s first half, was recorded live at three o'clock in the morning in the ballroom of St. Catherine's Court. The intricate series of five-beat lines that Jonny plays at the beginning is quickly backed by Ed's tasteful 12-string picking. Within seconds, the rest of the band comes crashing in, but at what seems

*Incidentally, it's worth noting here that the great majority of Radiohead's songs are in major keys, which are generally considered by most listeners to be uplifting, even as the band has been repeatedly accused of wallowing in gloom and misery. The ever-present ache in Thom Yorke's voice has a lot to do with this perception, of course, along with the frequent morbidity of his lyrics. But you can't discount the fact that this band also knows how to make the upbeat sound downbeat, a skill that's not easily acquired—ask any songwriter how tough it is to write a convincingly sad song in a major key.

like a completely random moment. The reason for this disorienting turn is that the song was originally recorded with Thom keeping time on acoustic guitar, but his track was later removed from the intro section, leaving Jonny and Ed's parts to hang enticingly in space. This studio arrangement choice would later give the band some problems when it came time to play "Let Down" live, as we'll see.

Once the rest of the band comes in, Jonny continues to play his 5/4 line over the simple 4/4 chord progression, a striking bit of complexity that Colin laughingly describes as "prog," despite his brother's earlier protestations to the contrary. (Colin also says it reminds him a little of Massive Attack's "Protection.") Thom begins singing a melody of drawn-out single notes in a low mumble; the clumps of bare-bones lyrics convey the emptiness of traveling—whether by car, train, or plane—and the malaise of "disappointed people clinging onto bottles." Yorke is writing as a witness here rather than as a participant, observing rather than emoting. This was a conscious choice; Thom has admitted that the first verse's line about not getting sentimental was directed at himself. "Sentimentality is being emotional for the sake of it," he said. "We're bombarded with sentiment, people emoting. That's the letdown. Feeling every emotion is fake. Or rather every emotion is on the same plane, whether it's a car advert or a pop song."[19]

Getting rid of excess emotion is certainly a worthy endeavor, but "Let Down" is not exactly a feeling-free musical zone. Indeed, as the song progresses, both its unemotionalism and its supposed objectivity get called into question. The second line of the chorus describes a bug crushed on the ground, and in the second verse Thom fixes on the image of that bug, its hard outer shell smashed, its wings twitching. But what seems initially like mere observation takes on a different cast a couple of lines later when he sings, "One day I am going to grow wings, a chemical reaction." Is Yorke transforming himself, like Kafka's Gregor Samsa, into an injured insect? The question isn't answered, of course, yet the growing urgency of the music indicates that some change is taking place. Thom's singing gathers momentum, losing its mumbliness and moving into a higher register, while Jonny's repeating guitar/piano line goes from five-against-four to three-against-four; the cycle is shrinking, gradually closing in.

After an atmospheric instrumental break featuring the burbling of what sounds like an analog synth's arpeggiator, the singing starts again. Now Thom is almost pleading, his voice climbing higher and higher, until he vaults into a falsetto, and then, thanks to a magical bit of double-tracking, the melody splits in two. One Thom continues to sing the verse, repeating the part about growing wings, while the other Thom repeats in high choirboy fashion the enigmatic closing line: "One day you'll know where you are." The song closes with another run through the chorus and a final turn for the burbling synth, which now bears an odd quality of triumph as it plays above the quiet acoustic guitar. Yet maybe that sense of triumph isn't so odd. After all, "Let Down" *is* a victory, a victory over the very emotionlessness it depicts. It may not be a happy song, but it does make you feel, which in this case is all that matters. Using pitch, dynamics, and rhythmic interplay to masterful effect, building subtly to a powerful peak, "Let Down" is a tremendous achievement and one of Radiohead's most intoxicating creations.

"Karma Police," probably *OK Computer*'s lightest moment, makes an appropriate contrast to the sublime sweep of "Let Down." Far less ambitious than its predecessor, centered around acoustic piano and guitar, it's also very reminiscent of late-period Beatles. That's especially evident in the lumbering "I Am the Walrus" thwack of the rhythm section and, as previously mentioned, the direct White Album lift in the chorus. The lyrics castigate a bunch of annoying people at parties, asking the titular karma patrol to give them what they deserve. Lines like "This is what you get when you mess with us" are a fine blend of the sinister and the comic, and Thom's vocal performance plays that blend for all it's worth. "I get stressed pretty easily," Yorke said in partial explanation of the song, "and having people looking at you in that certain [malicious] way, I can't handle it anymore. . . . That's what 'Karma Police' was about. Though it's a joke as well, you know, 'Karma police, arrest this man.' That's not entirely serious, I hope people will realize that."[20]

Jonny also stresses that, like "Paranoid Android" and "Subterranean Homesick Alien," "Karma Police" is "obviously not overly serious as a title or a subject," which reinforces his belief that *OK Computer* "feels like a comic album."[21] (To this, one might reply that the comedy's definitely in there, but most of it's a deep shade of black.) The lyrical theme of superfluous noise encountered earlier in "Paranoid Android" returns, as one of the song's main characters is likened to a "detuned radio." He also "buzzes like a fridge." In what may not be a coincidence, Thom has frequently compared the sound of American "alternative" rock radio to the sound of a buzzing refrigerator.

Most of "Karma Police" is structured fairly conventionally, going about its appointed verse-chorus-verse-chorus rounds with little variation. But at the end of the song, the band leaps into a new part in a completely different key, and all sonic stops are pulled out. Both Thom's voice and acoustic guitar are adorned with neopsychedelic delays, while wordless backing vocals rapidly rise and fall in the mix. Finally Ed, who's had very little to do so far other than sing backup through heavy processing, plucks a few notes on his guitar, which feed back and distort, lowering in pitch and increasing in volume, forming an exploding cloud that eventually self-destructs, taking everything else with it.

Ed explains that this imposing sound was produced by overloading one of Nigel's AMS digital rackmount delay units (to produce the feedback) and then turning the delay rate knob down (to change the pitch of the feedback signal). "It's not supposed to distort for that long," he says. "It actually takes on a life of its own, making its own beeps and such, because it doesn't understand what it's supposed to be doing. After a while, I'm not even touching the guitar, and the knobs [control] the feedback and the speed. I don't know whether that part's annoying or it's great. I know lots of people who think"—here he splutters with laughter—"that's the part that ruins the song, and maybe they're right. But the five of us like it. Otherwise, one of us would have said something."

Thom adds that when Ed was recording this part, "he didn't really know what he was doing, for various reasons." When it's suggested that the band seems to like having Ed not know what he's doing (take "Bullet Proof," for instance), Jonny cackles: "Confusion is power. *Nobody* knows what they're doing."

"He can handle it, you see," Thom says approvingly of his tallest bandmate. "He doesn't give a fuck. And especially when you're recording, there's nothing more boring than everyone knowing what the fuck they're going to do."

From the guitar explosion of "Karma Police," we cut directly to the computer monotone that dominates the disturbing soundscape called "Fitter Happier." An inhuman voice tells the fragmented two-minute story of a person who has conformed to the world's expectations to such a degree that he (or she) has been stripped of all personhood and is now little more than a robot, comfortable but vacant, "a pig in a cage on antibiotics." (This last line is adapted from Jonathan Coe's satirical novel *What a Carve Up*.)

Thom explains that at the time he wrote these words, "I was having real trouble writing anything. But I was walking around a lot, endlessly walking around each day. One particularly bad day I wrote this list. I set down items like a shopping list, and it turned into this thing. I showed the words to everybody, and everyone thought it was really good." The only question was what to do with it. Yorke certainly didn't want to read or sing "Fitter Happier" on tape. Always self-conscious about the quality of his voice, he felt that if he took on those words himself, the result would sound too serious, too miserable. So he tried typing them into the band's Macintosh using the SimpleText application and having the computer's onboard speech processor read them back to him. The effect was perfect. "I really responded to the way it mispronounces things," Yorke says. "And the computer voice just seemed a logical extension of this list mentality."

Behind the voice of the Macintosh is a swirl of loops, effects, and a pensive piano line that Thom singles out as his favorite part of the track. One of the loops—you can hear it in the right channel—is sampled from the 1974 film *Flight of the Condor*. "It's the sequence where all the people have been killed and he's calling the office to tell them," Thom says helpfully. Yorke recorded this sample off a hotel TV with his MiniDisc recorder late one night while Radiohead were on tour.

Interviewed by *Option*, Thom called "Fitter Happier" "the most upsetting thing I've ever written. The reason we used a computer voice is that it appeared to be emotionally neutral. In fact, it wasn't, because the inflections that it uses made it to me incredibly emotional. It brought out something that I thought was essentially flat, it brought it to life in a really fucking eerie way."[22] Again, Radiohead successfully convey deep emotion by removing overt sentiment.

On the next track, "Electioneering," Yorke and company finally summon up a little high-volume three-guitar clangor. (Not so long ago, guitaristic excess had been a band trademark, but on *OK Computer*, it was a rarity.) Supported by Thom and Ed's twisted riffing—in double dropped-D tuning, with both top and bottom strings tuned down a whole step from E to D—and Phil's cowbell-powered backbeat, Jonny unleashes his most aggressive soloing on the album. Yorke has characterized this song as "a preacher ranting in front of a bank of microphones,"[23] but it could also be seen as a metaphor for the life of the touring musician as politician, a long bleary round of drinks, handshakes, and promotional appearances in an attempt to court both the industry and the audience. "I trust I can rely on your vote," Thom snarls in a strident voice that wouldn't have sounded out of place on *Pablo Honey,* before wailing a chorus—"When I go forwards, you go backwards, and somewhere we will meet"—that reflects on both political and artistic compromise.

Like "Let Down," "Electioneering" is an example of more aloof, reportorial lyric writing from Thom. He says a partial influence here was John Lennon's (again) pithy news-report style on "A Day in the Life": "What can you say about the IMF, or politicians? Or people selling arms to African countries, employing slave labor or whatever. What can you say? You just write down 'Cattle prods and the IMF' and people who know, know. I can't express it any clearer than that, I don't know how to yet, I'm stuck. That's how I feel about 'Day in the Life,' Lennon was obviously stuck and said, 'I'm going to write a song because I've got to get this down,' and it's everything that he didn't say by doing that. . . . That was what I dreamt of doing on this record."[24]

It's unlikely that Thom would ever claim anything he's written as the equal of "A Day in the Life," but let's plainly state once and for all that "Electioneering" doesn't come close to measuring up to that Beatles perennial in any way. On the whole, the lyrics don't say more by saying less—they just say less. They also seem carelessly tossed off, with little sense of commitment to them. And there are certainly no dazzling flights of fancy here, no speculation on how many holes it takes to fill the Albert Hall or such like. On the upside, the melody is solid and the band plays with an admirable fury, but the song still sounds unfinished. To be fair, the loud, up-tempo, rocking side of Radiohead had to be represented somewhere on *OK Computer,* yet it's a shame that this not-quite-worthy contender has to bear that burden almost solely (with just a little help from "Paranoid Android").

Sonically, "Climbing Up the Walls," which follows "Electioneering," is a stunner. Phil's drums ring like metal trash barrels, partly because of EQ manipulation and partly because the main signal we're hearing is the sound of the drums bleeding into the other instrument mikes in the room. "If you were to isolate each instrument, you'd hear other stuff on [its track] as well, and that's what's so interesting," Ed says. "That's one thing about this album that's really great, that eighty percent of the performances are live and in an unorthodox studio environment, so there's lots of bleeding on the tracks." Thom's acoustic guitar was recorded at an extremely loud level, overloading the board, while his voice is filtered to the point that you can barely tell it's him singing. Ed's delayed guitar parts creak like the floorboards of a haunted house. Tape loops, random noise recorded off a transistor radio, and the album's craftiest use of strings—a 16-piece violin section, each musician playing a quarter-tone apart at the song's end—add further to the foreboding ambience. And Colin's bassline, played on a Novation Bass Station synthesizer, is the final masterstroke of doom.

According to Colin, Jonny was intimately involved in devising this keyboard bass part. "Jonny got some stickers," he recalls with a surprisingly straight face, " 'cause I don't know what a keyboard looks like. And he put on [the keys], 'Play this one, and then this one next.' It was great. The Novation's got a natural sort of squelchy, breaking-up sound. I do like it, but the frequency it fills up, I wish it wasn't quite so . . . *fat,* 'cause it kind of squashes everything else in the track. It's one of those Mark Morrison *Return of the Mack* bass sounds. I think we could be seeing some more of that swing bass thing on a new Radiohead album someday." Ed quips in response, "We could be seeing some of that on Colin's solo album."

Not only does "Climbing Up the Walls" sound spectacular, but the creepy vibe the music conveys also perfectly matches Thom's lyrics, which conjure a scene of domestic abuse and murder. "Do not cry out or hit the alarm," he coos chillingly, "we are friends till we die." Later on, he advises his addressee to make sure the kids are safely tucked in, and muses on the effect of "fifteen blows to the skull." As a mood piece, it's brilliantly effective; as a song, however, it leaves something to be desired. It does feel finished, unlike "Electioneering," but it's similar to that song in that it doesn't go much of anywhere, except volume-wise. "Climbing Up the Walls" starts quiet and ends up terrifyingly loud, but that buildup doesn't boast the emotional power of, say, "Let Down"—it sounds more like the band just decided to turn everything up. Still, within the context of the album, this song does do a good job of capping off what could be called the Armageddon section of *OK Computer,* starting with the guitar explosion at the end of "Karma Police" and progressing through the bleak vistas of "Fitter Happier" and "Electioneering."

After the aural firestorm of "Climbing Up the Walls," it's a shock to hear the lightly strummed guitars and tinkling xylophone (played by Jonny) of "No Surprises," a shock that was surely intentional. Written while on tour with R.E.M. in '95, the song boasts a gorgeous pop melody but harbors dark undertones. "I'll take a quiet life," Thom sings, "a handshake, some carbon monoxide," before ominously commenting that "this is my final fit, my final bellyache." Indeed, the almost sugary nature of the tune is pungently offset by the lyrics' apparent hopelessness; a friend of mine once mimed shooting himself in the mouth to the song's lush final chord, a move that aptly conveys the prevailing mood.

Originally, at least one member of the band (Ed) had intended "No Surprises" to have a Beach Boys feel, a kind of music-box quality similar to *Pet Sounds'* "You Still Believe in Me." But what came out in the end is more like the Velvet Underground's "Sunday Morning," tuneful but far from comforting. As on "Let Down," Thom begins singing the song in a low, almost gruff register, but on the second and third verses the melody moves upward, and the vocals take on an air of poignant resignation.

"No Surprises" was the first song recorded on the first day of sessions for *OK Computer* at Canned Applause; the version you hear on the album is the first take. "We did endless versions afterwards," says Thom with a laugh, "and they were all just covers of the first version. So we gave up and went back to [the original]. But then, everybody's always done that. That's what recording is, it's having the freedom to do that and not get freaked out. Something Nigel said all the way through the sessions was, 'It doesn't matter how we get there as long as we get there.' And he was right."

Similarly, because the next song, "Lucky," had already been released on the 1995 *Help* compilation, the band tried to remix it before including it on *OK Computer* but found that the original mix had a charm later ones lacked. And so the song was released again without a change, a somewhat surprising move. "We hemmed and hawed about it," Jonny confesses, "but it was released as a single [in the U.K.] and got to number sixty-something [actually 51], and it was embarrassing. The song deserved a bit better than that." Thom adds, " 'Lucky' was indicative of what we wanted to do. It was like the first mark on the wall."

It had also set the guidelines for how the whole album should be made, an example of recording ease that the band would subsequently strive for but rarely attain. Last but not least, it's a fine song. In its slow, mournful pace, it recalls mid-'70s Pink Floyd (a big influence on Jonny), while in its lyrics it echoes "Airbag."

Both songs seem to touch on some sort of rebirth arising from accidents. The singer of "Lucky" asks to be pulled out of a lake from the wreckage of an airplane, and the protagonist of "Airbag" survives what should have been certain death in a car crash. "I'm your superhero" is a recurring line in "Lucky," mirroring the chorus of "Airbag" and its theme of returning to Earth to save the universe. Thom has been keen to point out in interviews the "positive" aspects of the song, these suggestions of rescue or transcendence, but one has to admit the backdrop's still a gloomy one.

"Lucky" demonstrates once again the band's knack for distinctive sonic details. The song was partly inspired in the first place by the guitar part that Ed plays at the beginning of the song; he plucks his strings above the nut, producing high, ghostly overtones, a sound that Thom claimed was "like nothing we'd ever heard before."[25] And when Jonny found the right choirlike keyboard sound to use on the song's second verse, Yorke confessed he turned into "a gibbering wreck."[26] No doubt about it, "Lucky" is a beautiful piece of music. Yet it's still a tad disappointing that Radiohead chose to include on this album a song that many fans already knew and owned at the expense of other truly new songs ("Lift," for example). A minor quibble, but a quibble nonetheless.

OK Computer closes with "The Tourist," a lovely, laid-back number in waltz time, except for one extra beat thrown in toward the end of every other line in the verse (another trademark Radiohead rhythmic move). Singing in his most delicate voice, stretching notes nearly to their breaking point, Thom urges us to break away from the blur of speed and noise that has dominated the rest of the album, to stop traveling at "a thousand feet per second." His simple yet eloquent performance was done in one quick, rough take. Partly for that reason, it's one of his favorite vocal moments on the album. "It's the same with a lot of the vocals on *OK Computer*," he said. "They're first takes because after that I'd start to think about it and it would sound lame. . . . I don't remember doing it. It was something we left on the shelf for months. When I listened to it again it had obviously been, 'Go out and sing a rough vocal so we can work on it.' There's no emotional involvement in it. I mean, I'm not *emoting*, I'm just, 'Yeah, yeah, sing the song and walk off.' "[27] Again, the singing may not be *overtly* emotional, but the effect can still be moving to the listener.

Although "The Tourist" may seem like the perfect closing song for the album, it didn't always seem that way to the band. Sequencing *OK Computer* was a challenge, and the order of the songs changed drastically before mastering. Thom reported that for two weeks, he constantly shuffled and reshuffled tracks on his MiniDisc player, trying to find the right lineup. "I couldn't find the resolution that I was expecting to hear once you put the songs together," he said, "and I just went into a wild panic. . . . I couldn't sleep at all, because I just expected the resolution to be there—and it wasn't. There was all the trouble and no resolution. But that wasn't really true, as I discovered later. When we chose to put 'Tourist' at the end, and I chilled out and stopped getting up at five in the morning and driving myself nuts, we did find that it was the only resolution for us—because a lot of the album was about background noise and everything moving too fast and not being able to keep up.

"It was really obvious to have 'Tourist' as the last song. That song was written to me from me, saying, 'Idiot, slow down.' Because at that point, I *needed* to. . . . So that was the only resolution there could be: to slow down. If you can slow down to an almost stop, you can see everything moving too fast around you and that's the point."[28]

The song itself doesn't slow down, but it does the next best thing. After Thom's finished singing, the three guitarists construct a grand, multilayered chordal tapestry, which rises in volume and then is quickly stripped away, until all that's left is the shuffle of Phil's drums. The final note of the song is played on a high-pitched bell, like a dinner bell. It's a surprisingly bright, hopeful way to end an album that's delved into some pretty heavy emotional territory over the last 50-plus minutes, but in the end that sense of resolution feels appropriate, and not in the least contrived.

"When we started [recording *OK Computer*]," Thom told *Mojo* in 1997, "I really wanted to make a record that you could sit down and eat to in a nice restaurant, a record that would be cool and be part of the furniture. But there's no way you can eat to this record! You have to sit down and stop doing whatever you're doing."[29] This album is indeed meant to be paid attention to, and to be paid attention to as an album. According to Colin, "We always try really hard to combat the skip culture of the CD format by trying to make people sit down and listen in one sitting,"[30] and that has never been more clear than on *OK Computer*.

I would argue that as a collection of separate, discrete songs, *The Bends* is still Radiohead's strongest work, yet that album doesn't come close to forming the kind of cohesive whole that *OK Computer* does. The seamless flow from one song to the other is little short of magnificent, and though it would be too much to say this is a concept album, it does divide neatly into three separate sections: the introductory section that gradually establishes a mood of density, overload and disconnection (from "Airbag" to "Let Down"); the section that amplifies that mood and brings it to the brink of apocalypse (from "Karma Police" to "Climbing Up the Walls"); and the postapocalyptic section, less dense, more open, still somber but flecked with faint tinges of optimism (from "No Surprises" to "The Tourist"). When taken out of the context of the album, some songs—particularly "Electioneering" and "Climbing Up the Walls"—seem flat, but when taken together, every piece fits snugly, forming a whole that's well beyond the sum of its parts.

Asked his opinion of *OK Computer* shortly after its release, Radiohead's ex-producer Paul Kolderie said, "There are tendencies I don't like, such as Thom's tendency not to enunciate the lyrics properly—when I first heard the album I thought it was a little self-indulgent, but then, as the complexity of it revealed itself to me, I realized that it's really well put together. I think this music has a lot of beauty in it, a spiritual quality, and that's what people are grabbing on to."[31] It takes several listens to fully appreciate this beauty, this spiritual quality (it took me about ten), but given the time, *OK Computer* reveals that Radiohead have created something all too uncommon in the late twentieth century: a genuine, living, breathing, *feeling* work of art.

10

Few would deny that Barcelona is one of Europe's most beautiful cities. The dark, mazelike medieval streets of the Gothic Quarter contrast with the grand tree-lined nineteenth-century avenues of the Eixample, and both differ greatly from the rippling Modernist architecture of Antoni Gaudí, but the combination of all these elements in one place forms an urban environment that's alluringly unique. Set on a shimmering stretch of the Mediterranean, Barcelona is a piquant, cosmopolitan blend of European, Arab, and native Catalan heritage, bursting with great history, timeless art, and magnificent food. For all these reasons, when it came time to decide where Radiohead should begin its promotion of *OK Computer*, Barcelona was the obvious first choice.

On Wednesday, May 21, 1997,

I arrived in Barcelona to cover the official European launch of *OK Computer,* a four-day extravaganza for the band and its management including two club shows, many meetings with EMI reps from around the world, a smattering of Internet press conferences, and a seemingly nonstop round of interviews with newspapers, magazines, radio, and TV. Within a couple of hours, I was seated in a well-appointed room at the Hotel Meridien—just half a block away from the street performers, action painters, and knickknack sellers that line the world-famous boulevard known as Las Ramblas—waiting for Thom Yorke and Jonny Greenwood to arrive. On my way to the room, I'd run into Ed O'Brien, who greeted me warmly, renewing our acquaintance from the last time we'd spoken, a little over a year ago in New York. The specifics of what we said to each other on this particular day, however, have long been lost in a jet-lag haze.

Jonny was the first to enter the room after me. He also remembered our previous interview in New York. Brandishing a camera, he asked me if he could take my picture and went on to say that he was taking photographs of everyone he met on this trip. (Mightn't there also have been a hint of payback here for all the times they'd had to stand in front of someone else's camera?) After I agreed to Jonny's request, he told me to stand by the French windows overlooking the patio—more light that way— where he snapped several shots from a couple of different angles. Photo session concluded, I was thanked for my assistance, and we took our places on one of the light yellow patterned couches facing a long, low glass coffee table. Just about then, Thom flounced in, and with a few brief words of greeting, slumped in a chair across from us.

"We didn't want to start [the tour] in the U.K.," Yorke explained, "because we had a lot of obligations in Europe. So now, because we're a big band, you see"—here he broke into a grin— "we can say to people, 'Actually, we're *not* going to play all around

Europe for a month going through airport X-ray machines and getting sterile. So we'll choose a city, and our favorite city is Barcelona, so we'll go there.'" The band had been in town since Monday, after playing a warm-up show in Lisbon for "a few unsuspecting Portuguese people," as Thom put it. "They were all pretty terrified," he added succinctly.

We talked for a while about the making of *OK Computer*. After putting in so much work on the album, were they pleased with what they'd accomplished? "It's a bit too close," Thom said, "the tape is still warm, but yeah, it's cool."

"Journalists like it, which is always ominous," Jonny quipped.

Thom burst into laughter. "Yeah. Oh shit, now we're in trouble."

I didn't get as much time as I wanted with Thom and Jonny, but I quickly learned that this was a common complaint. From start to finish, the Radiohead appointment calendar over these four days was completely packed—German radio interview here, French magazine interview there, MTV spot in half an hour, Web site meeting 10 minutes after that—but perhaps that was the price they had to pay for being "a big band." All things considered, the fact that they were holding on to their good spirits was a surprise.

The Courtyard management team had requisitioned a number of rooms in the Meridien besides the one in which I interviewed Thom and Jonny. (None of them housed the band, who were staying uptown at the very space-age Hotel Claris.) Just down the hall in an adjoining suite, some other members of the organization were examining the first finished copies of *OK Computer*, complete with the bleak CD booklet collages executed by graphic designer and longtime band friend Stanley Donwood, who was also on hand for the festivities. Slipping into Spinal Tap mode, Colin commented upon his first glimpse of the final product, "It's all black. . . . you can see your face in it. . . . sorry."

Besides the arrival of the CDs, the most exciting news circling the Meridien was that MTV in America had agreed to air the video for "Paranoid Android," a cryptic piece of animation by Swedish illustrator Magnus Carlsson, despite the song's unusual length. The only obstacle had been set up by the cable network's censors, who ordained that the naked breasts of two mermaids appearing near the end of the video had to be covered up. No objection was made to an earlier sequence, in which a man comically but gruesomely mutilates himself. "To be perfectly honest," Colin said, "we could've understood if they had a problem with some guy chopping his arms and legs off, but I mean, a woman's breasts! And mermaids as well! It's fucked up."[1] (In the end, the mermaids donned bathing suits, but only for the U.S. broadcast version of the video.)

The next day, a warm, clear, sunny Thursday, I headed to the Claris to interview the other three members of Radiohead. Our chat took place on a luxurious roof deck overlooking the city. The area was awash in microphones, cameras, and the personnel necessary to operate them. In all the media frenzy surrounding the band, some of whom already seemed a tad bedraggled, the brightly tiled swimming pool and surrounding array of comfortable deck chairs were left empty. Directly following a fellow from the BBC, I took my seat next to Ed, Colin, and Phil at a round white metal table underneath a large canopy. Journalists and photographers encircled Thom some distance away; Jonny was nowhere to be seen.

Glancing around, I noticed that a man was, rather unobtrusively, peering into a movie camera in the corner behind our table, and that the camera was pointing straight at me. Wait a second, I'd already had Jonny take my picture yesterday—what was all this about? Ed explained that our entire interview was being filmed, along with most of the other events during the Barcelona trip; the band had hired a director named Grant Gee to follow them around on their *OK Computer* sojourns and document whatever happened. No one could say exactly what would be done with the footage, maybe a documentary sometime down the line. The only thing everyone was certain about was that this period of the band's existence had to be captured for posterity. "Nothing's been documented ever in our history," Ed said, "and this week is something we wanted to document."

Why? "Don't you think it's unusual? Whenever we've done promotion or anything before, we've gone to various countries, and this time people are flying in to see us, and we're here in this beautiful city. It's a pretty bizarre week for us, being in this position." Ed cracked that their record company had also displayed interest in this type of documentation, though that interest was, unsurprisingly, based more in straightforward mercantilism: "After the Beatles' *Anthology*, EMI keep on referring to 'anthologies for bands.' You know, it worked once, so they think, 'Heck . . .'"

"We only have to wait thirty years now, don't we?" quipped Phil.

"Yeah," Ed said, before turning to me and saying, "*You* could be on it in thirty years."

As it turned out, the results of Grant Gee's yearlong travels with Radiohead were released in 1999 as a 90-minute film called *Meeting People Is Easy*. The movie perfectly captured the mood of a '90s rock world tour—alternating between mind-draining activity and soul-sapping boredom—to such an extent that by the end, you couldn't help wondering why the band bothered putting themselves through such hell. (Oh yeah, that's right, because of the music. Say what you will about Radiohead, but you certainly can't accuse them of shying away from showing us how much they suffer for their art.) Some footage from Barcelona was included in the film, but for better or worse, yours truly ended up on the cutting room floor.

Of course, there was no way I could know this at the time. And I must admit the prospect of seeing myself playing the part of the tiresome rock journalist on the big screen left me feeling a little disconcerted—which I'm sure was part of the plan. Still, I managed to summon up my courage and carry on, bringing up the subject of the "Paranoid Android" video. Colin said that the animator, Magnus Carlsson, had spent about 12 hours straight listening to the song over and over again, and writing down what he saw in it; from those ideas, he'd put the video together. Its two central characters, a pair of pubescent boys, were "a sort of Swedish version of Beavis and Butt-head." The loads of symbology that they make their way through as the video stretches on had little to do with the actual song, but the band felt the images matched the music well, especially in the "rain down" section, where angels swoop down to earth in a helicopter.

I noted that the band itself barely figured in the video. "We are in it briefly," Ed said, "in the bar. Except Colin. You can't really recognize Colin."

"No," Colin responded, "I'm much more handsome in the video than in real life."

"If you freeze-frame it on video, the guy with the five strands of hair slicked back, that's Colin. It looks nothing like him."

"But that's cool. It's nice to just be in the background."

The band seemed to be appearing in their own videos less and less. "You noticed that?" Colin said with a giggle. Everyone laughed.

Talk turned to the album. I asked how the band planned to perform "Let Down" live, given the tricky rhythm of the intro. Who would count in, and where would he start from?

In response, Selway took a deep breath. The corners of his mouth curled up in a bemused smile. Slowly, he spoke. "Well, that's the whole mystery of it, isn't it?" The smile became a wide grin, and the sentence ended with a loud guffaw.

And that's when the argument started.

"We should try to have Thom play the acoustic guitar again at the beginning," said O'Brien, with a touch of heat in his voice. "I *really* think so."

"It sounds good without the acoustic on the album, though," Colin piped up.

"Yeah, but we didn't ever start the song like that before," Ed replied. "Doing it live, we need to establish that tempo."

"Otherwise, the drums might not lock on," Phil warned.

"Exactly—it's so dodgy. With the acoustic, we'd know when to come in." Ed was pushing the point hard. It was obvious this wasn't the first time this debate had raged, and it probably wouldn't be the last. For a few seconds, all three members were talking loudly at each other. Then, just as quickly as it had started, the conversation ended. Everyone stopped. Selway looked around at the other two, turned to me, and said with a smile, "So there's your answer." (Let the record show that "Let Down" was the one song off *OK Computer* that didn't appear in that evening's set.)

I ended the interview with what seemed like a frivolous question: What's it like to be in Radiohead these days? "I'll tell you in about six months," Colin answered. "Right now, we haven't got a clue. For all we know, no one could buy the record."

"Well, this is the thing that you realize," Ed continued. "The record company's got you. If a band has a successful album and then they start making records that don't sell, that's when they've really got you, because they've given you this taste of what it can be like, and they're like, 'Now you're not selling, we're going to tell you what to do.' It would be scary if that happened."

"We'd get put in prison," Colin said, "or be shot." He laughed as he said this, but the underlying uncertainty was real.

There was no detectable uncertainty in Radiohead's performance later that night at the under-1000-capacity Zeleste club, however. Before the adoring crowd, Thom confessed, "This is the most fucking nervous we've been in about two years." Honest as this remark may have been, it was in no way borne out by the playing. The well-paced set interspersed new songs with favorites from *The Bends*; only one song from *Pablo Honey*, "You," was aired. At least some of the *OK Computer* material was evidently translating to the stage in a pleasing way—the break back into the heavy guitar riff at the end of "Paranoid Android" got every member of the band smiling.

Catalonia's youth loved what they heard, yelling for no fewer than three encores. Of those, "The Tourist" was a standout, benefiting as so many Radiohead songs do from a fine guitar arrangement. For the final part of the song, Ed strummed chords, Thom played a melody line on the low end of the neck, and Jonny soloed up top. Always tasteful, never overbearing, it was a clinic on how to run a three-guitar band.

One stunned observer of the Zeleste show, *Mojo*'s Jim Irvin, called Radiohead in his review "emperors of their own beautiful universe."[2] For most of the band, however, that universe did not include the environs of the trendy Otto Zutz club, where the aftershow party took place. Typically, while the hangers-on drank their fill well into the night, Colin was the only band member to stay at the club for any length of time. The others retired as early as they could.

By the third day of the Barcelona experience, all concerned were getting worn out. As usual, the strain was most keenly visible in Thom's demeanor. Though most members of the Radiohead organization were careful to mention how much more emotionally well adjusted he was now than in years past, his mood shifts were still mighty and unpredictable. If nonmembers of the inner circle happened to unknowingly barge in on him at a private moment—when he was smoking a joint, for example—they could get their ears shouted off. And his attitude toward journalists varied wildly, for no apparent reason. My own brief dealings with him have seemed relaxed and straightforward, but others evidently haven't been so lucky. A writer for *Q* once described Yorke's interview stance this way: "He talks with his head bowed and eyes closed, covering his face with his hands and peering through his fingers, sometimes curling his limbs up into a tight ball, as if he is under physical attack."[3] One of Thom's last press appointments in Barcelona, with Jim Irvin of *Mojo*, came to a quick close after the singer began shaking uncontrollably.

Obviously, Thom Yorke is an extremely sensitive, high-strung individual. But spending so much time in the middle of the rock-biz promotional circus could frazzle just about anyone. Making this particular round even more unnerving than usual was the awareness of everyone involved with Radiohead that the work they were now putting so much time and money into promoting, the work that the band had slaved over for a year and a half, was not a guaranteed commercial success. In fact, it could very well wind up a disaster.

"We were immensely proud of the album when we did it," Ed O'Brien recalls. "We thought we were doing something incredibly special. But the longer the recording process goes, by the end you're not quite sure. You're not quite sure anyway, it's very difficult to be objective. Then, of course, tapes go to various record companies all over the world, and apart from the U.K., which was unanimous in thinking it was a fantastic album, people downsized the initial estimates of what it was going to sell. In Barcelona, we were well aware of that. You know, we want people to hear our music, so once the marketing people and people who sell the record come into it and they're not exactly optimistic, you start getting nervous." As the journalists, the TV crews, and the record company folks all got back on their respective planes and went home, the question of *OK Computer*'s fate remained unresolved. There was at least one promising sign, though: Even without much airplay, "Paranoid Android" debuted at Number 3 on the British singles chart, Radiohead's highest placement ever.

In the U.S., Capitol did its best to boost the album, coming up with a clever promotional gimmick in the process. Late in the spring of '97, the label sent an unusual mailing to about 1000 important U.S. press, retail, and radio types—Aiwa Walkmans with cassettes of *OK Computer* permanently bonded inside. If you wanted to use the Walkman, you had to listen to Radiohead. It was a pointed echo of the advice that Chris Hufford had originally given to Capitol's own doubtful executives: Stick with this album for a while and you'll come to understand how good it is. As time passed, more people were becoming receptive to *OK Computer*'s charms.

Meanwhile, it was time to shoot another eye-catching video with Jonathan Glazer, who'd directed "Street Spirit." The candidate this time was "Karma Police," and the video was a nightmarish retribution fantasy, shot with only a handful of cuts and relying on camera movement for most of its tension. In it, Thom sits sullenly in the backseat of a car driven by no one, chasing a breathless old man down a deserted country road. Eventually, the exhausted man turns and faces the car, at which point the car retreats, leaving a gasoline trail that the man promptly lights with a match. The video ends with a view from the interior of the car as it's consumed in flames; Thom has mysteriously disappeared.

Originally, the band had wanted to make videos for all 12 *OK Computer* songs. The videos would not be thematically linked in any way, and each one would employ a completely different method of filmmaking. But even by the time that "Karma Police" was shot, they were coming to the realization that this noble ambition couldn't be achieved. Due to lack of time and money, the plan was dropped. "It's kind of depressing," Thom said, "and we're going to have to leave it. We're just going to do videos for the ones we feel like doing or the singles. It's just a bloody mess."[4]

Three weeks prior to *OK Computer*'s U.S. release, the band made an appearance on June 8 at the Tibetan Freedom Concert in New York. The cause of Tibetan independence from Chinese occupation, endorsed by a growing number of rock stars, found a strong advocate in Thom Yorke, who had recently been doing a fair amount of research into Tibetan culture. "[E]veryone knows what the Chinese are doing," he told *Bikini*'s Rob Hill, "but no one will just stand up and say, 'You must stop!' All the governments have their hands tied by the fuckin' corporations. But musicians . . . we can give these corporations the big 'Fuck you!'"[5] Over time, like their idols in U2 and R.E.M. but far more quietly, Radiohead had become involved in the furthering of various noble causes, from Rock the Vote to Rwandan famine relief. But this was the first time anyone in the band had been so vocal politically, and with the Tibetan situation showing no signs of improvement, it wouldn't be the last.

Directly following the Tibetan Freedom Concert was the previously mentioned June 9 performance at Irving Plaza in New York. From there, Radiohead traveled to the West Coast, where they played the KROQ Weenie Roast, a multi-band, get-them-on-get-them-off affair that also included Blur and the Mighty Mighty Bosstones. The band's set was largely made up of new material, and the audience's response was only lukewarm, strikingly different from the praise they'd gotten in New York. By the end of the performance, Thom was lambasting the crowd, calling them "fucking mindless,"[6] and triggering a loud chorus of boos. The band professed not to care what the Weenie Roast's patrons thought—they hated playing radio shows anyway.

While in California, Thom took advantage of a two-day break in San Francisco to collaborate with one of his favorite techno artists, DJ Shadow, on a chilling number called "Rabbit in Your Headlights." The track wouldn't see the light of day for well over a year; it finally appeared on a 1998 album called *Psyence Fiction*, credited to UNKLE, a "band" of sorts led by DJ Shadow and James Lavelle, head of the respected dance label Mo'Wax Records.

Radiohead's remaining June live dates would all take place in front of audiences numbering at least five figures: the 21st at the Royal Showgrounds in Dublin; the 24th in Utrecht, Holland; the 26th at the Roskilde Festival in Denmark; and their first U.K. appearance of the year, the Glastonbury Festival, on the 28th. Thom, for one, wasn't happy about this plan. "I can't see why we're doing these big gigs," he groused. "Thing is, whoever it is up there, it's not the person sitting here. It's a completely different state of mind, that you have to spend a long time getting into. I can't switch it on and off. When even the logistics of these big gigs are discussed, I just fucking freeze up. It's not something I'm emotionally capable of dealing with yet."[7]

For a while during the band's headlining set at Glastonbury, it looked like Yorke's worst festival fears were coming true. The first few songs sounded fine, but just before "Talk Show Host," Thom's monitors, which allowed him to hear himself, stopped working. "[H]e lost his cues and fucked up completely," Chris Hufford remembered. "It bumbled to a halt and I could tell he was close to walking off then."[8] Though growing disgruntled, Radiohead continued to play. Occasionally, almost as if they were taunting the band, the monitors would re-engage and blast out a few more notes, only to go silent once again. Even worse, Thom was being blinded by two white floorlights pointed straight at him. "I couldn't see a thing, not a face," he said later, "until I screamed at the lighting guy to kick the lanterns round the wrong way so that they weren't in my eyes. Until then I hadn't seen the audience, it was a completely isolated experience. I'd played six songs to a pitch-black wall of nothingness."[9]

Up to that point, Glastonbury '97 had been a dismal affair for Thom. But when the lights turned away from the stage and on to the audience, everything changed. What he saw was a throng of humanity stretching as far as the horizon, and sparks from camp-fires illuminating the rolling hills off in the distance. What he heard was the ardent roar of countless thousands, all of whom had made their way to this muddy patch of the West Country to hear him play. For many of those in the crowd, it was a moment never to be forgotten. "When I've talked to people since who wit-nessed that performance," said *Mojo*'s Paul Trynka, "it's been galling to hear the odd person describe it as merely 'a good gig.' It wasn't. It was something far more profound."[10]

Onstage, the feeling was mutual. The sheer rush of seeing that enormous crowd respond with such awestruck enthusiasm made up for all the aggravation and technical snafus that the band had been suffering. Thom would later call what he experienced that June evening "not a human feeling . . . [but] something else, completely different."[11]

The only problem with such an experience, of course, is that it may raise your expectations to unreasonable levels. And sure enough, more than six months of touring later, in an exchange captured by Grant Gee's roving camera, Thom would tell a Japa-nese reporter, "Everything that's happened after Glastonbury has been a letdown."[12] The letdown commenced on July 1 in Ham-burg, followed by another gig the next day in Cologne and three festival appearances in France and Belgium to round out the week. After a short break, it was back across the water for the first U.S. tour in support of *OK Computer*. On July 25 in L.A., the band kicked things off by rampaging through "Electioneering" on *The Tonight Show*—not the most obvious song with which to introduce the new album to a nationwide TV audience, but for that very reason a perfect choice in the band's minds. (At times like this, Radiohead were growing predictable in their unpredictability.) The tour would end on August 29 in New York, with a potent rendition of "Karma Police" on *The Late Show with David Letterman*.

By now, it was clear that the critics adored *OK Computer*. Acclaim was widespread on both sides of the Atlantic. In the U.K., the album garnered 10 out of 10 in the *NME*, five stars in *Q*, and a "Masterpiece Award" from *Mojo*. British music buyers had seconded the prevailing opinion. *OK Computer* debuted at Number 1 on the U.K. charts, stayed there for two weeks, and lingered in the Top 10 for months thereafter; it would end the year as the country's eighth-biggest seller. In the U.S., *Spin, Request,* and *Details* all praised Radiohead to the stars. "A stunning art-rock tour de force," wrote *Rolling Stone*'s Mark Kemp in a four-star review.[13] As far as the American press was concerned, Oxford's finest had triumphed. But what would American audiences think?

The answer to that question roared across a string of sold-out summer sheds, as American rock fans demonstrated beyond any doubt that they loved the new music, to an extent that even surprised the band. "We talked to people after the shows," Ed recalls, "people who'd traveled long distances to come to the shows, and we realized that the album was actually incredibly pertinent and, if anything, it seemed to make more sense to the fans that we'd met in America than elsewhere. That was only probably because we did a lengthy tour and that was the first place that we toured. But it was exciting, and there was also an incredible sense of relief that people were actually getting it. People were describing not only the songs in themselves and the lyrics, but actually describing the sound of the album, and getting into the sounds, coming up and saying, 'That sound you got on your guitar, I didn't realize until the gig that was a guitar.' That stuff is very important. I mean, it makes us feel good. It kind of justifies our job."

Right from the start, due perhaps to the advance acclaim in

the press, *OK Computer* found a much larger audience in the U.S. than *The Bends* ever had (though it's arguable that *The Bends* did lay the groundwork to some extent). The album debuted in *Billboard* at Number 21, not necessarily the entry position Capitol had hoped for but still a record high for the band. From there, it slipped down the charts, but not quickly enough to keep it from being certified U.S. gold within five months, another group record. At this point, it seemed like the album's commercial life might be drawing to a close, but such was not the case. Like its predecessor, *OK Computer* would show admirable staying power in America, despite the pronounced absence of radio play. As 1997 turned to 1998, it gained a surprising second wind, climbing back into the Top 100 for another round.

In the meantime, Radiohead returned home for an eleven-date British tour in September. "Karma Police" had been released on August 25 as the next U.K. single, once again in two versions. Two remixes of "Climbing Up the Walls" backed the song up on one disc, including one very odd bossa nova take. The other disc featured two new B-sides, an ambient instrumental called "Meeting in the Aisle," based around a spare drum-machine beat and a tempestuous Mellotron line by Jonny, and the brief but outstanding "Lull." Above crafty guitar/Rhodes arpeggios punctuated by occasional xylophone interjections, Thom sings sweetly of being "distracted by irrelevance" and, in a touching moment, offers what sounds like a personal apology: "I'm sorry that I lost control." Blessed with a splendid melody and sensitive performances by the entire band, "Lull" is one of Radiohead's most overlooked gems. Its only flaw is that it ends too soon.

"Karma Police" performed respectably as a single in Britain, but it didn't match the chart placing of "Paranoid Android," peaking only at Number 8. Still, Jonathan Glazer's arresting video for the song would help keep it in the public memory and would also, eventually, aid the cause in America.

The band saw the fall out with a full European jaunt. By now, especially on the older numbers, they'd achieved a kind of looseness in their ensemble playing that only comes from long, intense rehearsal and a lot of concertizing. The tongue-in-cheek campiness of Thom's stage theatrics was escalating too, and appropriately enough, "Creep" was the most frequent beneficiary. On those nights when the band still felt like playing its old hit, Yorke would pull mock-heroic, Freddie Mercury–esque poses, stretching his arms wide or flexing his muscles. Sometimes he just let the crowd sing the song, which they did with gusto.

When Radiohead weren't playing shows, they could often be found putting new ideas down on tape. For the U.S. and European tours, the band had installed a mobile studio setup on their tour bus, oriented around a TASCAM DA-88 digital tape recorder. The only product of this setup that has so far seen the light of day, the abrasive "Palo Alto," features guitar and vocal parts recorded on the bus to a click track; Phil's drums were cut later in a "real" studio. "Palo Alto" was made on deadline, since the next single, "No Surprises," needed another B-side. "Nigel [Godrich] came out for a few days just to discipline us," Ed recalls, "because we were kind of, 'Ah, I don't know, we'll do it tomorrow.' He was like, 'Come on, come on, you've got to do your guitar,' which was good."

When I interviewed Ed O'Brien early in 1998, he strongly doubted that most of the other tracks cut on the road would end up on the next Radiohead album. At best, they'd probably be used as demos for songs that would receive the full studio treatment later. "It's a cool way of working," he said of the tour bus recording, "a different way of working, but it's nothing like playing in a room, in a rehearsal room or doing the takes. I think it's quite important to record an album within a certain time period, because it lends a certain cohesiveness to the whole thing. That way, there are themes running through it—Thom's lyrics will come to fruition at a certain time and you've got to grab that window of opportunity. Also, the way that we did it for *OK Computer*, a lot of the time there's five of us playing in a room. It's taken us twelve years to be able to play as a band. Finally we can do it, so once we're here, it's like, let's just enjoy it, let's do more recording like that, because Christ knows it's something that's taken long enough to get to."

Back in England in mid-November, Radiohead played five more major gigs, including an appearance at the fabled Wembley Arena. In December, the band continued recording, entering a London studio to work on a song they'd occasionally performed live in the past, "Man O'War," now renamed "Big Boots," for possible inclusion on the soundtrack of a new film based on the classic '60s English TV program *The Avengers*. A long day of sessions produced little that Thom was happy with; his dissatisfaction can clearly be seen in the studio sequence that appeared in *Meeting People Is Easy*, as he complains that they've been working for ages and *still* only two instruments—bass and one guitar—sound passable. According to some reports, the band has since scrapped the song entirely.

The year was coming to a close, but there was still time for one more trip to New York and a show at the Hammerstein Ballroom, broadcast live by MTV for their *Live at the 10 Spot* program. As Radiohead shows go, this one was a little shaky. Looking exhausted, possibly drunk, and badly in need of a shave, Thom performed as if he were merely fulfilling a tiresome contractual obligation. Ed claims that the band did actually want to play the Hammerstein show, but admits it was "a difficult gig for us." According to him, however, the problem wasn't Thom's recalcitrance but the insistence of the show's producers that the lights in the ballroom had to be kept on for the benefit of the camera crew. "Usually we kind of exist in a bubble onstage," Ed says, "so it was weird to have the lights on in the audience. It looked normal on TV, but the lighting killed the atmosphere in the hall. It felt uncomfortable. 'Talk Show Host' was rubbish. But heck, that's TV and that's what you deal with." One of the saving graces of the show was Jonny's visceral guitar improvisation, which transformed several of the *OK Computer* songs, particularly "Airbag." On this subject, Thom commented acerbically, "I don't think people coming to see us want to hear necessarily the same version of the song . . . unless they're anally retarded."

Off for the holidays, the band went back to England and watched the year-end plaudits pile up. Band of the Year, said *Rolling Stone* and *Spin.* Album of the Year, said *Q* and *NME.* The difference this year was that it wasn't just the readers and editors of music publications who recognized Radiohead's achievements; now the music industry took notice too. The band garnered a surfeit of nominations for the Brit awards and for music-biz awards all over Europe and Japan. (The Verve's *Urban Hymns* would beat *OK Computer* in every Brit category, but the band were consoled by wins in the Netherlands and Portugal, as well as two Ivor Novello awards honoring excellence in songwriting.) To top it all off, America's National Academy of Recording Arts and Sciences put them in the running for two Grammys: Album of the Year and Best Alternative Rock Performance.

In January, the next leg of the *OK Computer* tour began, covering Japan, New Zealand, and Australia. Record snowfalls hampered Radiohead's mobility during the Japanese trek, especially while traveling to a venue near Nagano for a show on the 15th. What was normally a three-hour journey took the band nine hours to complete on treacherous roads. "When we got there," Ed remembers, "when we played this hall that was supposed to take about two thousand, only four hundred people were able to make it, 'cause trains were delayed. I've never seen snow like it. But despite the fact that there were only four hundred people there, it was a bit of an event. You know, we as a band and crew were pleased to have got there, and the four hundred people who

were there had made it by any way possible. We were all the sur-
vivors. It was sort of a version of *Planes, Trains, and Automobiles*,
but in a band sense."

Because of a strict evening curfew, Radiohead's Japanese
shows started at what was for them a ridiculously early hour—
seven o'clock—with no opening act. "You're not forced to stay
up," O'Brien observed, "so it's been weird, getting up at seven
and being in bed by midnight. It's very un–rock 'n' roll." Even so,
Ed managed to connect more often than not with the rock muse
when it came time to hit the boards. "I came off stage last night
[in Tokyo] going, 'What a fucking great job to have, playing these
great songs. And this is what I do for a living.' We basically play
the songs that we like to play. There's no pressure on us now to
play songs that we don't like to play—we've got enough material,
we've recorded about sixty-odd songs in our career, and the fan-
base we have seems to be aware of B-sides and stuff like that, so
we're able to play those. We've done four gigs here, we've played
'Creep' once, and that's only because we wanted to. It's a lovely
position to be in."

Either the good spirits that Ed exhibited didn't last or they
weren't shared by other band members in the first place. In any
event, the amount of work that Radiohead had to put in besides
the gigs—the boring hours spent in transit or posing for photos,
the meetings with the record company execs who told them they
were "proud to be working your music," the taping of video
thank-yous to various countries for award presentations, the
phone and in-person press interviews conducted seemingly
around the clock—were soon taking their toll on the band's mental health once again. At one highly charged moment during the
Japanese tour, caught on film by Grant Gee, a flustered Thom
said to Jonny and Ed that the critical acclaim they'd won in the
past year was "bollocks," and that "we should get out while the
going is good."[14] By that time, however, everyone close to Thom

was used to such outbursts and knew enough to take them in stride. (It's been said that, depending on what kind of mood he's in, Yorke can erupt in a similar manner just standing in line at a bank or in a store.) The New Zealand and Australia shows all went on as planned.

The third U.K. two-part single from *OK Computer*, "No Surprises," was released on January 12, 1998. Part one featured live takes of "Airbag" and "Lucky" from the last European tour, while part two included two new B-sides, "Palo Alto" and "How I Made My Millions." The former, as previously mentioned, was recorded primarily on the Radiohead tour bus; why the song was named after a California city is unclear, but a hint may lie in the fact that Apple Computer's headquarters, which the band have visited in the past (they're all devoted Macintosh users), are located near Palo Alto. Sci-fi guitar and synth effects abound as Thom pictures "the city of the future," a place where any meaningful form of human contact has ceased to exist: "I'm too busy to see you/You're too busy to wait." The thematic connection between this song and the songs on *OK Computer* is strong, reinforced by the bone-crunching, feedback-squawking chorus, which exposes the shallowness of people's everyday dealings with one another. Yorke's words take as their basis a common exchange between two individuals—Q: How are you? A: I'm okay—that is often completely meaningless, born solely of societal habit; the questioner isn't looking for a real answer, and the respondent has no interest in giving a truthful reply. The sly chromatic guitar line that Jonny plays following the chorus harks back to, of all songs, "Pop Is Dead." "Palo Alto" stands along with "Lull" and "Pearly" as the most well-developed and artistically successful of the *OK Computer* B-sides.

As for "How I Made My Millions," it's a solo Thom vocal and piano performance recorded at home on his MiniDisc machine. Thom's girlfriend, Rachel, can be heard washing dishes in the background. Except for the last line of the song, "Let it fall," the words are completely incomprehensible; in fact, they may not be words at all, just vocal sounds. All the signs point to "Millions" being a simple demo of an idea that Yorke wanted to get down quickly and only later decided to release as-is. It's by no means a finished piece of music, but its stately melody has an air of wounded dignity that's surprisingly moving.

The video for "No Surprises," directed by Radiohead's faithful cameraman Grant Gee, has to stand as one of the most disturbing clips in the history of the form. It's a single three-minute, fifty-second shot of Thom Yorke's face, encased in some sort of clear plastic space helmet. The words to the song run, backward, across the bottom of the helmet as Thom lip-syncs them. After the first verse, the helmet begins to fill up with water. At first, Thom raises his head to avoid the water and keep singing, but eventually he can't keep it up any longer and plunges under. For over a minute—beginning at the point in the song when the word *silence* is repeated twice—Thom's face, submerged under water, is completely motionless. Finally, the water recedes and Thom reemerges, breathing heavily but singing once again, a look of relief, even triumph, in his eyes.

Watching *Meeting People Is Easy*, which includes several anxiety-laden outtakes from the video session, one begins to understand that look much more. Countless takes had to be ditched because Yorke was unable to hold his breath for the necessary duration, and as the day wore on and Thom grew more frustrated, the task just got harder. It was, Gee said, "possibly the most horrible day of my life,"[15] but the final result is undeniably gripping, though not necessarily something you'd want to see over and over. With or without help from the video, the single reached Number 4 on the U.K. charts.

On February 26, 1998, Radiohead added another award to

their shelf, a Grammy for Best Alternative Rock Performance. (*OK Computer* lost to Bob Dylan's *Time Out of Mind* in the Album of the Year category.) The band didn't attend the ceremony, which Ed said was "a bit of a shame—it could have given Thom some fantastic material for lyrics." Originally, they'd wanted to play at the Grammys, but the offer never came through, though there was brief talk of a joint appearance with David Bowie. Rumor has it that Radiohead's prospective appearance was quashed by certain top members of the Academy, who apparently felt that such an unphotogenic bunch shouldn't be allowed to disgrace their stage. That being the case, the band chose to avoid the entire event.

Not long after the Grammy win, the *OK Computer* roadshow got under way once more. During the spring '98 American tour, which began on March 28 in Houston and ended on April 17 at New York's Radio City Music Hall, several new songs began creeping into the set lists, mostly plaintive, low-key numbers with titles like "Nude" and "How to Disappear Completely and Never Be Found" (the latter borrowed from the name of a 1994 book by one Doug Richmond detailing the many ways in which people on the run from creditors, the law, or irate family members can wipe out all traces of their previous identity and assume a new one). Was this a preview of the next Radiohead album? No one could say for sure. In fact, no one could say anything about when or how the next album would be made. "When you finish a record," Thom said, "you come up with all these grand theories of how you're going to do the next one and make it easier. But ultimately you know it'll be just as hard no matter how many bloody times you do it . . . although it *would* be good to not spend a year and a half on it."[16]

Information on the follow-up to *OK Computer* might still be anyone's guess, but if Yorke's comments were anything to go by, it would be done as naturally as possible. "I just read in a magazine in L.A. that [writer Charles] Bukowski was once asked, 'What's your philosophy of life?' and he said, 'Don't try.' And that's right. You can't try. If you try, you're fucked. 'Cause then you're like everybody else."

Maybe Thom wasn't trying, but Capitol certainly was, and to a large extent they were succeeding. Thanks in part to their ceaseless promotion, "Karma Police" had become an unlikely radio hit, and *OK Computer* had rescaled the *Billboard* charts, climbing from Number 179 in mid-December to a peak of Number 37 in mid-March. Now the Grammy win had prompted a demand for new product, a demand that was answered in April with the U.S.-only release of the *Airbag/How Am I Driving?* EP. In addition to the *OK Computer* version of "Airbag," the EP contained six tracks that had previously been available only as B-sides of the "Paranoid Android," "Karma Police," and "No Surprises" import singles. "Palo Alto" and "Pearly" were wisely included, but "Lull" was inexplicably absent. (A similar B-sides EP had been issued in Japan in December.) *Airbag/How Am I Driving?* debuted at Number 56 in *Billboard* the very same week that the RIAA certified *OK Computer* platinum, for sales of a million copies in the United States.

The final public appearance on Radiohead's 1998 schedule was the third Tibetan Freedom Concert on June 13 and 14 in Washington, D.C., an appropriate way to round off a year that had begun in New York at the second Tibetan Freedom Concert. The event took place at RFK Stadium in front of 120,000 people and raised $1.2 million for the Milarepa Fund, a nonprofit organization dedicated to the promotion of nonviolent social change in Tibet. The concert was plagued by bad weather, including a freak electrical storm that injured several spectators. Radiohead's original set on the 13th was canceled due to the chaos and rescheduled for the next day. But that night, the band rewarded the patience of 800 festival attendees with a rousing "secret" solo show at the jam-packed 9:30 Club, organized at the last minute.

At RFK on the 14th, given a welcome worthy of conquering heroes, Radiohead brought on R.E.M.'s Michael Stipe, who sang a duet with Thom on "Lucky." (Thom returned the favor by singing backup during R.E.M.'s set.) For old time's sake, the band even brought "Creep" out of the closet. They'd been playing it less and less frequently, and not at all on the last American tour. At Montreal's Molson Centre in April, the crowd had yelled for "Creep" incessantly until Thom deflated their efforts with a curt "Fuck you, we're tired of it." But today he relented, giving the fans what they wanted with a dramatic flair that showed just how much he and the band had grown since 1992. "[T]hey've taken that song back from the fans," Stipe commented, "and they've made it really beautiful."[17] The crowd, evidently in agreement with at least the latter half of the R.E.M. leader's opinion, roared its approval as Thom, Jonny, Ed, Colin, and Phil dazzled them one more time.

With that, Radiohead brought their *OK Computer* promotional schedule to a successful close. In terms of time actually spent on the road, the '97–'98 tour had been a far easier ride than the band's previous ones; they'd been able to dictate the terms of their engagement with the public to an unprecedented degree. Yet the scale and intensity of the tour experience dwarfed anything they'd previously been through: more fans, more press, more cameras, more people wanting some piece, *any* piece, of the band. Radiohead had entered the rock 'n' roll pantheon, but the entry had come at a price. If their commercial status continued to grow, they could risk losing the identity, the emotional balance, the togetherness that had enabled them to survive as a band through all their ups and downs, especially the success of "Creep" and the subsequent backlash. As the band dispersed in all directions for a well-deserved summer vacation, it was hard to say whether, in the future, they would want to continue paying that price.

In the end, according to Ed O'Brien, at least two important lessons had been learned during the last year. The first: "If the five of us plus our managers think that it's a really good album, then we should stick by that. We're the ones in the position to know." And the second: "People underestimate what the general public is capable of listening to. Everything is so heavily formatted, not just in America but in the rest of the world as well, and what's happened is that radio people are scared to be proactive. There's a lot of good music out there that never gets heard on the radio. It's not above people's heads. People get it. We're people making it, other people are capable of getting it. We just have to break away from those constraints, particularly the commercial constraints. People have to be braver." Guided by these lessons, Radiohead prepared themselves to face a post–*OK Computer* world.

EPILOGUE

On December 10, 1998, after
nearly six months out of the public
eye—the longest such period the
band had spent since they signed
to EMI*—Radiohead played their
only European show of the year,
the Amnesty International concert
in Paris to commemorate the 50th

*During the band's time off in 1998, Colin Greenwood be-
came the third member of Radiohead to get married, following the leads of Phil and his brother Jonny.

anniversary of the United Nations Universal Declaration of Human Rights. No new material was presented. In an interview with Britain's Channel Four prior to the concert, Thom Yorke offered these words: "Radiohead very much came out of the culture of complaint. I think we've grown up and it's dawned on us that our problems are utterly, utterly irrelevant."[1] Might these remarks have some bearing on the tone of the group's new music? Perhaps, but not necessarily.

Meanwhile, across the Atlantic, Radiohead picked up another Grammy nomination for Best Alternative Rock Performance. The *Airbag* EP wasn't as strong a contender as *OK Computer* had been the year before, however, and so it wasn't much of a surprise when the Beastie Boys' *Hello Nasty* ended up taking the award.

In February 1999, the band entered a Paris recording studio to begin laying down tracks with Nigel Godrich, who, since the release of *OK Computer,* had become one of the industry's most in-demand producers, working with Beck, Natalie Imbruglia, R.E.M., and Jason Falkner, among others. Outsiders weren't welcome at the sessions, but sources close to Godrich said that Yorke and company had at least 20 tunes ready and that no drastic stylistic departures were expected. Among the songs being considered for the new album, several would be familiar to die-hard fans from previous live performances: "I Promise," "True Love Waits," "Nude" (also known, though supposedly not by the band, as "Big Ideas"), "Motion Picture Soundtrack," and "How to Disappear." Some of these songs had also been in contention for inclusion on *OK Computer;* a couple dated from the *Pablo Honey* era. No one gave any indication as to whether the most surprising deletion from *OK Computer*, "Lift," might make it back into the lineup this time around.

Once the Paris sessions and a subsequent two-week stay at a studio in Copenhagen were concluded, the band planned to return to England for further recording and mixing. EMI would obviously have been delighted if the new album had been ready in time for a pre-Christmas release, but the company has learned through experience not to impose firm deadlines on Radiohead. Their wisdom in this matter seemed to have been demonstrated once again when it was announced, shortly after recording began, that the band were taking a week off, effective immediately. No reasons were provided, but if the history of previous albums is anything to go on, one can construct a likely scenario: The band entered the studio believing that they'd worked out all their session gremlins and that this time they'd be able to work quickly, smoothly, and efficiently, but they soon learned otherwise, and as tempers flared and the stress level increased, it was decided for the good of all that a short break was required. Mind you, this is only a guess.

"They're the kind of band that always takes ages in the studio," John Harris comments. "That's partly because of the level of ideas. It isn't like Oasis, where it's pretty obvious it's going to be straight-ahead, heads-down twelve-bar rock 'n' roll. Everyone in Radiohead is sufficiently creatively minded that there might be eight suggestions as to what a single song should sound like. They're also very scared of themselves. I remember Jonny said to me that when Thom plays him a song, it's often difficult knowing if he should do anything on it at all or whether he should just leave it as [Thom] on acoustic guitar. So there's a lot of paranoia about 'Ooh, are we really worthy of playing on this song?'"

"I'm sure they feel the same pressure to produce a hit as always," says John Leckie. "It's just that now it's all left unsaid. But they know. Of course, they don't *have* to do anything—every band in England and the U.S. right now seems to want to sound like Radiohead."

April saw the band back in England, settled in a Gloucestershire mansion for the next stage of tracking. Even at this point, experimentation was the norm, as several songs were treated to as many as nine different versions, few of which were completed, leaving "lots of stuff for future Radiohead box sets," as Ed quipped to *Select*.[2] The sessions were further prolonged by the arrival of Phil and Cait Selway's first child in mid-June (a boy) and by Jonny and Thom's departure for Amsterdam on the 13th of that month to play a duo set for the 1999 Tibetan Freedom Concert. (One new song was attempted, provisionally titled "Nothing to Fear.") But the principal delay was the band's seeming inability to agree on what constituted a successful song arrangement. Thom continued to bring new songs into the studio, making the problem even worse.

Concerned fans couldn't have been reassured by the tone of Ed O'Brien's frequent diary postings on the official Radiohead Web site (www.radiohead.com). Originally intended to be a sort of continuing progress report on the sessions, they had instead become a record of an astonishing lack of progress. "We've been working on this since January and nothing substantial has come of it," he wrote on August 4, "except maybe a few harsh lessons in how not to do things. It's like, how do we start this? When we made our last three albums, there were time restrictions—we no longer have these. Are we going down Stone Roses territory?" Another entry two days later was similarly cheery: "It's taken us seven years to get this sort of freedom, and it's what we always wanted, but it could be so easy to fuck it all up."[3]

By the end of the summer, Radiohead had brought their mobile operation back home to an undisclosed location in the Oxfordshire countryside and had decided to basically start over from scratch. "After only two months' rehearsal and three months' recording," Ed wrote on September 3, "it's been concluded that what we should be doing now is trying to get basic arrangements. We're like fucking lasers, us."[4] In a lighter moment, O'Brien noted that the new songs were being influenced, intriguingly enough, by old-school hip-hop, funk, and soul. Among the current possible contenders for inclusion were such titles as "Optimistic," "Knives Out," "Say the Word," "Lost at Sea," "You and Whose Army," "Up the Ladder," "Cuttooth," "Follow Me Around," and "Life in a Glass House." (The last two can be heard briefly in *Meeting People Is Easy*.)

Following yet another short break from activities, the band reconvened for work on September 27. In the interim, some of Ed's Internet postings wound up being printed in the latest issue of *Select* magazine. On October 2, O'Brien noted that he now found himself in the uncomfortable position of "unofficial spokesman for the band—which is bollocks, quite frankly, as this is obviously not the [diary's] purpose." Regardless, Ed pledged to continue with the updates, claiming that it was actually helping the band realize that there was a pattern to the way they worked and that they shouldn't become despondent when things didn't go as planned.

That October 2 posting also suggested that the main source of struggle over the last several months had been the question of how best to use the recording studio: "[T]he way we worked on the last record was to rehearse everything up to such a standard, where most of the parts have been so finely tuned, that recording was largely a matter of capturing the best performance. And that's fine, but recording in this way tends to mean that the songs have a certain way of sounding—i.e. pretty good in a live/band context. Well, that's not enough now, and I think there is a feeling that unless we change our approach, then we're just going to become parodies of ourselves and ever so dull." For each successive album Radiohead have made, the studio itself has become a more important part of the creative process. It seems likely that this trend will continue.

Reports made after the recommencing of sessions in September were largely positive. Ed's October 8 posting mentioned that the band had done "a 'head count' on songs and their current status; it's pretty encouraging as there are about five or six which could be finished fairly quickly. But of course," he concluded with customary sarcasm, "we don't want to do that yet—that would be far too pragmatic." In the end, recording wasn't completed until the following April, with mixing, track selection, and mastering still to come. EMI's official statement that Radiohead were "not in a rush" to finish their fourth album still held true, obviously; the new release wasn't expected until at least 2000.

In a relatively short time, Radiohead have undergone a remarkable transformation from pop flavor of the month into perhaps the most important rock band working today. "They're one of the few out there now that are trying to do something new with rock music," John Harris says. "Nearly every time out they've advanced the boundaries, but not in a way that's forced or self-conscious. Didn't John Cale say something about 'making music because you haven't heard it yet'? Well, that's what Radiohead do." Will they be the ones to maintain rock's relevance in the twenty-first century? Most who are in the know agree that that will depend mainly on the mood swings of the band's creative catalyst, Thom Yorke.

If there's one thing Thom can't stand (or one thing he can't stand more than anything else he can't stand), it's the "fridge buzz," the plague of crunchy guitars wielded by bands who sound completely interchangeable, that to this day infects mainstream rock radio. One reason he has such hatred for this style of music is because, having written "Creep," he feels partly responsible for its perpetuation. Those close to Thom say he never wants to put out another "Creep," and when he finds himself writing something in that vein, he edits himself mercilessly.

Like Nirvana's Kurt Cobain, Thom Yorke is a hypersensitive, ultracreative person who's had a hard time adjusting to pop success. Also like Cobain, he got tagged early in his career as a spokesman for his generation and has spent much of the time since trying to shed that unwanted mantle. But the differences between the two artists are as striking as the similarities. Cobain never was able, maybe never allowed himself, to develop and alter his art over time in the drastic way that Yorke has (although Nirvana's 1993 *Unplugged* performance, with its hints of haunted folk music, suggested that such change might have been in the offing). Cobain became a heroin addict; Yorke has dabbled with drugs, but he hasn't allowed them to rule his life. Most importantly, and most obviously, Cobain killed himself. Yorke's still here, and for all his morbidity, it seems unlikely that he will ever do something so despairing and at the same time so narcissistic. At heart, Thom's a fighter, not a quitter—he won't be pushed around by anyone or anything. In this, he's joined by his four bandmates. For them, artistic freedom has been too hard-won to relinquish lightly.

Another thing Thom can't stand is celebrity, being famous for its own sake. "That whole idea of being Thom Yorke the personality . . . I don't want to die having been just that," he told the *NME* in 1995. "I want to be remembered for doing pieces of work that people liked, and other than that I don't really want to know. I'm not into this for immortality's sake. Sixty years from now, I'm going to be dead, and that will be that."[5] Indeed, the band as a whole is very wary of viewing their music as culturally significant in any way, at least in public. Ed O'Brien once claimed that if Radiohead really believed they were an important band, they'd have to split up. After all, how could they go on when every step they took could be a potential disappointment, a step down from the apex they'd reached?

Paul Kolderie, who co-produced Radiohead's first album, said in 1997, "In terms of the band's commercial future, the negative factor is that Thom is going to shoot himself in the foot, although none of the others will. The positive factor is what they've got up their sleeves in terms of music."[6] Kolderie's suspicion of Yorke's penchant for self-inflicted injury seems to be borne out by comments Thom has made himself in the past, for example: "I'm really into this theory now that anything that's worthwhile is really difficult, and if it's becoming easy, it's time to fuck it up."[7] Though this "theory" may have some basis in Radiohead's actual experiences, it doesn't qualify as a prescription for future band harmony or success.

Yet it seems the members of Radiohead have turned the corner in accepting one another's idiosyncrasies. They've managed to keep the band together through some trying times, and the key appears to have been the realization that hanging on to their friendship is more important than anything else. "[W]hen we started our little band, when we were kids at school, it was never really being about friends or anything," Thom once said. "We were all playing our instruments in our bedrooms and wanted to play them with someone else and it was just symbiotic. We never really thought about it."[8] That's not the case anymore.

Colin says, "I think the main reason why we survived the experience of having a big success with one single and then having people sort of fall away from us after that was that we'd been together as a group and played music together since we were like fourteen years old. . . . When we signed to EMI in the winter of 1991, we thought that at the time the most important thing was the fact that we were signed to a major record company with a contract as professional musicians, and that the friendship thing, which we'd had before then . . . would be a secondary thing. But the longer we do this and the more we meet people whose music we love and admire, like U2 or R.E.M., groups of people who've known each other for a long time, we realize now that the friendship thing . . . is the more important thing to keep you going, and successful and happy and sane."[9]

Being friends doesn't mean being constant companions, however. Radiohead have learned well how to draw the line between being a band and being individuals, for the sake of everyone's sanity. As Randee Dawn astutely observed in *Alternative Press,* "No one's individual identity hinges on being part of a group 24 hours a day; like five straight, infinite lines they are on their own course, and scatter in multiple directions when there is no reason to be a band. But where all the lines intersect, where all five guys, five personalities—five wires cross—that juncture is Radiohead."[10]

As for how long those wires will keep crossing, how long Radiohead will continue to make music, and what that music will sound like, who can say? "I always find it very suspicious when bands start to become concerned with things like careers," Jonny Greenwood says. "I sort of more admire bands like the Pixies, who always said their whole outlook was to make a few good records and then piss off and leave it alone. Which is great. I admire that more in a way than bands who've made twenty albums, and are still going, and still have integrity, which is fine too. The Pixies had it right, though, I think."[11]

One thing's for certain: No one, not even the band themselves, could ever have predicted that five artistically inclined misfits from Abingdon School would rise to such a staggering level of international success and acclaim. Radiohead have beaten the music-biz odds many times—first by sticking together, then by getting signed, then by racking up a big hit, then by surviving that big hit. Working within an industry that fears unchecked artistic growth, they've stood out by constantly reinventing themselves, and they've gained respect for doing so. In a sense, whatever they choose to do now, it doesn't matter much. They've already won the game.

"Hopefully we'll carry on making albums that reflect diversity and reflect the different pieces of music that we listen to," Ed O'Brien told me in 1998 on the phone from Tokyo. "We are heavily influenced by what we've been listening to the preceding year or two years running up to the recording of an album. We'll be the first ones to say that we try and rip off other sounds, but because of our limitations as musicians, we can't do everything exactly right. We can't do *anything* exactly right. But that's what makes our own sound."

This comment reminded me of something Thom said back in Barcelona, that "aiming and missing is the whole premise."

"Absolutely," Ed responded with enthusiasm. "It really is. I remember reading something that Brian Eno said in some magazine about the importance of limitations, and I was thinking, 'Oh God, I'm not sure whether maybe that's just justifying his own position,' but he's absolutely right. There's nothing more the kiss of death vis-à-vis a musician than if he can do everything by the age of sixteen and can play every lead guitar riff to every song. It's very, very dangerous, unless you approach it in the way that, say, Picasso did as a painter. At age nine, he was a child prodigy, but then he decided, 'Enough, I'm putting down my tools, I'm going to approach it in a totally different way.' So I think you've got to be careful. Virtuosity is one thing, but if you've learnt all the rules—which we haven't—you've got to go, 'Right, hang on a sec, I can do this one way now, I've got all this background, forget all that and start anew.'"

Ed paused for a moment, then laughed.

"So," he concluded, "we're fortunate in limitations."

ACKNOWLEDGMENTS

Many people have made invaluable contributions to this book. Principal among them are the members of Radiohead themselves, who agreed to be interviewed by me on four occasions between 1995 and 1998. I spoke to Jonny Greenwood first in November 1995, then to Jonny, Ed O'Brien, and Thom Yorke in March 1996. In May 1997, I interviewed all five members of the band in Spain, and in January 1998, I talked to Ed on the phone while Radiohead was on tour in Japan. For arranging these interviews, thanks are due to Daralyn Adams at Capitol Records. Jenny Bendel, the band's independent U.S. publicist at the time, fearlessly escorted me around Barcelona for much of that crazy *OK Computer* Memorial Day weekend, for which she deserves a round of applause.

Of the other individuals who agreed to talk to me or assist me in my research, I owe the greatest debt of gratitude to the folks at Oxford Music Central, an organization that lives up to its name in every respect. Ronan Munro, Dave Newton, and the venerable Mac were remarkably generous with their time, providing countless pieces of useful information and indispensable early press notices of the band, while Pat Loughnane stepped up with some priceless photos. Thanks also to Lesley Bosley and Jeff Drummond-Hay at Abingdon School; James Lister-Cheese, Tim Jordan, and Dai Griffiths at Oxford Brookes University; Richard Haines, John Harris, Paul Kolderie, Carol Baxter, Uzi Preuss, Aaron Axelsen, Peter Clements, and John Leckie.

Jim Irvin helped me in two ways: first by writing one of the most informative features ever done on Radiohead in the September 1997 issue of *Mojo,* and then by graciously putting me in touch with several of the people he'd interviewed for that piece. For further research assistance, thanks to Howard Massey, David Farinella, Helen Haste, Tina Cartwright, Catherine Hitchens at the Oxfordshire County Council Registry, and the staff of the Center for Oxfordshire Studies at the Central Public Library in Oxford.

Radiohead fans are a notoriously rabid lot, and so it should come as no surprise that there are literally hundreds of personal Web sites devoted to the band. Several of these are immensely informative and were helpful to me in my preliminary research, particularly *Green Plastic Radiohead* (www.greenplastic.com) and *Planet Telex* (www.underworld.net/radiohead/).

It was Chris Paton who first suggested the idea of a Radiohead book to me, and it was Bill Flanagan who encouraged me to follow up on that idea. In a roundabout way, Baker Rorick, Chris Butler, Richard Barnes, and Chris Charlesworth helped as well, leading me to see that of the many vague concepts floating in my head at the time, this was the one to pursue. A big thank-you to all those with whom I toiled at *Musician* between 1989 and 1997—especially Ted Drozdowski, Keith Powers, Mark Rowland, Ted Greenwald, Dev Sherlock, Dan Gingold, and Michael Gelfand—and to Dave DiMartino and the whole crew at *Launch,* both in New York and Santa Monica, for their seemingly infinite understanding and support.

Special thanks to my agent, Dave Dunton, whose enthusiasm for this project never wavered; to Jacob Hoye, Mitch Hoffman, and Kathleen Jayes, my ultra-cool editors at Dell; and to the fabulous Robin Malik for her help in photo research and design. Finally, extra special thanks to the love of my life, Laurie Jakobsen, and to my parents, without whom none of this would have been possible (obviously).

NOTES

INTRODUCTION
1. Colin Greenwood, June 1997 interview with unidentified journalist, available commercially on CD as *Radiohead Interview*, Baktabak, 1998.

CHAPTER ONE
1. These and subsequent statements made by Thom from the Irving Plaza stage in this chapter have been transcribed from a bootleg recording of the show, available under the title *New Yorke Stories*.

CHAPTER TWO
1. Phil Sutcliffe, "Death Is All Around," *Q*, October 1997.
2. Ibid.
3. Ibid.
4. Ibid.
5. Steve Malins, "Scuba Do," *Vox*, April 1995.
6. Ibid.
7. Ibid.
8. Jon Wiederhorn, "Static Electricity: Radiohead Transform Emotional Turmoil into Kinetic Pop," *Rolling Stone*, September 7, 1995.
9. Steve Appleford, "Under Pressure: Just What Do You Want from Radiohead?" *Option*, January/February 1998.
10. Tom Doyle, "Party On!" *Q*, June 1997.
11. Wiederhorn, "Static Electricity."
12. Mick St. Michael, *Radiohead* (London: Virgin Sound and Media, 1997), 9.
13. Sutcliffe, "Death Is All Around."

14. St. Michael, 10.
15. Jonathan Hale, *Radiohead: From a Great Height* (Toronto: ECW, 1999), 16.
16. St. Michael, 15.
17. This concert took place on December 1, 1995, and was bootlegged.
18. Appleford, "Under Pressure."
19. Victoria Harper, "Rock Rebels? No, Oasis with Brains," *The Mail on Sunday*, August 3, 1997.
20. Spring 1995 interview with Jonny Greenwood and Ed O'Brien, available on a CD packaged with Mick St. Michael's *Radiohead* (Virgin Sound and Media, 1997).
21. Gina Morris, "You've Come a Long Way, Baby: The Secret Life of Radiohead," *Select*, April 1995.
22. Jim Irvin (with Barney Hoskyns), "We Have Lift-Off," *Mojo*, September 1997.
23. Morris, "You've Come a Long Way."
24. *The Abingdonian*, vol. 18, no. 2, July 1984.
25. Doyle, "Party On!"
26. Morris, "You've Come a Long Way."
27. Radio interview conducted in the spring of 1993, packaged as *Radiohead: The Interview* (Talking Music, 1998).
28. Doyle, "Party On!"
29. *Answerphone 01*, fanclub magazine issued simultaneously with *The Bends*.
30. Tony Harkins, "Welcome to the Instrumental Asylum," *Melody Maker*, November 27, 1993.
31. Morris, "You've Come a Long Way."
32. Ibid.
33. *Radiohead* (Virgin) interview disc.
34. Morris, "You've Come a Long Way."
35. *Radiohead* (Virgin) interview disc.
36. *Radiohead Interview* (Baktabak) disc.
37. Ibid.
38. St. Michael, 15.
39. Doyle, "Party On!"
40. Morris, "You've Come a Long Way."
41. Doyle, "Party On!"
42. St. Michael, 15.
43. Wiederhorn, "Static Electricity."

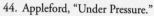

44. Appleford, "Under Pressure."

45. *The Abingdonian,* vol. 19, no. 2, December 1990, 14.

46. Doyle, "Party On!"

47. Dave Newton (uncredited), "Sounding Off: On A Friday," *Local Support,* February 27, 1988.

48. Dave Newton (uncredited), "Reviews: On A Friday, Old Fire Station," *Local Support,* March 26, 1988.

49. Appleford, "Under Pressure."

CHAPTER THREE

1. St. Michael, 17.

2. Ibid.

3. Sutcliffe, "Death Is All Around."

4. Doyle, "Party On!"

5. 1995 interview with Chris Tetley, available commercially on CD as *The Rockview Interviews: Radiohead* (Rockview Records, 1997).

6. Hale, 34.

7. *Radiohead: The Interview* (Talking Music) disc.

8. Andrew Mueller, "Shiny Unhappy People," *Melody Maker,* October 28, 1995.

9. Sutcliffe, "Death Is All Around."

10. St. Michael, 17.

11. The Stud Brothers, "Fame Fatale," *Melody Maker,* March 11, 1995.

12. Doyle, "Party On!"

13. Irvin, "Lift-Off."

14. Clark Collis, "Can Pop Stars Share a Flat Without Murdering One Another?" sidebar to "Pulp in Residence," *Select,* July 1995.

15. Ibid.

16. Ibid.

17. Ibid.

18. Nick Johnstone, *Radiohead: An Illustrated Biography* (London: Omnibus Press, 1997), 6.

19. Morris, "You've Come a Long Way."

20. Ronan Munro (uncredited), "In Your Neighbourhood: Courtyard Studios," *Curfew,* February 1992.

21. Ibid.

22. Irvin, "Lift-Off."

23. Ibid.

24. Doyle, "Party On!"
25. Ronan Munro (uncredited), "Reviews: On A Friday, Jericho Tavern," *Curfew*, September 1991.
26. St. Michael, 21.
27. Irvin, "Lift-Off."
28. Ronan Munro (uncredited), "On A Friday," *Curfew*, December 1991.
29. Irvin, "Lift-Off."
30. Ibid.
31. Johnstone, 7.
32. Irvin, "Lift-Off."
33. Ibid.
34. Quoted in Johnstone, 8.
35. Ronan Munro (uncredited), "Radiohead," *Curfew*, February 1993.
36. Munro, "On A Friday."
37. Johnstone, 8.
38. St. Michael, 24.
39. *Radiohead Interview* (Baktabak) disc.
40. Morris, "You've Come a Long Way."
41. *Radiohead: The Interview* (Talking Music) disc.
42. Morris, "You've Come a Long Way."

CHAPTER FOUR

1. *Radiohead: The Interview* (Talking Music) disc.
2. John Harris, "Live! On A Friday," *Melody Maker*, February 22, 1992.
3. Irvin, "Lift-Off."
4. *Radiohead* (Virgin) interview disc.
5. *Radiohead: The Interview* (Talking Music) disc.
6. Johnstone, 10.
7. Irvin, "Lift-Off."
8. *Radiohead: The Interview* (Talking Music) disc.
9. Ibid.
10. *Radiohead* (Virgin) interview disc.
11. St. Michael, 50.
12. Irvin, "Lift-Off."
13. Ibid.
14. Ibid.
15. Ibid.
16. Ibid.

17. *Radiohead: The Interview* (Talking Music) disc.

18. Ibid.

19. St. Michael, 25.

20. Ibid.

21. Quoted in Johnstone, 11.

22. Irvin, "Lift-Off."

23. Quoted in Hale, 50.

24. *The Rockview Interviews* disc.

25. Andrew Collins, "Super Creep," *Select,* May 1993.

26. Peter Paphides, "'We're Going to Save Pop Music,'" *Melody Maker*, February 6, 1993.

27. Ibid.

CHAPTER FIVE

1. *Radiohead* (Virgin) interview disc.

2. Ibid.

3. Irvin, "Lift-Off."

4. *Radiohead: The Interview* (Talking Music) disc.

5. William Stone, *Radiohead: Green Plastic Wateringcan* (London: UFO Music Ltd., 1996), 23.

6. Irvin, "Lift-Off."

7. Quoted in Stone, 23.

8. *Answerphone 01.*

9. Morris, "You've Come a Long Way."

10. Ibid.

11. Wiederhorn, "Static Electricity."

12. *Radiohead: The Interview* (Talking Music) disc.

13. Quoted in St. Michael, 36.

CHAPTER SIX

1. Johnstone, 12.

2. *Radiohead: The Interview* (Talking Music) disc.

3. Irvin, "Lift-Off."

4. *Radiohead: The Interview* (Talking Music) disc.

5. Johnstone, 17.

6. *Radiohead: The Interview* (Talking Music) disc.

7. Ibid.

8. Irvin, "Lift-Off."

9. St. Michael, 40.

10. Ibid.

11. St. Michael, 41.

12. *Los Angeles Times*, quoted in Johnstone, 18.

13. St. Michael, 40.

14. Sandra A. Garcia, "Radiohead: Decompression" *B-Side*, July/August 1995.

15. Doyle, "Party On!"

16. Malins, "Scuba Do."

17. Irvin, "Lift-Off."

18. Wiederhorn, "Static Electricity."

19. Doyle, "Party On!"

20. St. Michael, 44.

21. St. Michael, 49.

22. Randee Dawn, "Modulation Across the Nation," *Alternative Press*, October 1995.

23. Doyle, "Party On!"

24. Ibid.

25. Ibid.

26. Ibid.

27. St. Michael, 45.

28. Irvin, "Lift-Off."

29. Doyle, "Party On!"

30. St. Michael, 54.

31. Garcia, "Radiohead: Decompression."

32. *Radiohead: The Interview* (Talking Music) disc.

33. Ibid.

34. Irvin, "Lift-Off."

35. Steve Malins, *Radiohead: Coming Up for Air* (London: Virgin Publishing, 1997), 50.

36. Garcia, "Radiohead: Decompression."

37. Irvin, "Lift-Off."

38. *Answerphone 01.*

39. St. Michael, 51.

40. St. Michael, 53.

41. Jack Rabid, "Radiohead," *The Big Takeover*, Issue 38, 1995.

42. Irvin, "Lift-Off."

43. St. Michael, 59.

44. Peter Howell, "Paranoia Will Destroy Ya," *The Toronto Star*, December 7, 1995.

45. Irvin, "Lift-Off."

46. St. Michael, 54.

47. St. Michael, 53.

48. Irvin, "Lift-Off."

49. Tom Doyle, "Diary of an LP," *Melody Maker*, April 22, 1995.

50. Stone, 41.

51. Morris, "You've Come a Long Way."

52. According to Thom Yorke as quoted in *Vox*, April 1995.

53. Irvin, "Lift-Off."

54. Ibid.

55. St. Michael, 59.

56. Doyle, "Party On!"

57. Irvin, "Lift-Off."

58. Stone, 50.

59. Doyle, "Diary of an LP."

60. *Radiohead Interview* (Baktabak) disc.

61. Clark Collis, "Videohead," *Select*, October 1994.

62. St. Michael, 65.

63. Garcia, "Radiohead: Decompression."

64. Ibid.

65. Johnstone, 25.

66. Garcia, "Radiohead: Decompression."

67. Malins, 59.

68. Ibid.

69. Andy Richardson, "Boom! Shake the Gloom," *New Musical Express*, December 9, 1995.

70. Ibid.

71. Quoted in Johnstone, 25.

72. Stone, 51.

CHAPTER SEVEN

1. Malins, "Scuba Do."

2. Rabid, "Radiohead."

3. Ibid.

4. Ibid.

5. Irvin, "Lift-Off."

6. Garcia, "Radiohead: Decompression."

7. Ibid.

8. Malins, "Scuba Do."

9. Ibid.

10. Quoted in Steve Lowe, "Back to Save the Universe," *Select*, December 1999.

11. Malins, "Scuba Do."

12. *Radiohead Interview* (Baktabak) disc.

13. *Radiohead* (Virgin) interview disc.

14. *Answerphone 01.*

15. Malins, "Scuba Do."

16. *Answerphone 01.*

17. Ibid.

18. Malins, "Scuba Do."

19. Garcia, "Radiohead: Decompression."

20. *Answerphone 01.*

21. Garcia, "Radiohead: Decompression."

22. *Radiohead* (Virgin) interview disc.

23. Ibid.

24. *Answerphone 01.*

25. Malins, "Scuba Do."

26. *Answerphone 01.*

27. Appleford, "Under Pressure."

CHAPTER EIGHT

1. Rabid, "Radiohead."

2. Johnstone, 31.

3. Craig McLean, "Albums of the Month: Radiohead," *Vox*, April 1995.

4. Stone, 50.

5. David Roberts, review of *The Bends*, *Q*, April 1995.

6. Dave Morrison, review of *The Bends*, *Select*, March 1995.

7. Quoted in St. Michael, 78.

8. Quoted in St. Michael, 74.

9. Dave DiMartino, "Give Radiohead to Your Computer," *LAUNCH*, February 5, 1998.

10. Ibid.

11. Richardson, "Boom!"

12. Dawn, "Modulation."

13. Garcia, "Radiohead: Decompression."

14. Dawn, "Modulation."

15. Ibid.

16. Ibid.

17. *Radiohead* (Virgin) interview disc.

18. Thom Yorke, "That's Me in the Corner" (tour diary), *Q,* October 1995.

19. Johnstone, 38.

20. Richardson, "Boom!"

21. Doyle, "Party On!"

22. Stone, 60.

23. *The Advocate,* September 1995, quoted in Johnstone, 36.

24. Richardson, "Boom!"

25. St. Michael, 89.

26. Quoted in Johnstone, 39.

27. Mueller, "Shiny Unhappy People."

28. Doyle, "Party On!"

29. Irvin, "Lift-Off."

30. Ibid.

31. Doyle, "Party On!"

32. Stone, 60.

33. Ibid.

34. Johnstone, 39.

35. DiMartino, "Give Radiohead."

36. Stone, 60.

37. Richardson, "Boom!"

38. Stone, 62.

39. Irvin, "Lift-Off."

40. Appleford, "Under Pressure."

41. Quoted in St. Michael, 99.

42. Morris, "You've Come a Long Way."

43. Appleford, "Under Pressure."

44. Johnstone, 40.

45. Doyle, "Party On!"

46. Mark Sutherland, "Rounding the Bends," *Melody Maker,* May 24, 1997.

47. Caitlin Moran, "Everything Was Just Fear," *Select,* July 1997.

48. Doyle, "Party On!"

49. Johnstone, 43.

50. Hale, 109.

51. DiMartino, "Give Radiohead."

52. Ibid.

53. Appleford, "Under Pressure."

54. Irvin, "Lift-Off."

CHAPTER NINE

1. DiMartino, "Give Radiohead."

2. Ibid.

3. Ibid.

4. Thom Yorke, interview by Jim Irvin, review of *OK Computer, Mojo*, July 1997.

5. DiMartino, "Give Radiohead."

6. Irvin, interview.

7. *Radiohead Interview* (Baktabak) disc.

8. Irvin, interview.

9. Sutcliffe, "Death Is All Around."

10. *Radiohead Interview* (Baktabak) disc.

11. Ibid.

12. Sutcliffe, "Death Is All Around."

13. DiMartino, "Give Radiohead."

14. Ibid.

15. Appleford, "Under Pressure."

16. DiMartino, "Give Radiohead."

17. Irvin, interview.

18. Cameron Adams, "Is Radiohead the New Pink Floyd?" *Rolling Stone Australia,* October 1997.

19. Sutcliffe, "Death Is All Around."

20. Ibid.

21. DiMartino, "Give Radiohead."

22. Appleford, "Under Pressure."

23. Irvin, interview.

24. Ibid.

25. Sutcliffe, "Death Is All Around."

26. St. Michael, 89.

27. Sutcliffe, "Death Is All Around."

28. DiMartino, "Give Radiohead."

29. Irvin, interview.

30. *Radiohead Interview* (Baktabak) disc.

31. Irvin, "Lift-Off."

CHAPTER TEN

1. *Radiohead Interview* (Baktabak) disc.
2. Jim Irvin, "Live Shows," *Mojo,* July 1997.
3. Tom Doyle in *Q,* June 1997.
4. DiMartino, "Give Radiohead."
5. Quoted in Hale, 116.
6. Keith Cameron, "Notorious Pig," *NME,* June 28, 1997.
7. Doyle, "Party On!"
8. Irvin, "Lift-Off."
9. Sutcliffe, "Death Is All Around."
10. Irvin, "Lift-Off."
11. This comment is transcribed from the Grant Gee film *Meeting People Is Easy* (Capitol Video, 1999).
12. Ibid.
13. Mark Kemp, "Deep Blue," *Rolling Stone,* July 10–24, 1997.
14. *Meeting People Is Easy.*
15. Personal communication from journalist Paul Biel, who interviewed Grant Gee in 1998.
16. DiMartino, "Give Radiohead."
17. *Spin,* January 1998, quoted in Hale, 123.

EPILOGUE

1. "What Goes On," *Mojo,* February 1999.
2. Personal communication from that magazine's editor, John Harris, July 1, 1999.
3. Quoted in Steve Lowe, " 'It's Great to Be in Our Band!' " *Select,* November 1999.
4. Ibid.
5. Richardson, "Boom!"
6. Irvin, "Lift-Off."
7. Richardson, "Boom!"
8. Ibid.
9. *Radiohead Interview* (Baktabak) disc.
10. Dawn, "Modulation."
11. DiMartino, "Give Radiohead."

ABOUT THE AUTHOR

Mac Randall is the East Coast editor of *Launch* and former senior editor of *Musician* magazine. His work has also appeared in several other publications, including *Rolling Stone*, *Time Out New York*, *The Boston Phoenix*, and *Guitar World*. He has interviewed the members of Radiohead several times and was one of only two American journalists present at the official 1997 unveiling of their *OK Computer* album in Barcelona, Spain.